*Popular Music History*

Series Editor: Alyn Shipton, journalist, broadcaster and lecturer in music at Oxford Brookes University

This new series publishes books that challenge established orthodoxies in popular music studies, examine the formation and dissolution of canons, interrogate histories of genres, focus on previously neglected forms, or engage in archaeologies of popular music.

Published:

*Handful of Keys: Conversations with Thirty Jazz Pianists*
Alyn Shipton

*The Last Miles: The Music of Miles Davis, 1980–1991*
George Cole

*Jazz Visions: Lennie Tristano and His Legacy*
Peter Ind

*Chasin' the Bird: The Life and Legacy of Charlie Parker*
Brian Priestley

*Out of the Long Dark: The Life of Ian Carr*
Alyn Shipton

*Lee Morgan: His Life, Music and Culture*
Tom Perchard

*Being Prez: The Life and Music of Lester Young*
Dave Gelly

Forthcoming:

*Gone in the Air: The Life and Music of Eric Dolphy*
Brian Morton

*In Search of Fela Anikulapo Kuti*
Max Reinhardt and Rita Ray

*Soul Is Stranger Than Fiction*
Kevin Le Gendre

*Trad Dads, Dirty Boppers and Free Fusioneers: A History of British Jazz, 1960–1973*
Duncan Heining

# Lionel Richie
## Hello

SHARON DAVIS

equinox
LONDON　OAKVILLE

The book is lovingly dedicated to

Milan Williams – a true Commodore

# preface

This book was meant to happen. When Lionel Richie left the Commodores in 1982 I was fortunate enough to be the journalist on the *Blues & Soul* team who interviewed him on the phone – several times too! I finally met him in person in 1987 at London's Mayfair Hotel. Needless to say, I was a little nervous. Well, for god's sake, it was *the* Lionel Richie! Anyway, he greeted me as a long-lost friend – or at least that's what it felt like – and we sat in his hotel lounge talking about everything and anything. The conversation was easy; the atmosphere homely. He asked me questions about the music business and my life, and we swapped anecdotes about musical situations. Subsequent interviews were phone calls, and when *Blues & Soul* and I parted company, another writer took over. However, Lionel was responsible for some of my finest moments in journalism and for that I'll be forever grateful.

One of the questions I aimed at him was if he had trouble with his ego. He laughed loudly: 'Hah! Everyone thinks I'm now enjoying instant success but that success has taken fifteen years, so my ego is the least of my problems. I'm overworked but I've been very lucky. I love performing and I love being in the studio. No one can take that away from me. If I get tired on the road, the best place for me to go is in the studio. I am lucky because what I make my living doing is really my hobby.'

Anyway, it's time for me to offer well-deserved thanks to several people who've helped me achieve this book. Firstly, Wayne Imms and Robin Quinn, who invited me to become involved in their radio programme about Lionel, which gave me the idea to put pen to paper. Thank you, guys! Then to Silvia Montello, Daryl Easlea and Harry Weiner at Motown/Universal for willingly providing the music as reference material. What a way to write a book – music and words. I can highly recommend it! A big thank-you to the folk at *Blues & Soul* magazine for their tireless work in promoting soul music for the last forty years; to my gang including Gerry Constable and John Pawsey, my agent. And last but not least, to the Equinox team for sharing this project with me. Mr Richie has the final word – of course.

'I can't envisage ever giving up this business. I must explain, I never thought I'd get this far. I don't really know how I got here in the first place. I am just an extremely lucky man who thanks God for the success I've had and am still enjoying.'

Sharon Davis
West Sussex, 2006

It was an emotional finale to the XXIIIrd Olympiad at the Los Angeles Memorial Coliseum in June 1984. All the participating athletes gathered in the arena for the official closing ceremony, which ended with the lowering of the Olympic flag and the extinguishing of the Olympic flame. A magnificent, dazzling laser light show followed, while a giant spacecraft hovered over the stadium for at least five minutes. A huge gasp was heard from the Coliseum as a blinding searchlight swept across the 92,000 spectators, and with the full moon as its backdrop the spaceship joined in the celebrations!

Landing instructions were relayed to the ship from the arena, accompanied by complementary music from composer John Williams. Sensing the invitation to land was a friendly gesture, the spaceship replied in music, prompting a wave of cheers from the crowd. A ten-foot-high alien was then deposited near the Olympic flame. His arms were outstretched in a gesture of friendship, as the dancing laser skipped over the arena before coming to rest. It illuminated the centre stage, where a massive spot revealed – Lionel Richie being raised up on a platform in the centre of the stadium! Needless to say, the spectators went wild, screaming and clapping, not able to believe their eyes.

With two hundred break-dancers and three hundred assorted acrobats and dancers, Motown's biggest star paid a spectacular salute to the athletes. To an estimated TV audience of 2.6 billion in 120 countries, Lionel Richie sang 'All Night Long (All Night)', including a special verse in honour of the occasion. As the song ended, athletes from all nations joined him on stage before a magnificent firework display brought the glorious and colourful celebrations to an end.

'It was just a magnificent moment!' gushed Richie's manager Ken Kragen. 'Lionel was really out front doing things that nobody else had done!'

And an extremely happy and privileged artist glowed, 'To have the entire world watching "All Night Long" was just the best combination in the world to have. To sing that song on that stage in front of the entire world was just the best!'

It was Lionel Richie's finest hour – and this is his story.

# 1 keep on dancing

'I was always "little Richie" or "Alberta's son" and I couldn't get away with anything.'   Lionel Richie

'It took a lot of head sessions to really get to know each other properly.'   William King, of the Commodores' membership

'When [the Jackson 5] picked up a cheque for about $180,000 it didn't take me long to decide that I should take this career seriously.'   Lionel Richie

With the phrase 'we want to be more successful than the Beatles', one of the world's most accomplished black groups was born. These few words inspired a handful of enthusiastic young freshmen from the Tuskegee Institute to form a music group, the Commodores. After chasing their dream with determination and an iron will to succeed, the six musicians eventually realized their ambitions and became international artists. They were absolutely unstoppable as they slowly but courageously climbed the shaky ladder to success. With the later, inevitable fortune and fame, they kept their nerve and followed their soul to sustain and enjoy their elevated position in the music world. But, as it came so it went, when the Commodores lost its heart.

Born on 20 June 1949 in Tuskegee, in east-central Alabama, Lionel Brockman Richie, Jr, was the son of Lyonel, a retired army captain and systems analyst, and Alberta, an elementary school teacher. Raised in a religious environment, the young Richie was an altar boy at the family's local Episcopal church, and later sang in the choir there. Holding the church elders in high esteem, in particular Father Jones, who was a steadying influence on him, Richie admitted he originally wanted to pursue a career in the ministry. 'I couldn't think of doing anything better with my life than being like him.' That is, until his Uncle Bertram gave him a saxophone and introduced him to secular music. A professional musician from New York, Richie's uncle was a gifted musician who played with the big bands and had, at one time, worked with the great Duke Ellington. With this introduction and Richie's growing interest in secular music, his grandmother Adelaide, a classically trained piano teacher, became relentless in her efforts to direct his growing interest in music by teaching him her art. 'During lessons I kept trying to make up my own songs and it annoyed her', Richie recalled years later with a smile.

As for his family life in general, he acknowledged his upbringing was rather stifling because he rarely strayed far from his neighbourhood without his parents. His family background was strictly middle-class: 'Especially since my father was a military man. So, it was always about getting a respectable career...We don't stray too far from the basics...The notion of being an entertainer would not have gone down well with my family.' His formative years were spent on the campus of the Tuskegee Institute, founded by Booker T. Washington. The noted black educator had founded the Institute in 1881 to enable blacks to benefit from a solid education, and to uphold moral and work principles. Richie's grandfather had worked for Washington in the Institute's enrollment office, and lived with his wife in a large house practically in the shadow of the Institute itself. Lionel Richie, his younger sister Deborah and their parents lived with them. Living in a sheltered, intellectual community, among people from diverse backgrounds, who advocated different ideas and philosophies, his inquisitive mind thrived. However, the often claustrophobic community had its downside because everyone knew when he misbehaved. 'Because I was raised in a village, everybody knew me. I never knew I had a name. I was always "little Richie" or "Alberta's son" and I couldn't get away with anything.'

When young Richie left high school and started studying economics at the Institute, where he planned to stay for two years before enrolling at the Wyoming Seminary, he was exposed to many varied forms of music. The local radio station played country and western, and he developed an interest in gospel, soul and African music. Those college days, he readily accepted, shaped him for the future, giving him his first break as a professional musician. He was also attracted to the Institute's musical programmes, including ballet and symphonic performances, yet his most vivid personal memory of college life was his painful shyness, which would, of course, undermine his confidence as a performer. He readily accepts that being a member of a group helped him meet girls, even though he carried his saxophone around the college campus not because he could play it, but rather as a ploy to attract the women he was desperate to know and who were more inclined to date musicians. He later admitted, 'I couldn't say the words of love to a girl face to face [so] I wrote them down in a note and [would] be halfway across campus before she could read it. I was not a ladies man.' And further,

> The funny thing about me was I was never a part of the in-crowd at college. And I was hopeless when it came to dating girls. The first time I saw Brenda Harvey,

who was to become my wife, she was marching as a majorette at a football game and I didn't even know how to go about asking her out. I [was] the guy who was too short to play basketball, too slow to run track and too short to play football.

(Yet, he had gained entrance to the Tuskegee Institute on a tennis scholarship.) Brenda Harvey was his third girlfriend, introduced to him by a mutual friend, but it took him three years to declare his love. As he said, 'I played it straight with no funny business. We fell in love before the hits, before the fame, before the fortune. She was there before the Commodores were known around the world, before anyone knew who I was.' However, when the group later became a Motown act, Brenda and the other group members' girlfriends were not involved, let alone discussed, because it was more productive to promote six hot-blooded guys who were single and available.

It was 1967 when budding guitarist Thomas McClary (born 6 October 1950) arrived from Florida and met Lionel Richie in a registration queue at Tuskegee Institute. 'I heard this guy whistling Eddie Harris's "Listen Here",' McClary remembered, 'and we started talking.' Richie, who boasted he was a saxophone player, introduced his new friend to his jamming pals — bass player and lead singer Railroad, drummer Andre Callaghan and trumpeter William King (born 30 January 1949), who was newly recruited from the Institute's marching band. Known as the Mystics they entered one of the Institute's talent contests, which in themselves were quite extraordinary. William King said of them,

> You go on stage and perform and it doesn't matter if you're good or not the audience throws things at you. If you're really excellent they may applaud you but somebody way in the back will throw something at you. We decided we were going to change things around and that it wouldn't be that way with us...We were going to get a standing ovation, to tear the house down.

Unfortunately, all his high hopes were dashed before the seven-piece group could actually perform their two rehearsed James Brown songs. 'When the curtains were pulled back only Callaghan and I were to be seen. Richie had left ... and Railroad had got scared and left too. Needless to say, it was not one of our better performances.'

Undeterred, the Mystics continued to play at school prom dates and college gigs until they encountered stiff competition from another high-flying Institute group known as the Jays, who had worked for two years and enjoyed a loyal local fan base. Keyboardist Milan Williams (born 28 March 1949) played with this unit and, of course, it was inevitable that the two groups would clash. An underhand tactic decided the fate of the groups, as McClary explained, 'I thought I had set up a secret meeting with the Jays to discuss the possibility of joining them, but when I got there, Lionel and

William were already in the basement. The Jays were trying to recruit them.' From the shambles a new group was actually formed with Lionel Richie and Jimmy Johnson on saxophone; William King on trumpet; a four-piece rhythm section of Thomas McClary playing guitar, Milan Williams on keyboards, Michael Gilbert, bass and lead vocals, and drummer Andre Callaghan. This appears to be the first unofficial line-up of the future international superband. Now they needed a name, and several were tossed around, including the Mighty Wonders, but nobody could agree. In actual fact, the competition between the membership was so intense that the new group very nearly disbanded because no decision could be reached! In sheer desperation they decided to choose a name by throwing a dictionary into the air and from whatever page was open when it landed, someone would 'blind pick' a word. 'It was "commodore",' said William King. 'It's an old navy rank from the old days: they don't use it any more. I guess we were lucky really because we could have ended up being anything. The "commode" was nearby! Can you imagine us coming out in paper tissue suits. And we were so headstrong that we had made up our minds to stick to whatever came down.'

The new band built up a solid reputation in and around the Tuskegee Institute, earning between $12 and $20 a night. On Tuesday nights they played nearby Montgomery, with gigs in Mississippi and New Orleans on other weeknights. Lionel Richie: 'We had a built-in energy source on campus. A lot of the groups break up because of the hassles on the road. We kind of germinated right there on campus.' Their local success prompted the Institute to send them to play at a benefit concert at New York's Town Hall, which was promoted by their future manager Benjamin Ashburn. An unusual combination of Harlem street politician and marketing genius, Ashburn had a master's degree in marketing from New York University, and headed his own public relations firm specializing in politics and products. After seeing the Commodores' performance he was pleasantly surprised with their raw professionalism and energetic mash-ups of R&B cover versions, but decided to bide his time before approaching them professionally. As fate would have it, Milan Williams would contact him a year later, in 1969.

As their confidence grew, the Commodores realized they had to branch out, away from their immediate locality. So, during the 1969 summer vacation they headed for 135th Street and 7th Avenue, in New York City, to a nightclub called Small's Paradise, where they told the owner Pete Smalls they wanted to perform in his club. 'He stood back and just stared at us,' recalled William King. 'We were all young, short-haired with those little waves that were fashionable at the time. We said to him, "Whatever you need, we got it." So he pointed to the door and said, "There you go, use it!"' While the guys were squaring up to an astonished club-owner, their stage gear and instruments were stolen from their van parked outside the venue. It was a well-used city scam of the time, with the stolen items later being returned at an inflated price. This amused William King: 'Because we would beat the hell out of the guy when he showed up, which he did some thirty minutes later. And he was six foot six tall and weighed two-twenty. Anyway, we got the majority of it back. This was our introduction to New York!' And the Commodores learned their lesson the hard way.

Staying in one room at the nearby YMCA on 135th Street, it took three days for the group to realize that all keys fitted all doors, when their clothes and what remained of their instruments were stolen. Stranded, with no money and no work, the Commodores were absolutely destitute in an unfriendly city which had shown them nothing but grief. They were on the verge of abandoning their dream when Milan Williams remembered Benjamin Ashburn, and persuaded him to visit them in their tacky YMCA room, where, incidentally, they had turned the bed lengthwise to enable them all to sleep on it. Taking pity on the downhearted group, Ashburn immediately offered them accommodation in his own apartment on 135th Street and Lenox Avenue. They remembered, 'We knew this guy had to be all right because he was willing to take us in and he didn't know us from Adam.' Not only that but he also persuaded Pete Smalls to give them a slot on his forthcoming Monday audition night. Many Tuskegee students lived in New York and the Commodores burned the phone wires begging them to bring themselves, families and friends to Small's Paradise to support their act. The ploy worked because, when the owner arrived at his club, he was greeted by hundreds of youngsters. William King recalled, 'It was one of those magical nights when everything went perfectly so Mr Smalls cancelled the act he had planned and kept us over for three weeks. It was our first bite.' Milan Williams said, 'What we did that night sold us to Benny Ashburn. We knocked his socks off and he agreed to manage us.' They were also earning money. According to Lionel Richie, 'I kept some...from that very first show and that's how I got the nickname "Jack Benny" after the comedian who was known for his miserly ways!'

From Small's Paradise, the Commodores moved to the Cheetah Club until the end of the summer, when another term at the Tuskegee Institute started. Although Benny Ashburn was not officially working with them, he did secure weekend club engagements which often meant eighteen-hundred-mile round trips. But such was their determination to succeed, the miles were immaterial and their tiredness was pushed aside once the first chord was struck at the start of their act.

Also in 1969 Benny Ashburn struck a deal with Jerry Williams at Cotillion Records, a subsidiary of Atlantic Records, for the Commodores to record an album. 'Swamp Dogg' Williams had visited Tuskegee but the only thing William King could remember was that 'he was wearing an all-green bright suit! Shoes, socks, pants, shirt and jacket – all lime green. And that shocked me!' Shocked or not, the Commodores recorded the Williams-produced single 'Keep On Dancing', an irresistible, tuneful song previously recorded by Alvin Cash. The B-side 'Rise Up' was reminiscent of the Bar-Kays' 'Soul Finger'. These tracks were lifted from an R&B album of cover versions spanning 1966 to 1968 like Johnnie Taylor's hit 'Who's Making Love', the Temptations' '(I Know) I'm Losing You', Sly & the Family Stone's 'Sing A Simple Song', and the Intruders' 'Cowboys To Girls'. 'We recorded everything at one time', recalled King. 'There were no overdubs or anything like that. At the time we thought that was the way to do it. We didn't know any better. Anyway, we were happy enough because we thought it was only an audition at first. That was our first experience in a recording studio.' Lionel Richie's memory was sketchy. 'I think we played all the songs for the audition at the Atlantic recording studios... "Keep On Dancing", that was the hit, or was at least what Atlantic put out. That's when Michael Gilbert was singing. We did a lot of stuff [and] this was the beginning of the Commodores, the very first group.' Although the single bombed and the album was shelved, the group promoted their work in Britain by performing at Ronnie Scott's Club in London's Soho district.

While the Commodores recorded seriously for the first time, the Beatles, whose career Lionel Richie had avidly followed since 1962, were on the verge of splitting up. Although 1969 wasn't their last year together, it signified their last joint recording session where two albums' worth of material was completed. It was also the year in which Paul McCartney married Linda Eastwood and John Lennon wed Yoko Ono, leaving George Harrison and Ringo Starr as the helpless spectators while the two couples argued constantly over the group's future. By the time the Commodores released their first single for Motown, the Beatles had been disbanded, with its membership pursuing solo careers, and John and Yoko had moved to New York to live.

Not only did the Commodores' recording career stop before it had started, but the group shuffled its membership. Michael Gilbert and Andre Callaghan were drafted into the army for the Vietnam War, while Jimmy Johnson left because he felt the group was a non-starter. The departing trio was replaced by bassist Ronald LaPread (born 4 September 1950) from the Tuskegee blues outfit the Corvettes, and Walter 'Clyde' Orange (born 10 December 1947), who had headed his own band, the J-Notes, in which he played drums and sang lead. He continued to do this in the Commodores until Lionel Richie stepped into the spotlight to sing his self-penned ballads. For now, though, he was relegated to the background to play his saxophone (which he did badly) and assist on vocals. He was also, apparently, the only group member who couldn't read music, so he memorized by heart the group's material. 'The Commodores needed a drummer and I needed a more dedicated band,' Clyde Orange said. 'Plus, I had a ten-piece drum set while their drummer had three.'

Thanks to regular rehearsals in Richie's grandmother's basement, the Commodores were soon the most popular group on campus, and what a mixed membership it was too! Lionel Richie was studying economics, while Clyde Orange (the only one who did not attend Tuskegee Institute as an undergraduate; he was a graduate of Alabama State University, with a Bachelor of Arts degree as a music major) studied business. Milan Williams and Ronald LaPread studied engineering; Thomas McClary and William King studied business management. While it's true to say the membership of the Commodores was accidental, their subsequent rise to fame was not. They plotted their career carefully and shrewdly in much the same way as a lawyer prepares a complex court case. Responsible for the mathematics of their plan, Richie said he felt more at home behind a calculator than a microphone because he believed the music business was a game of numbers. All he needed to find was the right combination. They drew up a seven-year management plan, based on William King's 200-page essay on the Beatles and what made them such a phenomenon, and, with Benny Ashburn, they formed the Commodores Entertainment Corporation. Music, management and personalities were considered to be the three most important aspects in an entertainer's world, and the Beatles successfully managed to blend all three. The Commodores therefore decided they had to develop the same camaraderie. According to King, 'It took a lot of head sessions to really get to know each other properly. I had to know if I loved or hated the guys and if it isn't love, we don't need to be in the same group together...You form a bond and that was what the group had from 1969 to 1974.' It was also at this time that Richie decided to tell his parents of his career move. His father was dumbstruck. 'I'm sitting there with an Afro, mile-high platform shoes, standing by five other guys in my second seminar of my senior school, "Dad, we want to take over the world." I can't even describe the words my father used. They were on another level!'

As the Commodores pursued their dream, their musical heroes, like Motown Records' Smokey Robinson and the Miracles, the Temptations, and the Supremes, were million-selling recording stars. Yet these, and other black groups, regularly failed miserably on the touring circuit because, as good as they were, they were unable to fill 25,000-seater stadiums on their own. Acts like the Beatles or Led Zeppelin could easily do so – and without a current hit single. This was an obstacle the Commodores intended to overcome, no matter how long it took. Meanwhile, Benny Ashburn beavered away securing them bookings where he could, including around Europe where – following performances on the SS *France* liner – they played at the Acu-Acu club near Cannes. Later on they became favourites at a resort club in St Tropez on the French Riviera. William King said, 'It did a lot for us because it let us know that we could bridge the gap. We were also playing for an older audience, so France was good for us.' Ed Sullivan, the American chat-show host, saw them perform in France and signed them for two appearances. Unfortunately, his programme was taken off air before this could happen, thus probably denying the Commodores a speedier transition to stardom.

Motown Records was the brainchild of Berry Gordy Jr, whose family had migrated from the South to Detroit in search of a better life. The seventh of eight children, Gordy attended Northeastern High School before becoming a professional boxer, a sport that attracted quick money. He then served in the Korean War and, upon returning to Detroit, worked at Ford's Mercury plant, earning $85 a week (good money at that time). In his spare time, Gordy wrote songs, some of which were recorded, but he yearned to open his own record company. Inspired by his friend William 'Smokey' Robinson, composer and lead singer of the Miracles, Berry Gordy borrowed money from his family in 1959 to purchase a property, 2648 West Grand Boulevard, Detroit, which became Hitsville USA, the Home of Young America. Against great odds, success came relatively quickly. In 1962 Gordy presented his first Motown Revue; his major acts toured the USA in a battered bus for three months, performing 94 dates. It was the simplest way to expose his artists and music, ultimately selling more records, and it was also to show mainstream America what was happening in Detroit. It was a good move because the tour not only sold records but gave Motown an identifiable image. It was also an eye-opener for many of the artists who had not previously travelled outside Detroit. For instance, they had their first encounters with the segregated South from which their parents had relocated to Detroit for a better way of life. In Alabama, following a show before a racially mixed audience, the artists were boarding their coach when gunshots rang out in their direction. Thankfully, nobody was injured this time.

As Britain was Motown's second biggest market, Berry Gordy sent a Revue to tour during March 1965, which included the Temptations, the Supremes, Martha and the Vandellas, the Miracles, Stevie Wonder, and Earl Van Dyke and the Soul Brothers. It was a financial disaster but did give audiences the chance to see the faces behind the music, and led to the British television show *The Sound of Motown*, organized and presented by Dusty Springfield, herself an enthusiastic fan and tireless promoter of the company's music. The tour also coincided with (and promoted) EMI Records introducing the Tamla Motown label, combining the names of two of Berry Gordy's American labels. Through EMI's international network, the product was available on Tamla Motown in most territories of the world except the USA, which, incidentally, was the only country not to use the new logo. The label's first single was the Supremes' 'Stop! In The Name Of Love' (TMG 501). Prior to this, selected Motown records had been released in Britain since 1959, the first being Marv Johnson's 'Come To Me' on the London-American label. In November 1961, Motown's releases switched to the Fontana label with the Marvelettes' 'Please Mr Postman', and during September 1962 the Oriole label issued its first Motown single, 'You Beat Me To The Punch', by the company's first lady of song, Mary Wells. Motown and Oriole stayed locked until September 1963 when Stateside (an EMI Records subsidiary) took over with Martha and the Vandellas' 'Heatwave' in October 1963. The Tamla Motown label was launched two years later. Not every record was successful, of course, but on average the TM outlet held its own, helping the company's climb to international success. As the music was no longer R&B/black/soul-based and aimed at a particular purist market, EMI Records could promote much of it as mainstream music, thereby making a profit and recouping its initial advances.

In the USA the hits continued. By 1966, three out of every four Motown releases were hits for artists like Mary Wells, Marv Johnson, the Marvelettes, Martha and the Vandellas, the Velvelettes and, of course, the three groups idolized by the Commodores. Motown was a hit factory and grew to be the largest independent record company in the world. It was a family-based company where everyone helped each other; secretaries became recording stars and successful groups provided backing vocalists for their struggling colleagues. As the Motown family grew, Berry Gordy hired composers and producers, notably Brian and Eddie Holland, and Lamont Dozier, who, with the studio musicians known as the Funk Brothers, were responsible for creating the glorious 'Motown Sound'. By hiring outsiders, competition within the ranks grew; Berry Gordy's demands for million-selling discs escalated, and the studios were in operation around the clock. Artists sang what they were given and the results were passed to the assigned producers and engineers to transform into hit records, after passing through Berry Gordy's Quality Control Department. If a particular song was rejected at this point, it was returned to the originators for an immediate re-working. This practice was still in operation when the Commodores joined Motown, and would, of course, be a wrangling point because they considered themselves to be a self-contained unit.

Meantime, from Tuskegee the fledgling Commodores once again had to hit the performing circuit of Boston, New York, through Virginia, the Carolinas, and along Interstate highways 75 and 85, before Benny Ashburn considered they were ready to be properly showcased in New York before an audience of record company people, publicity companies and anyone else who could be enticed to attend.

The audition was staged at Lloyd Price's Turntable Club on Broadway and 50th Street, and, as the group was still at Tuskegee Institute, they planned to set out the previous night for the seventeen-hour drive. When they reached Atlanta one of the van's tyres blew and was changed. A second tyre was then ripped into pieces and had to be replaced, while a third burst in Richmond, Virginia, leaving the travellers no choice but to push their van to a nearby petrol station. There a fleet of state troopers appeared from nowhere, screeched to a halt and surrounded them, demanding they stand arms up and legs astride against a nearby wall. It was explained that three black guys bearing an uncanny resemblance to three Commodores had robbed a bank and were on the run. Eventually it was sorted out; the state troopers sped off, leaving the shaken and tired Commodores, with their last $20 spent on yet another new tyre, to continue on their way. When they eventually reached the New Jersey Turnpike they had no cash to pay the toll, the needle on the petrol gauge was locked on zero, and they had been travelling for twenty-four long hours. Not the best start to one of the most important performances of their professional life!

Thankfully, their luck changed when a kindly attendant at the New Jersey Turnpike directed them to another, toll-free, road but they still had no petrol to continue their journey. Pushing their van to the nearest petrol station, they traded their instruments for petrol. As a last resort, Milan Williams phoned Benny Ashburn, who spoke to the station manager and somehow persuaded him to let them have not only the petrol and their instruments back, but money to get them to New York. Six hot, sweaty, hungry and extremely weary Commodores arrived thirty minutes late at Lloyd Price's Turntable Club. But once that first note was struck, they said, 'We smoked, man, we smoked!'

One member of the audience who clearly agreed with them was Motown's Suzanne de Passe.

> I was, at the time, Berry Gordy's creative assistant, and a friend of my mother's, by the name of Benny Ashburn, said, 'I have this group and I'm trying to get them a record deal.' What struck me more than anything else about the group was they were energetic and very versatile. This was a very special group of guys...We were about to take the Jackson 5 out on their first tour and we needed an opening act. The Commodores seemed perfect for that.' (BBC Radio 2, *The Lionel Richie Story*)

Lionel Richie told me, 'I think she was really amazed at how we ran our show, how we looked and how we performed. The whole thing. Because if anyone was [to be] instrumental in our success – and during our success – it was Suzanne, along with our manager, Benny.' After negotiating a mutually acceptable deal, the group went on to stay with the young Jackson boys for two and a half years, covering three major tours.

Raised in Gary, Indiana, the original members of the Jackson 5 were the three eldest sons of Joe Jackson, a steelworker and ex-member of the Falcons, namely, Jermaine, Jackie and Tito, and two cousins, who were later replaced by the two youngest Jackson brothers, Michael and Marlon. Groomed by their father to be entertainers, the young group won a prestigious talent show where eight-year-old Michael sang a version of the Temptations' 'My Girl'. This achievement led to club dates outside their locality and they began to build up a solid reputation. At one of their early professional gigs at Mr Lucky's, a local nightclub, Keith Gordon, owner of a Gary-based recording studio, offered them a recording deal. This led to a late-1967 single 'Big Boy' being released on the Steeltown label; it sold well enough for a second release 'Some Girls Want Me For Love' in 1968. During the brothers' appearance at Chicago's Regal nightclub they were spotted by Motown artist Bobby Taylor (of the Vancouvers), who was sufficiently impressed with their high-octane act to recommend them to Berry Gordy. He shared the enthusiasm, called them the Jackson 5 and took a personal interest in their career. He desperately needed the brothers to succeed, so he assigned them to a newly formed writing/producing unit called the Corporation. When the time came to present his young protégés to the world he used his superstar Diana Ross to showcase them at a gala party held at the Daisy, one of the more chic nighteries in Beverly Hills, before introducing them to television viewers on her *Hollywood Palace Show*. Declaring she had also discovered the brothers, Motown played the promotional game by using her name on their debut album, *Diana Ross Presents The Jackson 5*. An angry Michael Jackson observed years later, 'Motown decided to use Diana Ross's name to introduce us to the public. But she never discovered us. We were an established professional act before we ever signed to Motown!' The album spawned their first million-seller 'I Want You Back' in 1970, and heralded the beginning of J5-mania the world over, which would monopolize the 1970s in the same way as the Beatles had dominated the 1960s. Never before in the history of Berry Gordy's company had an act made such a huge impact on the world. The rest is HIStory.

The first tour with the Commodores as support act kicked off in 1970, when Motown celebrated its tenth anniversary and as the Jackson 5 were riding high on a trio of American chart-toppers – 'I Want You Back', 'ABC' and 'The Love You Save'. It was, of course, the Commodores' first glimpse of living in the fast lane, of experiencing the way Motown worked, and it was a lesson they'd never forget, as William King explained:

> It was the first time we had seen showbusiness at its best, not only on stage but backstage too. We learned the importance of being on time, for example, and in having the right people working for us. A person may not do the job exactly right at first but if he has the spirit and love inside him to aim for better things, he is more use to you that the guy who has the ability but won't put himself out for you. Everything is relative to everything else but we looked at things differently after that first tour.

According to Lionel Richie, 'Motown trained their acts in a kind of discipline and it paid off. You'd never hear anyone say anything about their acts not showing up or being late. The whole experience of being around the Jacksons and Motown affected me a great deal in the way I related to myself as a professional entertainer.' The tour's opening night also stayed in Richie's mind, as he further explained:

> We had a Commodores meeting, and we decided to lighten up and not do a hard set. We played a couple of warm-up numbers and did a few good tunes, nothing spectacular. We didn't want to embarrass the Jacksons! We came offstage and here was little Michael running around playing pattycake and pinching people. Then the stage darkened and the lights came back on, and there was this same little kid tearing the place down! So, the Commodores had another meeting that night because the kids killed us, and we had to pull out all the stops to compete.

To be fair, the Commodores were hardly known outside Tuskegee and, unlike the Jackson 5, didn't have the music catalogue to pull from. To compensate they performed their versions of other people's hits like the Temptations' 'Cloud Nine', Three Dog Night's 'Liar' and Glen Campbell's 'Wichita Lineman', with Richie on lead vocals. Hardly riveting stuff but educational nonetheless, as Clyde Orange, hidden behind his drum kit, remembered.

> We learned how to play in front of thousands of people dancing around and blowing them away. By the time we did our first headlining tour with KC & the Sunshine Band opening for us, we had arena performing down cold. Our slogan was 'Once you've been exposed to the Commodores, you'll refuse to accept anything less than the best.'

William King said,

> I have never seen an act to visually better the Jackson 5. When Michael hit that stage, he was not a little boy. He was a superstar. Marlon, Jackie, Tito and Jermaine were all supporting him and they were stars too. No matter how hard we worked or how good a show we put on, they always topped us.

With this in mind, Clyde Orange admitted his group needed a focal point, someone to work the audience, and the only one who was not indispensable as a musician was Lionel Richie. 'So, we said, "Richie, since you stand in the centre of the stage, you've got to sing." He'd say, "No, man, I'm a horn player." We talked him into doing two songs. Ronald and I would do the rest.' He was bullied into submission. 'They really pushed me. Pick up that microphone. Go over and kiss the girl. "But I don't know her," I'd say. "Just do it." I'd get a scream, so they'd say, "Do another one". So I developed all of my skills from the guys pushing me out there.'

The second Jackson 5 tour spanned 42 days from July to September 1971, with stadium performances from Hawaii to New York. Jacksonmania was at its dizzy height, capturing the imagination, love and money of America's youth. The tours were total mayhem, but exciting and thrilling beyond words, as the J5 touring circus rolled in and out of theatres, causing unimaginable havoc, winding its way around the USA. At this juncture, Lionel Richie admitted he was a member of the Commodores 'just for the fun of it' and certainly was not contemplating a lasting career in music. However, he was literally shocked into changing his mind when he saw first-hand the financial rewards of a hit-making touring group.

> When the Jackson 5 picked up a cheque for about $180,000 it didn't take me long to decide that I should take this career seriously. I majored in economics and I knew how long it would take me to earn that kind of money as an accountant – too long! Madison Square Garden was the turning-point. I remember standing with Michael Jackson at the corner of the stage and peeking out from behind the curtain at the crowd. Michael looked at me and said, 'We've sold out Madison Square Garden.' Just the two of us – the Jackson 5 and the Commodores. And all I could say was 'yeh'.

Of course, Richie was aware it wasn't the Commodores who had sold out the world-famous stadium, but he was touched by Michael's unselfish generosity. It was moments like this that led to them enjoying a future lasting friendship. Amid the frenzied and unprecedented success of this tour, there was one aspect that continued to vex Michael. 'I wish we could finish a show and not have to leave before the end because of the crowds rushing to the stage. We have a real good ending but we never get the chance to do it!'

As well as being able to promote themselves before huge audiences – an incredible opportunity for an untested band – Lionel Richie, on behalf of the Commodores, networked with music business personnel, publicists, managers and so on. He grabbed every opportunity to converse with Motown personnel who mingled and served, while enjoying the luxury of touring with a successful group. It worked both ways because the

Commodores were also being watched and listened to, with their music being honed more towards the current R&B/funk vein made popular by groups like the Ohio Players – using a solid, heavy bass, sporadic horns, wah-wah guitars, which often mirrored the work George Clinton had forged with Funkadelic. To date Motown hadn't become involved in this type of music but felt the Commodores could possibly spearhead the move on their behalf. So, it was with this in mind that in the spring of 1971, six young men from the Tuskegee Institute were invited to become a Motown act. It would be a further year before they released a single.

# 2 machine gun

'The joke at Motown got to be "OK, Commodores, we've reached the end of the roster, now it's your turn."'   Lionel Richie

'I said I'd like to put Lionel behind the microphone.'   Gloria Jones, writer/producer

'It's as drippy as you might imagine.'   A reviewer about Lionel Richie's first composition

Motown may have taken the motor city's name, but the company had outgrown its Detroit roots. With its numerous subsidiary labels like Tamla, Soul, VIP, Motown and so on, Berry Gordy was richer than he could have anticipated. Between 1968 and 1970 he, as sole company shareholder, earned over $5 million in dividends. Not only did the recording side of Motown generate vast sums of money but so did its management company, Grapevine Advertising, and Jobete, the in-house publishing arm to which most of Gordy's composers were signed to a fee-paying deal. Artists like Marvin Gaye, whose international chart-topper 'I Heard It Through The Grapevine' transformed him into an A-list performer, the Marvelettes, Stevie Wonder, Smokey Robinson and the Miracles, the Temptations, Gladys Knight and the Pips, all continued to fly the Motown flag, while new signings or one-hit wonders came and went. One major upheaval suffered by Motown was Diana Ross leaving the Supremes, although the move had been planned several years earlier. Fans were devastated; it was the end of a musical era that had covered 28 US hits (including three with the Temptations), sell-out tours, international stardom and all the trappings of a luxurious lifestyle.

Berry Gordy desperately wanted to expand into television and films, but being unable to do so from Detroit began transferring the Motown offices to Los Angeles in 1970. His company moved into executive offices at 6255 Sunset Boulevard, where a new television wing, Motown Productions Inc, was opened alongside a new recording studio. Gordy had already opened a West Coast office during 1967 but now had an effective East Coast/West Coast operation. However, Detroit still played an integral part in his company's operation, because at least three-quarters of its records were cut there in two large studios. In his determination to join the movie mogul set, Gordy intended to push his artists into films, and while the industry dwindled in Hollywood, television investment and video cassette software peaked in Los Angeles. Motown's production wing immediately went into action to store up video tapes of artists' performances, particularly those featured on television, plus tapes of acts in the studio, on location and at concerts, in order to assemble an extensive library. As Motown was expanding into an entertainment complex, what of the music? The raw rhythms and scratchy vocals of the Detroit Sound gave way to a sophisticated, up-market style: white music for the mass market which, on most occasions, lacked the depth and natural feel of the Detroit sessions. This was a time of change and transition for the Motown Sound, and it lost many fans as well as gaining new converts.

For the Detroit-based artists the company's move was devastating. By 1972 a few had relocated to Los Angeles, leaving the remainder to face the same situation they were in during the 1960s, stranded in Detroit looking for a recording deal. The move, too, was a spiritual blow for the city's black community, since Motown symbolized black success. Producer/writer Hank Cosby felt Motown lost its whole creative structure when it moved west.

> They had to change the whole thing and their costs zoomed way up. When they were in Detroit they were able to do business at a very moderate rate. In LA everything skyrocketed and it never came down again. In Detroit we had our own little village, but what we really had then was a warm feeling and when it became a big corporation that feeling had to go.

'When Motown moved away it left most of their business behind in a right state and there was no one for me to speak to,' recalled Martha Reeves. 'I wasn't asked to go along with them so I felt I owed them nothing. They didn't seem that bothered with the way I felt. I loved being with Motown and they'll always be a part of me, but I felt disheartened in the way they treated me towards the end.' When Reeves later managed to ask Berry Gordy what her future held, he refused to give her a straight answer.

> He told me something about self-contained groups like his latest discovery the Commodores, and a lot of new acts. He then promised to call me real soon...little did I know I had officially left Motown. The man who was once my hero had turned his back on me.

Likewise with his musicians, who were the company's very backbone, responsible for creating that glorious Motown Sound. They were also the last to know of Motown's move, noted percussionist James Jamerson, who with three other musicians turned up for work one day to find the Detroit studio was closed down. 'Even people who didn't work there felt like they had been stripped of a precious jewel that gave the city a special flair. Motown was Detroit's child and was supported by the entire city. Its closing sent shockwaves around the country.'

Despite its move, however, Motown's business was booming, with hit singles from Gladys Knight and the Pips – 'Didn't You Know (You'd Have To Cry Sometime)', 'The Nitty Gritty', 'Friendship Train' and the Grammy Award-winning 'If I Were Your Woman', written by Pam Sawyer and Gloria Jones, who would become instrumental in the Commodores' early Motown recordings; Jr Walker and the All Stars had 'What Does It Take (To Win Your Love)', which happily marked the start of a new career for the 1960s sax man, while new signing Yvonne Fair was behind one of Motown's raunchiest albums, *The Bitch Is Black*. Ex-Temptation Eddie Kendricks recorded his aptly titled first album *All By Myself*, and Smokey Robinson worked with Marvelette Wanda Rogers on a solo album, shrewdly released under the title *The Return Of The Marvelettes*. Established acts continued to play their part in ensuring Motown remained the top-selling black company, while the company itself branched out further with more subsidiary labels catering for different musical styles because, for instance, a country and western song would not be accepted by the media and record-buying public on the Tamla or Soul labels. Also, with more labels Motown was guaranteed more radio airplay and press exposure.

As the company moved into its second decade songwriters and producers took on an even more vital role within the company structure, as did the introduction of the new labels. It seemed logical, therefore, that when Berry Gordy moved to Los Angeles, a new label be introduced. Mowest – an abbreviation for Motown/West Coast – was opened to cater for records emanating from the Los Angeles nerve-centre; the music was commercial and introduced both new acts and seasoned performers to a curious public. The label opened in Britain nine months after the first US release, issuing the Devastating Affair's 'I Want To Be Humble' in January 1972, with a launch party at Ronnie Scott's Club in London, where new signing Thelma Houston was guest of honour. 'What The World Needs Now Is Love – Abraham Martin And John' was the new label's first US number-one title. The brainchild of radio DJ Tom Clay, who assembled material that would 'get across the idea of what we needed was love even though we were up to our armpits in hate, war and killing', the single sold over three million copies but its follow-up 'Whatever Happened To Love' didn't: then it was a case of whatever happened to Tom Clay!

'When we signed to Motown, we were number fifty-eight on its roster,' Lionel Richie told Joe Smith in an interview.

> In front of us you had the Temptations, Supremes, Gladys Knight and the Pips. When we got ready to do our recording session, we were bumped because the

Temptations had priority over us. Over the next two years, acts started leaving Motown one by one. The joke at Motown got to be 'OK, Commodores, we've reached the end of the roster, now it's your turn'.

The time wasn't wasted on Richie, though, because he discovered a talent for songwriting, and watched and learned from the masters like Holland, Dozier and Holland, and Norman Whitfield, who was steering the Temptations into the expanding psychedelic market with 'Cloud Nine' and 'Papa Was A Rolling Stone', a new and exciting adventure for a group who excelled in tight harmonies and masses of sweet-talking vocals. Richie also remembered, in a *Blues & Soul* interview,

> We did some work with Norman Whitfield [but] not a whole album. That's why nobody has heard it and we'd probably have to go back and do some patching here and there. But there definitely is an album sitting there. Norman is amazing, [he] was just the best teacher in the whole world. He taught me how to sit down with no pad, no pencil, no nothing and write a song, just hum it. Just hum the frigging song...I also watched Berry Gordy dub Diana Ross on a Marvin Gaye record, and it gave me the opportunity to study what these people were doing. When they finally asked me, 'What do you have in the way of material?', I had two years' worth.

William King remembered working with various producers like Jeffrey Bowen, Willie Hutch and Hal Davis, but nothing gelled. In simple terms, the Commodores wanted to record and produce music that was alien to Motown's hit-making staffers.

> Motown had a set pattern they followed whereby they cut the tracks and you just go into the booth and sing what they tell you and in the way they tell you. That was the Motown sound and it had worked for the Temptations and the Supremes and all of the other groups. But we didn't want to do it that way; we didn't want to just sing on a track that had been cut for the Jackson 5. That's not us.

Following the release of Thelma Houston's 'No-one's Gonna Be A Fool Forever', the Commodores finally debuted on the Mowest label with 'The Zoo (The Human Zoo)' in March 1972 with the intention of infiltrating the new funk market that had grown within the American R&B faction. It was written and produced by company staffers Pam Sawyer and Gloria Jones, about whom William King raved,

> Boy, were they crazy – two of the wildest ladies I have met in my entire life but I am so glad that I was able to meet them. They were always happy. Everything was always up with them and there was never a dull moment. Even if you sang a wrong note, they'd put it to you in such a way that you didn't feel you were being downed. I would not have missed working with them for the world.

Wild lady and widely talented Gloria Jones told Adam White,

The talent was always there. They were from the south and here they were in Hollywood. They had this rawness, this freshness and energy that was just amazing. They were actually a band that could perform right there in the studio. Walter was doing all of the lead vocals so I suggested to Suzanne de Passe that I wanted to change the sound. I said I'd like to put Lionel behind the microphone. (*The Billboard Book of Number One Hits*)

With traces of (the group) War's fusion of R&B, rock splashed with funk, 'The Zoo (The Human Zoo)' failed to attract record buyers; it was released in Britain not on the Mowest label but much later on the mainstream subsidiary, in November 1974, and was their second single to reach the top fifty. EMI Records' international network of countries followed the British move, although the different territories could, at any time, request for release a single more suited to its home market. By and large, though, they and Britain would follow America's lead.

An early 1973 pose of Lionel Richie, whose only ambition at this time was to have a hit single. Little did he know what the future held!

In the USA a second Mowest single, a Tom Baird production titled 'Don't You Be Worried', followed early in 1973, while their third, 'Are You Happy', was their first on the Motown proper label in April 1973, with 'There's A Song In My Heart' as the B-side, which was also the flipside to the May 1974 release 'Machine Gun'. More importantly at this stage in the group's career, 'There's A Song In My Heart' was Lionel Richie's first composition to be recorded, resulting from a session with Terry Woodford and Clayton Ivey. However, as the song didn't represent the group's intended sound, it was relegated to a flipside, prompting one reviewer to write, 'It's as drippy as you might imagine.' Richie wasn't happy either: 'The sounds that we were making just weren't us. Motown knew they didn't have any acts comparable to folks like Earth, Wind & Fire who were just starting out at the time and they simply didn't know what to do with us.' Milan Williams said, 'Something had to happen 'cos if we couldn't come up with a way to continue at Motown, I personally thought we were going to be dropped.' On the upside, though, he enthused about his early company memories, calling it the University of Motown. 'There was Marvin Gaye at one end of the hall, Stevie Wonder at the other and Smokey Robinson wandering out of reception. All of them walking with pen and paper in hand. It was incredible...surrounded by all those people, it was a great place to polish your craft.' Further, 'It was a family, but it was also rivalry. In other words, one brother makes it and the other brother has to say, "I can do that and I'm gonna do better than you".'

As 'Are You Happy' disappeared without trace, hopes were raised when a fiery little instrumental 'Machine Gun' was issued in April 1974, in between releases by Yvonne Fair and the Jackson 5. Originally titled 'The Ram' and written by Milan Williams, the song zipped from R&B into mainstream funk to chart in the US top thirty, earning the Commodores their first gold disc, while in Britain it soared into the top twenty. The song was the result of Suzanne de Passe introducing the Commodores to Alabama-born James Anthony Carmichael, who had previously produced Gladys Knight and the Pips and had worked as arranger on the Jackson 5's recordings. It was intended to restore the Commodores' faith in Motown, but the meeting of minds clashed angrily. Lionel Richie's most vivid flashback was when Carmichael screamed at them to turn down their music. They played louder. 'Our amps were turned up to twelve and the windows started to rattle. Those windows at Motown were definitely not supposed to rattle!' he told David Nathan.

> James was having a fit, grabbing his coat, ready to walk out, saying 'Gentlemen, gentlemen, my career!' ...James was this real conservative guy – neat shirt, pressed pants and all – and we were jeans and sneakers, funky and 'down home'. We played him some records by The Ohio Players and Earth, Wind & Fire, so

he'd get some understanding of what we were trying to do. But, he shook his head and told us 'Motown will never accept this kind of music.' So we kept working with him until he saw that it was possible to sell the company our sound. (*Lionel Richie: An Illustrated Biography*)

'I felt like I deserved better,' James Carmichael told Steven Ivory.

> I didn't have anything against the guys, but I'd paid my dues at Motown. I was hoping to work with someone like Diana Ross. The Commodores? The guys opening for the Jackson kids? It just didn't seem fair...They thought I understood self-contained groups. They needed someone in with the Commodores who understood [them] as well as the art of making a commercial record. (*Can't Slow Down*, CD notes)

Milan Williams had actually written 'Machine Gun' with lyrics but Carmichael insisted it be recorded as an instrumental because Williams had created perfect funk music with its biting rhythm. 'It was cutting edge so to speak,' he said at the time. 'We used the synth to carry the melody and we also used the clavinet as the basic and most dominant rhythm instrument. It was a new sound.' He called in Calvin Harris, nicknamed 'Razor Black', who had worked as engineer in the Detroit studios, to assist the single's recording sessions. That one-off situation led to a long-term relationship with the group. 'These were great sessions, always packed with people, particularly women. The Commodores liked working with an audience in the control room while they performed. They would start late in the afternoon and go into the wee hours. Their songs tended to run long!' The 'Machine Gun' session lasted three days, an experience that educated Lionel Richie, for whom the recording side of the business was uncharted territory. 'I thought we just went into the studio, turned up the amps, played, sang and that was it. I found out that there was a lot more to it than that.' 'Machine Gun' was a single that also stuck in Berry Gordy's mind, as he remarked upon his introduction to it in his memoirs *To Be Loved*:

> Piggy-backing this brand new group on tour to open for the Jackson 5, we gave them great exposure even before they had a hit. The story about their first record success began in the least likely of all places – on the island of St Maarten, where I had gone to play in a backgammon tournament and to sneak a long overdue vacation. In my party was Suzanne de Passe, who wasted no time in promoting the new group.

She insisted her boss hear one song which she chanced to have with her on tape, an instrumental called 'The Ram'. Gordy had never favoured instrumentals and was reluctant to release it. However, when he realized he had little choice, he instructed her to change the title. 'It doesn't sound like a ram to me. Those darting sounds remind me of gunshots. Why not call it "Machine Gun"?'

The runaway success of the record spread across North America, Africa and South America, but the group whined it did little to promote their name because it was an instrumental. They decreed its follow-up would have lyrics, but meantime Motown capitalized on its unexpected good fortune by releasing the *Machine Gun* album. Not having any newly recorded material, the producers resurrected tracks from numerous recording sessions, including some from the aborted Mowest album, to release this pot-pourri of music in July 1974, the same month as company heavyweight Stevie Wonder's Grammy-winning *Fulfillingness' First Finale* and following *Marvin Gaye Live!*. With high hopes of good, steady sales, the *Machine Gun* album was released in Britain in September 1974 and, surprisingly, died without trace. The clavinet-led instrumental title track kicked off an album of varying sounds but did include eight Commodores compositions, including two by Lionel Richie – 'Superman' (the next British single) and the twice-used 'There's A Song In My Heart'. 'Rapid Fire', similarly slanted towards the title track, was outpaced by 'Young Girls Are My Weakness' and 'The Bump' boasted a main riff that could easily have been swiped from "Flashlight" by the Parliaments. With its chunky funk and Milan Williams breaking through on the keyboards, Clyde Orange held the beat with his compulsive drumming. Taken as a whole, the album was energetic, vital and, in spite of the musical variance, commanded regular listening. Not many people in the western world did listen; however, it passed gold status in Japan and Nigeria, where, following the national anthem,

One of the Commodores' first publicity shots, used as the front cover for *Machine Gun*, released in 1974 (Lionel Richie, middle/foreground).

'Machine Gun' was played as the 'close-down' track on the country's radio and television networks. It made sense to cash in on this unexpected (and somewhat peculiar) success, so the Commodores toured the Far East for the first time, performing in Japan and playing to 40,000 people in Manila alone. 'It's funny, they don't know the lyrics to much of what we're singing, but nevertheless the people all sing along and they're so warm. It really is fantastic!' raved Thomas McClary at the time.

'I Feel Sanctified' followed 'Machine Gun' in October 1974; its British release was March 1975, and it sank without trace, prompting William King to say, 'We knew we couldn't duplicate "Machine Gun" because it was one of a kind. The problem with "Sanctified" was that it was too R&B and didn't do well on the pop charts. We hadn't planned it that way because we wanted to solidify ourselves in the R&B market first.' This failure didn't prevent the release of the group's second album, *Caught In The Act*, in February 1975 (and three months later in Britain). Greeted as Motown's only significant donation to the funk market, the album was regarded in some quarters as the best album the Ohio Players didn't record! Illustrating changing styles, it was hard to judge at this time whether the public preferred another hard-hitting, frenetic, non-stop funk set, or a change of pace, slipping into the slow lane. Sure, 'Slippery When Wet', 'Wide Open' and 'I'm Ready' represented their recognizable sound, while Lionel Richie tested a different market by shifting gear with 'Let's Do It Right' and 'This Is Your Life', a slow, drawling ballad. Generally speaking then, *Caught In The Act* offered more than the one-tiered *Machine Gun*. Because of its wider potential, increased sales were expected – and achieved, when the album passed gold status to peak in the US top thirty. Not so in Britain and Europe, alas.

Next out was 'Slippery When Wet' in April 1975, and two months later in Britain, which not only topped the US R&B chart, replacing the O'Jays' 'Give The People What They Want' and holding off Van McCoy's monster dance track 'The Hustle', but crossed over into the mainstream listing to peak in the US top thirty. It went on to win the Bronze Award at the 1975 Tokyo Music Festival, indicating the group's growing popularity in Japan. In August, the poor-selling 'This Is Your Life', displaying Richie's balladeer composing talent, was US-released only. Motown/UK preferred the deep-throated, old Sly & the Family Stone take, 'Let's Do It Right', which, unfortunately, they didn't. It bombed. Promotional copies of their next outing 'Wide Open' were distributed to radio stations for preview purposes. When the reaction was lukewarm, the single was pulled. Meanwhile, the Commodores headlined their first US tour, before supporting the Rolling Stones on the 1975 US leg of their world tour. Lionel Richie was keen to perform before the British group's audiences to determine whether their music would be accepted by mainstream/rock fans.

> The first night we did two shows with them in Philadelphia. Working with the Rolling Stones was like working with the Jackson 5 in one respect. The people had come to see them, and not us. They wanted to see Mick Jagger and the Rolling Stones, and whoever else was on was just killing time. As with the Jackson 5, it took us two shows to realize what was happening and we came back with what the people wanted. We took the ten top songs of the day and packed them into one forty-minute show. Our reviews were fantastic. On the second night Mick Jagger asked us to stay on the tour with them, and then go back to Europe and do that tour. But we didn't feel it was the right time to do it. We wanted to substantiate ourselves in America, first. (*B&S*)

The Commodores' stage act was designed to exemplify the energy ploughed into their recordings because, as Richie went on to explain,

> Both things are important. The music itself and the visual effect it gives. Each compliments the other in terms of records and appearances, and we try to base a new show on each album we do. We feel it's necessary to really give a good show because people are paying their money to hear what they've bought on record. In fact, we want to give people more than what they want! (*ibid.*)

Eight months after *Caught In The Act*, a third album was released, with a November 1975 release date in Britain and throughout EMI Records' territory. Titled *Movin On*, it did just that by storming into the US top thirty. 'We intended that our lyrical content got heavier,' William King explained in 1975. 'And with each successive set, we're moving up another rung on the ladder into the direction we want to go.' *Blues & Soul*'s reviewer noted,

> The album kicks off with 'Hold On', a funky rhythm item that has the same flavour as 'Slippery When Wet'. Then it's into 'Free', a multi-rhythm-ed item that's typically Commodores, [and] back into that guitar fronted funk for 'Mary Mary' before side one phases out on the unusual marathon cut 'Sweet Love' – basically a ballad but the group utilizes several tempos and rhythm patterns. '(Can I) Get A Witness', another brash, brassy rhythm item that typifies the group and the same pattern is retained for 'Gimme My Mule', a pulsating chant. 'Time' is another basic ballad that's built around several rhythm patterns before the album closes on its only instrumental 'Cebu', an interesting and haunting mid temp track.

Once again all tracks were penned by the group and although the album rose no higher than the top thirty in the USA, it represented their changing fortunes. Within Motown's walls they were being hailed as one of the most successful company teams to secure themselves a niche in the funk/R&B market, against heavy competition from the likes of the rapidly rising Kool & the Gang, formed in Jersey City in 1964 by bass player Robert 'Kool'

Bell and signed to De-Lite Records. This was an achievement for a relatively new Motown group, but it wasn't enough for its impatient membership. They craved total independence as a recording unit followed by world acceptance. Unbeknown to them, the time was fast approaching when the next phase of their detailed game plan was due. However, their first move was to expand their musical direction, because being known as a black R&B/funk act was limiting in terms of promotion, public exposure, and those all-important record sales, which in turn led to packed arena performances. William King was aware of the dilemma.

> It's very hard to break away from that stereotype situation. We have played to many predominantly white audiences at colleges, even before we began recording. But it's getting the airplay and recognition that can be a problem. What we want to do is ease our audiences down into the more mellow music.

And this they did with the Lionel Richie composition 'Sweet Love'.

# 3 three times a lady

'Why should we have to sell 800,000 copies in the R&B chart before we get accepted as pop?'    Milan Williams in 1976

'So long as they can stand up and talk, that's fine by me.'    William King, on his choice of women

'It seems the whole world really does love it, and it's a great feeling.'    Lionel Richie, of 'Three Times A Lady'

Although they were now established Motown artists and recognizable record sellers, not many people realized the Commodores were still students at Tuskegee University and regularly returned there to complete their degree courses. While they toured, they studied. It was a clash of the arts, but as none of them wanted to abandon their studies, this was their lifestyle until graduation day arrived. By the time their next single was slotted for release in 1975, Diana Ross had starred as Billie Holiday in her first full-length movie *Lady Sings the Blues*. She was nominated for the 'Best Actress' Oscar, but lost out to Liza Minelli for her role in *Cabaret*. Smokey Robinson had left the Miracles to pursue a solo career, and the Jackson 5 were contemplating leaving Motown for CBS Records. This was also the time when the disco explosion was bubbling with an assault on the charts, involving artists like Gloria Gaynor, Silver Convention, KC and the Sunshine Band, the Tymes, and Disco-Tex and the Sex-O-Lettes. Motown's British strength was poor, with Stevie Wonder and Syreeta being their only charting acts, while in the USA Wonder was their only crossover top-ten act, until Diana Ross released the title track from her second movie *Mahogany* towards the end of 1975. An abysmal showing for the top black independent record company. But help was at hand from the Commodores.

'"Sweet Love" talked about so vividly how we shouldn't only have love for the person that you're with, but for the world as a whole society,' William King pointed out. 'A way that's very simple and uncomplicated for us all to get along. The lyric content was just so pure.' Released as a single in November 1975 and pressed in yellow vinyl to promote sales (British release was in January 1976), 'Sweet Love' also signified its composer finally marrying his college girlfriend Brenda Harvey, a commitment he intended to take seriously, although, he admitted to David Nathan, the early days weren't exactly wedded bliss.

> We went through every kind of change together; some good, some painful. I was this young kid, with stars in my eyes, ready to conquer the world. And it wasn't easy living with this guy who doesn't have time to spend with you because he might be in New York or Paris at any moment. (*Lionel Richie: An Illustrated Biography*)

When he returned from a touring stint, the singer admitted he often misread signs and situations because all he wanted to do was relax. Brenda, on the other hand, had stayed at home during his absences and wanted to do other things, like go on holiday. 'I did a lot of things wrong,' he sighed. But he pledged total faithfulness always, resisting the temptations offered by the hundreds of willing groupies who shadowed the group on tour. 'If a girl came up to me and said, "I want you to take me to bed," I couldn't go through with it. That's the kind of guy I am. I wasn't interested in disrespecting Brenda or the vows I had taken.' He was destined years later to change his mind.

Peaking in the top five in the USA, 'Sweet Love' was Lionel Richie's first serious step into solo recognition with his highly distinctive voice and styling. Although he continued to play the saxophone and split lead vocals with Clyde Orange, the song signified the start of the group's funkless material. The musical changeover that Thomas McClary had previously spoken of to the press was happening, they were leaving behind solid R&B/funk fans who would not accept their commercial slanting towards blue-eyed soul. The withdrawn 'Come Inside'/'Time' single made way for the release of 'High On Sunshine' in Britain only, where, surprisingly, 'Sweet Love' bombed, while both territories agreed on the next title, 'Just To Be Close To You' in late 1976. The beautifully conceived and executed ballad was a top-ten US charter and top seventy in Britain, which prompted Motown/UK to be silently confident they could break the Commodores, thereby recouping some of their promotion expenses to date. To capitalize on the single's success, the group was the O'Jays' special guests on a nationwide trek from February to April 1976, which took them to venues not previously visited. The exhausting 64-date tour was sold out, cementing both groups' growing popularity but this was more likely in response to the O'Jays' past hits like 'Back Stabbers', 'Love Train', 'Put Your Hands Together' and the current 'Give The People What They Want', issued via Philadelphia International Records, one of Motown's fiercest competitors in the black music field. However, the tour paved the way for the Commodores' 1976 album *Hot On The Tracks*; British release was in July 1976.

With a dull, incongruous album sleeve – the wheels of a locomotive – one wondered whether the music within was better or worse than the artist's imagination! Lionel Richie took it upon himself to fend off criticism about the album's artwork. 'If we'd had it our way, every sleeve would have been different, but then we can't do everything and we've had to rely on others to take care of some things.' Even more worryingly, he often didn't see the sleeve concept before the album was released, yet pointed out he had no real argument with Motown about this, rather the opposite.

> Our relationship couldn't be better and I wouldn't like them to think we're complaining behind their back. That's the way they honestly felt we would be best represented and we have no complaints. It's been a learning process for us and Motown, and we've both come out of it just fine – and it's the place we'd like to be for the rest of our career.

Motown historian Dave Godin was delighted with *Hot On The Tracks*:

> Not just the brilliant 'Just To Be Close To You' but the whole of this elpee sets a standard of excellence that makes the Commodores a name to be reckoned with. But let's not forget that setting those standards is a habit with Motown and this is exceptional. Perhaps *Right On The Tracks* would have been a more appropriate title. (*B&S*)

It was possibly the best album to date to highlight the individual group members as composers, and the first to feature four Lionel Richie-penned tracks. A raving slice of disco, 'Let's Get Started', invited listeners into the album, only to be defused by a slower-paced 'Girl, I Think The World About You', considered to be Richie's finest track with the group so far, with its tempo change towards the close, coupled with cool vocals adding that extra sparkle. Where other acts may be content to leave the musical backdrop to chug along, the Commodores added a guitar riff, or a delicate touch of the synthesizer, and it is this attention to detail that made them a cut above the competition. A chat-introduction led into 'Just To Be Close To You', while Motown's listening recommendations were 'High On Sunshine' and 'Fancy Dancer' – funky, brassy, with the slickness controlled. 'Thumpin' Music', 'Come Inside', 'Quickdraw' and 'Can't Let You Tease Me' supported the group sound that remained excitingly vibrant and crammed with carefree enthusiasm. And it was this that took the album to number 12 in the US chart. Prior to its British release, Motown tested the market with 'High On Sunshine'; it sold poorly, not an encouraging basis on which to issue its vinyl mother. Nonetheless, the company had no choice and swallowed the abysmal sales.

'Just To Be Close To You', the album's highlight, was then released, to top the US R&B chart and shoot into its mainstream top ten. British release was during October 1976, and when reissued in November 1978 the single was a disappointing top-seventy hit. The soft sweet ballad, written and performed by Lionel Richie, set the group's tone for the next five years at least. Melody replaced funk, but with the musical changeover the Commodores lost and/or abandoned their R&B audience who had been so loyal from the outset. The ballads were later classed as a middle-of-the-road product but, for the time being, Motown attempted to market it under mainstream music. The ploy failed because the single was banned from American pop radio stations for being 'too black'. 'If that was too black to be played on a pop station, then how the hell did it get to number seven in the national chart?' moaned Milan Williams in 1976. 'Why should we have to sell 800,000 copies at number one in the R&B chart before we get accepted as pop?' According to Thomas McClary,

> When people make those kinds of statements it's because they're usually afraid to make a step. It's not that white audiences can't accept certain types of music. We heard a tune by the Bee Gees. Now years ago that would never be played on an R&B station because black people never would listen to it. Now they hear these tunes today and they can tell you a lot of the pop tunes that are on the pop charts merely because they've been exposed to them. So, to make a statement saying that certain tunes are 'too black' for pop stations is like stepping out of the deep end... Statements about music being 'too black' are hindering the people that are listening to the music, and they are also hindering the artist. Whatever I create should be accepted or rejected by the people – and not by radio stations! (B&S)

Lionel Richie was more upbeat with his opinion:

> The single was a gamble that paid off. In life there are two kinds of people – the safe ones and the gamblers. The gamblers, if they win, win big. In our case, if we win we are called unique or trendsetters or whatever the word of the day might be. If we fail, nothing is said and we fade away...'Machine Gun' was a safe beginning. But now that we have progressed, we come up against the heavies of the business and the competition is stiff so we have to be original. We know we haven't reached the status of a Stevie Wonder – he could sneeze on record and start a whole new trend.

Despite his positive attitude, Richie despaired at what he called 'age-old problems of people's hang-ups'.

> In the music business you'll find that musicians are universal people. We can go to Japan, Colombia, South Carolina and I can meet someone I've never seen before in my life and immediately we have something we can identify with, and that's music. The problem is musicians are very open-minded people dealing with a very closed-minded society.

During November 1976, the same year as the Temptations left Motown for Atlantic Records, *Hot On The Tracks* passed platinum sales – the group's first – and earned them their second consecutive gold disc. At a New York ceremony they were presented with personal discs by Barney Ales, then president of Motown Records. It was a grand affair because the Commodores were now one of the company's A-list acts, although Clyde Orange confided to Adam White that they didn't actually feel part of the Motown family. 'I felt they had their little clique and there were certain groups that would always be a part of that clique that was the original Motown' (*Billboard Book of Number One R&B Hits*, 1993). Family feeling or not, the Commodores now commanded respect from within the company and would, rightly or wrongly, be promoted as a Motown success story!

'Fancy Dancer' followed 'Just To Be Close To You' and was, Richie said,

> as heavy a disco-funk item as you are likely to find in November 1976. It was Ronnie LaPread's idea, he came up with the track. I added the lyric and the actual melody. So, with Ronnie being into rock and funk, you're left with a funky bass track because that's what he plays. The melody and lyric are rather straight because that's the way I am.

As with all songs, each Commodore added a personal touch of individuality to retain some modicum of continuity in the group sound, after which James Carmichael took over and with engineer Cal Harris transformed the

The Commodores pose in stage gear. These autographed photos were handed out to fans attending their concerts (Lionel Richie, middle/foreground).

Commodores' skeleton into a finely honed song. Regrettably, the honed 'Fancy Dancer' only struggled into the US top forty and bombed altogether in Britain on its early 1977 release. Once again this proved that the record-buying public preferred the group's ballads to uptempo sounds, pushing them further into the pop/mainstream market, away from their black roots.

Hit or not, during March 1977 the Commodores embarked upon their own headlining tour that included a third visit to the Far East and their first British stint, which kicked off at Birmingham Odeon followed by dates in London, Leeds and Manchester. To coincide with the visit, Motown/EMI rush-released a three-track single – 'Easy', 'Machine Gun' and 'I Feel Sanctified'. Each concert review overflowed with praise and excited acclaim for Motown's top group. With support act Muscles, the Commodores, sporting large Afros and wearing boldly coloured, sparkling catsuits with ballooning sleeves and elasticated waists, confidently burst onto the London stage with 'Let's Get Started' and the party began – spraying confetti, dense dry ice, flashing lights, gunfire, spitfire lyrics, jagged dance routines, and heavy music. Apart from the named group members, to ensure the sound balance was nigh-on perfect, there was support from three other musicians and vocalists, called the Mean Machine, comprising Darrell Jones, Harold Hudson and Gary Johnson (who was in time replaced by Winston Sims). Later on David Cochrane joined when the unit was expanded. The more popular repertoire like 'This Is Your Life' (later recorded by soul master Jerry Butler), the smoothie 'Just To Be Close To You', 'High On Sunshine' and everyone's favourite 'Sweet Love' led to the build-up of what the group called 'Commodore County – the land of love'. When the first notes of 'Machine Gun' were heard, the audience rose to dance; the party was well under way. 'I Feel Sanctified' kept the high-octave pace before the weary group left the stage for a few minutes before returning to the uproar of the hand-clapping, foot-stomping audience. 'Slippery When Wet' was the fitting finale, which left the London audience in no doubt that the Motown act was here to stay. Although this performance was sold out, others weren't and by the time word had spread about the visually exciting act, the Commodores had moved on. However, inroads into British acceptance were being made, and certainly, with the type of act the group was presenting, future tours were assured. On 26 March the tour was suddenly abandoned when Ronald LaPread's wife, Kathy Faye, was taken ill at their Tuskegee home. After performing one date without him, the group took the (professionally) surprising, yet (personally) understandable, step of also returning to the USA. Sadly, Kathy Faye later died from cancer, prompting their next album *Commodores* to be dedicated to her.

After the successful London concert, readers of *Blues & Soul* voted the group into sixth position in the Top Vocal Group category in the magazine's annual poll, beating the Temptations but not the Supremes. The Capitol Records signing Tavares was top. Diana Ross walked away with the Top Female Vocalist award; Stevie Wonder the Top Male, holding off Marvin Gaye. *Hot On The Tracks* was fifth Top Album; Wonder's *Songs In The Key Of Life* held the pole position, while 'Just To Be Close To You' was fifth Top Single. Candi Staton's delicious 'Young Hearts Run Free' was a worthy number-one title. Life was definitely changing for the Commodores; all they had to do was maintain the glorious momentum.

The aborted tour also managed to boost sales of the fifth album *Commodores* (subtitled *Zoom* for British release), from which 'Easy' had been extracted for single release to become a runaway top-ten hit; in the USA it was their first single to go straight into the pop chart's top five. Milan Williams said, '"Easy" like Monday morning. We had so many elements in that. First of all, the piano intro by itself. Out of all the songs Richie has ever written that song is one of the greatest in terms of people wanting to re-do the song.' The simple, beautiful ballad boasted such a memorable melody that it was as vital three decades later, thanks to being the musical backdrop to television commercials for the Halifax Building Society. Still stinging from the media criticism that 'Just To Be Close To You' was 'too black' for pop radio stations, Lionel Richie slanted 'Easy' towards

The Commodores larking around in this shot for their 1977 *Zoom* album (Lionel Richie, second from right).

three times a lady

country & western although it wasn't accepted by that market at the time. As lead vocalist on their biggest hit so far, he found he was the group's focal point, being sought out by fans and journalists alike. It appeared he was confidently slipping into the role of spokesman because he was an easy conversationalist and highly opinionated; he meticulously explained situations, and was passionately fluent about music generally. His engaging manner demanded attention, while his flattering techniques were clearly rehearsed for impact. The remaining Commodores, although grateful for Richie's money-spinning compositions, were, naturally enough, slighted when he was singled out, only accepting it because they knew the value of positive publicity. Behind the scenes, however, they felt differently, because Richie's music was totally alien to their original intentions, as summed up by Clyde Orange:

> I didn't come up listening to Elton John. If Elton was around, he wasn't in the mix with James Brown, Otis Redding, Wilson Pickett, Sam Cooke and the Motown Sound. I came from the black side of things. I'm from Jacksonville, Florida, and at the time there was a station called WOBS. They played everything from country to Blues to pop to R&B, and I was well versed. But it was basically black music [and] that's the craft I wanted to bring into the group.

Years later 'Easy' was regarded by its composer as more than a runaway pop hit; it represented his late father's words of wisdom.

> When I wrote the song I had no idea the words would mean more to me after he had passed. ...I think what my father was saying to me was live your life, be who you want to be, and that's his philosophy that I wrote, based on talking to him a lot. Now that he's passed, I'm trying to live that philosophy of being true to myself.

'Easy' was the perfect launching pad for the *Commodores* album in March 1977, and as Dave Godin wrote, 'Drop the needle anywhere on this album and you'll know why I continue to acclaim the constant demonstration that the Commodores give of their talent. One of Motown's hottest and most potent of acts.'

'How a group can offer an album that goes off into nine different directions and yet stay right on course beats me, but that's just what this amazing group have attained on this, their most impressive album to date,' wrote *Blues & Soul*'s reviewer.

> As in the past, they tend to concentrate on basic rhythms, adding horns for support more than as a front line – which they tend to use vocals for. Starting out with the driving 'Squeeze The Fruit', the heavy, pounding funk item never lets up and typifies their past work and, whilst it isn't the album's most creative track, it is a natural continuation to the group as we know them. 'Funny Feelings' is a string-laden and rather complicated piece of music that appears a little too

predictable, [while] 'Heaven Knows' is the first real ballad and although it isn't another 'Just To Be Close To You', you'll find it makes refreshing listening. The slightly uptempo chorus line actually spoils the mood but it again underlines the group's ability to come up with the unexpected. Side one closes with the impressive but uncommercial 'Zoom'. 'Won't You Come Dance With Me' is another track that utilises a variety of rhythms but this time it's all a little too disjointed. 'Brick House' is the album's most consistent hunk of funk and is the natural successor to 'Fancy Dancer'. Slightly slower but equally effective is 'Funky Situation' which is built around a very gritty riff but that breaks down when the rhythm pattern changes. 'Patch It Up' is worthy of almost the same comment. Finally, you're left with 'Easy', a very clever and subtle pop song…All credit to them since they not only co-produced the album but also wrote all nine songs.

Lionel Richie felt the album was now an extension of their basic sound, more relaxed and more experimental because 'we had it drilled into us that we can't even think of revolutionizing our sound until we have a firm following and that is was we did with the *Machine Gun* and *Caught In The Act* albums. We built a following for ourselves.' And with their Commodores logo soaring like a spaceship into a pale-blue sky on the album's front sleeve, the designer was also feeling more experimental!

It's true to say that Ronald LaPread's arrangement on the 'Zoom' track was one of the album's most moving, and years later he explained his feelings about this to A. Scott Galloway:

> The group was coming to terms with my wife dying of cancer. She and I had started working on some music. As I played, she wouldn't know what to say technically, but she'd go 'take it up here, bring it down there'. For years the band couldn't listen to 'Zoom' because it brought back memories of crying in the studios. We had received our first decent royalty cheque from Motown but there was absolutely nothing we could buy to save her life. (*Commodores Anthology*, 2001, CD notes)

Admitting the track was his favourite at the time, James Carmichael elaborated by saying, 'It expressed how we all feel. We'd like to fly away. It could be due to dissatisfaction, romantic interest, any number of things can make us want to fly away and zoom quickly.' And fly it did – *Commodores* hit second platinum status in the USA! By now, the group was the most popular black unit in the USA, not only due to their music but their sold-out spectacular live shows. Maurice White's Earth, Wind & Fire, with lead singer Philip Bailey, had graciously conceded defeat and accepted second place. However, the two groups were identical in principle: both had distinctive lead singers, and both loved elaborate performances that included pyrotechnics and energetic routines. In Britain, the competition was quite different. Punk and New Wave emerged with high-profile groups like the

Sex Pistols, Iggy Pop and the New York Dolls. Disco music was in its infancy as Rose Royce, the Trammps, Joe Tex, Tavares and Van McCoy, among others, made chart inroads, although Donna Summer was the only chart-topping artist. Mainstream music was represented by a whole host of British acts in a year when fans also mourned the deaths of Elvis Presley and Marc Bolan. So, it was a pot-pourri of musical tastes that competed against the Commodores and other Motown acts.

*Commodores* went on to spend a year on the US album chart, and a delighted William King told journalists this milestone release represented a group that was 'a huge melting-pot' before explaining, 'We had Milan who was jazz and country and western, Thomas which was acid rock to the max, and we had Richie, a little bit more laid back, and we had Walter which was big band and jazz. So we had this huge amount of music in so many different directions.' Milan Williams added that there was no one person controlling the group; all decisions taken had to have a majority vote. 'You can hum a melody to someone and if someone can hum you back the melody next day, you got a hit song.' The policy worked because, as Richie confirmed, disagreements were rare.

> We never have those great musical arguments whether [a song] should be an F-minor or C. There was nothing like that. We went for 'How does that sound?' We dealt with the word 'simplicity' but better than most acts. It was all about 'How do we look and how do we sound?' in the simplest form.

He also believed this current album took them straight into the pop market because of the success of 'Easy' while insisting 'There are things on there that can be related to our past so that the continuity can be kept intact. I think our next step could be on to double albums. There are six guys in the group and we each come up with forty songs for an album, and then we cut it down from 240 to nine!'

Motown was now an extremely powerful and successful record and film company, and had made huge inroads into television films thanks to Suzanne de Passe, who had originally trusted her instincts to sign the Commodores to Berry Gordy's company. With this expansion and development came the inevitable personal and professional upheavals, with some artists being ignored altogether. The Supremes, for example, floundered and would never enjoy the same success as they did when Diana Ross was lead singer, but through the determination of support singer Mary Wilson, the group's career was secure for several years yet. Motown, as a company, also suffered with the departure of the Jackson 5 and the Four Tops, yet publicly these losses seemed to make little difference to its financial situation. Established names like Stevie Wonder, Marvin Gaye and, of course, Miss Ross, moved with Motown, and had, along the way, secured personal control of their careers, away from the restrictions of previous company departments. All these changes meant the beloved 'Motown Sound' lovingly created by musicians and artists during the glorious 1960s was merely a memory that was fading fast. Motown's new policy was dollars, sophistication, supply and demand, which, sadly, was destined to overtake the quality of the music itself.

Two slices of Commodores' funk closed 1977; both were US hits. First out 'Brick House', a pulsating hunk of disco funk with Richie's slurred vocals, where the horn player filled the gap between 'brick' and 'house'. The story goes that when one further song was needed to complete *Commodores*, William King was sent home to write one in double-quick time. Stressed out, he fell asleep, and when he awoke there was a notebook on his chest with the lyrics written in it. Apparently, his wife had penned them while he slept. From a male perspective 'Brick House' related to the female form, as Lionel Richie attempted to explain. 'Brick house means she's stacked...She's built like a brick shithouse means she's strong. Shit is not a negative thing. It just means the brick house is not gonna fall down...I know that sounds bad.' William King added, 'The song described how every man feels about every woman, and the 36–24–36 was just a generic number. There are some men that like small women. There's some, like myself, that like all women. I don't care. So long as they can stand up and talk, that's fine by me.' Twenty-six years later, Lionel Richie recorded a new version of the song with Rob Zombie for his horror film *House of 1000 Corpses*. An odd pairing by any stretch of the imagination, but as Zombie so succinctly told the press, 'The movie is so fucked that we needed something equally as fucked to go with it.' The singer also recalled to *Rolling Stone* magazine's Andrew Dansby, the first time Rob Zombie had visited him at home, 'My housekeeper answered the door and said, "There's a Mr Zombie at the front door." And he had showed up. This long hair, dark glasses, dark beard, blue jacket, ripped pants, red-toed combat boots. And I loved the question – "Where would you like me to *put* him?"' Richie also spoke about the first time he heard the re-worked song.

> When Rob called me on the phone he was so nervous. I asked why? He said, 'Just come over.' He played this track to me and it blew me away, because he Zomba-rized it. Under no circumstances was he thinking the Commodores...As a compliment to what he did, I said, 'Give me the microphone, man.' He said, 'What are you gonna do?' I said, 'Well, you can't have "Brick House" without some *howse* in it. You're not saying *howse* right!' Well, he fell about laughing. The next thing we knew, we were slapping hands and he said, 'Man, this is gonna scare people to death!'

The single went on to appear in other films, like *The Associate* (1996), *Muppets from Space* (1999) and *Undercover Brother* (2002).

While 'Brick House', with its various connotations, shot into the US top ten, its follow-up 'Too Hot Ta Trot' struggled into the top thirty. On its British release during January 1978, it notched up the group's fifth chart placing, but it stalled in the top forty. However, on the upside the single and group appeared in a Motown/Casablanca Filmworks movie *Thank God It's Friday*, which boasted acts from both record companies involved. Casablanca's glamorous disco diva Donna Summer held the starring role and won an Oscar for Paul Jabara, who penned the film's hit 'Last Dance', while Diana Ross and Thelma Houston completed Motown's contingent. Neither appeared in the film but could be heard singing 'Lovin', Livin' And Givin'' and 'Love Masterpiece' respectively. Other contributing acts included Cameo, Sunshine and Pattie Brooks. 'Too Hot Ta Trot' was hastily conceived because it was written in one day. The group was midway through a US tour set to gross them $6 million when Benny Ashburn instructed them to fly to Los Angeles, where they would spend three days filming and recording. Upon their arrival, a studio executive told them, 'Go to the studio, gentlemen, you're going to write; make up something and put words to it.' The film's lukewarm storyline was based around a young woman who, in Clyde Orange's words, was 'too hot to trot', so he wrote the lyrics around the plot, which didn't impress the remaining Commodores one iota! 'They weren't thinking about writing lyrics and getting deep and heavy. So at the end of the day we had no choice but to go with mine. And then Richie said, "You're writing it, you sing it".' It wasn't the group's greatest performance, rather a singalong funky throwaway, but they got away with it because they were such a bankable act at the time. 'It was one of those songs that was surrounded by a great product, a movie,' Orange told Adam White. 'All these things helped. Nobody's going to go back and record "Too Hot Ta Trot" or any of those funk songs because they come and they go. They're just fad songs, and that's the way I wrote it.' Happily, the tune lasted longer than the film, which, a *Rolling Stone* reviewer claimed, was '*Saturday Night Fever* Earache...a plotless, pointless derivative of *Car Wash*. The music just keeps droning, wiping out what dialogue there is.' Climbing into the US top thirty in November 1977, the single peaked in the British top forty two months later.

Motown cashed in on their triumphant sell-out US tour by rush-releasing a double album (*Commodores Live!*) as a 1977 Christmas gift from the Commodores to their fans – 'the ultimate souvenir for fans who'd caught the shows and a fine consolation for those who missed them'. An interesting marketing ploy which worked; the album became a top-three seller, and was their long-delayed debut in the British album chart, peaking in the top sixty. Culled from standout performances at the Omni Auditorium, in Atlanta, Georgia, and the Landover in Washington, DC, and supported by the Mean Machine (David Cochrane, Darrell Jones, Harold Hudson, Cecil Willingham), the release captured the excitement and fever-pitch conditions of the two concerts, as reviewer David Nathan glowed:

> ...the band is every bit as good on stage as on record. They really do manage to capture the identical sound and this double set bears testimony to my statement. On a couple of slower tracks, where they are allowed to elongate and rap, you'll come across the rare occasion when a 'live' recording can actually be an improvement on the original studio cut. As with 'greatest hits' albums, 'live' sets are hard to review because you'll already know every track since they do represent the band at their best. It's perhaps a pity that 'Machine Gun' was omitted but the inclusion of the studio-recorded 'Too Hot Ta Trot' perhaps makes up for it.

Despite the runaway success of the album, Lionel Richie wasn't satisfied with one aspect:

> Although we understand the company's desire to cut out our rapping, it is an integral part of our show. It makes it look as though all we did was a 'live' album whereas the idea was to capture our 'live' show on record, and there's a lot of difference between the two. And by missing the little gestures in our normal show, it makes our act appear disjointed.

Hot on the album's release, two Commodores tracks, 'Zoom' and 'Too Hot Ta Trot', became Motown's first British 12-inch single in February 1978. This type of disc was originally pressed as a promotional tool for club DJ use only because 7-inch singles were impractical. The 12-inch was usually far superior in mastering, production and clarity, and was pressed to achieve maximum quality over a nightclub's massive sound system. These records also contained full-length versions of songs, lasting between 12 and 20 minutes, whereas the 7-inch was an edited track ideal for radio play. Club promotion has always been imperative in a dance record's life, and usually begins before the official release date of the 7-inch single. Sales of both versions contributed to chart placings and in 1978 12-inch singles reputedly outsold the 7-inch ones. Prior to the release of the Commodores' 12-incher, other British record companies were beginning to venture into this field, encouraged by successful results in the USA. However, one drawback was that the 12-inch singles were manufactured on album presses and, since more money could be generated from albums, companies were reluctant to commit these facilities to the singles. In time, though, special presses were allocated to the singles because the market became a huge money-spinner.

Behind the scenes, the group attempted to bolster their own company's finances by signing two acts to their Commodores Entertainment Corporation, a holding company for all their activities. Platinum Hook and 3 Ounces

The Commodores in relaxed mood circa 1978 (Lionel Richie, first left).

Of Love were also both signed to Motown and, because the group was so wrapped up in its own career, Motown hired outside producers to work with it. Benny Ashburn had spotted Platinum Hook performing in a New York club, but, as his time was fully taken up with the Commodores, they had a two-year wait before joining their ranks. The self-contained group released their first eponymous album in June 1978. A well-received but poor-selling release meant their career with Motown ended within two years. Three young Detroit girls, known as 3 Ounces Of Love, supported the Commodores on their US and European tours. They too released one self-named album from which the singles 'Star Love' and 'Give Me Some Feeling' were extracted, but they suffered the same fate as Platinum Hook. David Nathan reported that the Commodores Entertainment Corporation, with a working staff of eight, operating seven working companies, also maintained a fan club, a rehearsal hall and recording studio in Tuskegee, property in Alabama, Houston and Los Angeles, and the group's investments in African art and rare coins. Ten acts, including the Mean Machine, were signed to the management operation, while five third-party composers were signed to the publishing section, which was also responsible for the group's own compositions. Through the Commodores Moving On Company they owned three buses, two tractor trailers, seven Mercedes-Benz cars and two limousines, all of which were hired to other artists when not used by the group. The touring arm catered for sound and light crews; there was a licensing department for group merchandise, and a sponsorship division for their work with companies like Schlitz Beer. By now the Commodores were probably the busiest black act in the business; each year not only were they obliged to record two albums, but were committed to tour the USA and overseas. That left little time for personal issues, but somehow they managed.

Back to the music and after cutting short their 1977 British tour owing to the death of Ronald LaPread's wife, the group returned for a spring 1978 trek with the 3 Ounces Of Love as support act. This was part of a world tour that started in their home country, playing at major venues holding in excess of 10,000 people, where their stage act comprised twelve or so songs over 90 minutes. William King smiled when remembering the clothes they wore.

> We had these huge things all over our costumes – plexiglass – and these were heavy. We had to have special hangers made. We would get so involved in the lights and the music, the playing and performing, that we would sweat like pigs...I can remember walking out at Madison Square Garden, the roar from that crowd was just so loud that you couldn't hear the music. If I was playing in the wrong key nobody knew it.

The April and May UK dates included Brighton, Birmingham, Newcastle, Manchester and three in London, and all were sold out, with audiences screaming for more. Lionel Richie said, 'The crowds were wonderful to us, so very warm, we all love the country...thirty thousand people a night around the world is everything, especially when they know all the lyrics to the songs. It becomes one big performance.' One song that the world sang as one eclipsed all prior achievements. It was another Lionel Richie ballad (written for Frank Sinatra – 'but it never happened'), recorded and released in the middle of the disco explosion no less, but which became one of the most enduring love songs of all time following its initial release in 1978. 'Three Times A Lady' shot to the US top position in June 1978, and five months later achieved the same in Britain, before becoming an unstoppable worldwide number-one title. While newspaper headlines proudly declared the Commodores were 'The Black Beatles', the single passed two million sales in the USA, and one million in Britain, where it was Motown's top-selling single of all time, staying at number one for five weeks. Clyde Orange laughed, 'It was one we didn't have to argue about. Richie sang the first two bars and we said "That goes on the album" and that was that.' He also explained that they still worked the system whereby each group member was pushed to write a song for their albums.

> That was our security, thanks to Benny Ashburn and to James Anthony Carmichael, who saw that everybody had something to offer... The thing was to pick the best songs from each person that would make that album stand up and be real strong when you put the whole package together. It was always a fight, but the fight came for the seventh and eighth song because that meant somebody was going to have two songs on the album. And [that] kept you razor sharp...it was a competition.

With no resistance to the beautifully melodic 'Three Times A Lady' being included on *Natural High*, the album was simultaneously released in the USA and Britain during May 1978. However, unlike the USA, the track wasn't immediately lifted as a British single – even though it was the best on the album and radio play was extensive – because people wanting to own the song would have to purchase the album, which generated more money for Motown, while other potential buyers, who followed record company politics, knew it would be released as a single at some point, and opted to wait. Instead, 'Flying High' was issued, to struggle into the top forty; hardly worth the bother!

Anyway, the easy-listening 'Three Times A Lady' was conceived, Richie explained, after he had attended his parents' wedding anniversary.

> My father made a speech about how much he loved my mother and appreciated the way she had stood by him for thirty-five years. It was beautiful, but it started me thinking about my own life and how my wife Brenda stands by me, and how she does so many things without being asked, or thanked. So I wrote the song for her. I think my next-door neighbour summed it up when she said that if any man wanted to buy her a gift, all he need do was buy her this record and he wouldn't have to say anything else. But, personally speaking, the song has given me so much personal satisfaction, and I think it's a songwriter's dream to be totally accepted...it seems the whole world really does love it, and it's a great feeling.

James Carmichael said, 'With "Three Times A Lady" we knew we were in deep water because there were no waltzes being played in the seventies. So when you come along with a song in three-quarter time, you had better have spent a long time thinking about it.' It was also clear that when Richie presented the song to the group, he had to sing the single, as Carmichael continued, 'He had the best delivery. His voice was just mellow enough to carry the right flavour to give to people so's they could taste it. And it tasted good.' Inevitably, this sweet-sounding (or tasting) slice of romance firmly established Lionel Richie as the group's lead singer whether he liked it or not. The balance of the group had changed, and with that came mutterings of an uncertain future. For one thing, no matter what else the group went on to release, or Richie to compose, comparisons with 'Three Times A Lady' would plague them. Nothing was ever good enough, and nothing closely matched this monumental single. Over the years the song was, of course, re-recorded many times by artists like Johnny Mathis, but perhaps the most unusual was from André Kostelanetz, who recorded a classical interpretation with the New York Philharmonic Orchestra, which, a proud Richie pointed out, 'was a true honour. Having one of my songs done by such an illustrious musician was real important to me.'

While in the love mood, all the Commodores were married and during their long stays away from home they used Citizens' Band (CB) radios to keep in regular touch with their families. To this end, each had a call-name – Clyde Orange was Robin Hood; Lionel Richie was Jack Benny (because he was stingy with money, just like the comedian); William King, the Red Baron; Milan Williams used Captain Quick Draw, which inspired the 'Quick Draw' track on the 1975 *Hot On The Tracks* album. 'It's the silliest song in the world but it worked,' remarked Lionel Richie. 'I can't believe he did it, but we put it out.' Thomas McClary became Mr Magoo, and Ronald LaPread was Shaggy Dog. All still maintained homes in Tuskegee, a quiet town of 11,000 people who shared no cinema but two restaurants where, apparently, one could eat like a king for three dollars! Years later, Richie admitted he owned his student apartment and the home he had grown up in because they gave him a safe haven away from his whirlwind musical lifestyle.

> I fly…around the world but when I want to go home and reflect for a minute, I go in my car across town, get in my student apartment, close the door, and say 'Now, God, this is where I came from.' This gives me the incentive to figure out where I've gone and how far I would like to go. I sit in that room for hours at a time, making sure that when I leave that room I have a sense of direction.

The *Natural High* album was crammed with good musical ideas, although, as I wrote at the time, 'Flying High' sounded like three tunes thrown together 'with funky drums and bass, played at a disco tempo with disco strings and topped with Chicago-style wimpy vocal harmonies'. And further,

> Clyde Orange's 'Visions' was just as mixed up but more fun, a slowie that threatened to boil over into guitar/clavinet nastiness, but never quite made it.

'Say Yeah' was better than 'Three Times A Lady', and the hard funk is heavier than ever, with McClary debuting a new fuzzed-out, rubbery guitar tone on 'X-Rated Movie' and 'Such A Woman' while 'Fire Girl' stands out on its own.

To all intents and purposes, it was the perfect showcase for 'Three Times A Lady', although when it crossed over so strongly into the pop market, maybe fans weren't expecting such a heavy influx of funk and dance. William King said the album was constructed in such a way that it would lead up to and around 'Three Times A Lady'. 'It was to be the climax. Richie had to re-write the second verse a couple of times before it got through, though.' With the Commodores' logo stamped in the sky to reflect onto a landscape of different-coloured fields, the album's artwork ensured one couldn't escape the attempt to dominate from afar.

While 'Flying High' peaked in the US top forty in November 1978, and 'Just To Be Close To You' crept into the British top seventy – an abysmal placing for the follow-up to 'Three Times A Lady' – the group's first *Greatest Hits* compilation hit the stores. Spanning material from 'Machine Gun' through to 'Easy', the album passed platinum sales in the USA, while in Britain its sales hit gold status. 'Though we started in the disco field,' said Lionel Richie, 'we always felt we had more to offer. Right from rock to m-o-r, from funk to disco.' And this album had it all! So did Motown Industries: at the close of 1978, it was the top black-owned company in the USA for the fifth year running. Record sales rose from $43.5 million in 1975 to $50 million in 1976, placing the company $2.4 million ahead of its closest competitor, Johnson Publishing. But would this good fortune last?

Motown certainly enjoyed continued success. So did the Commodores – but only for another eighteen months.

# 4 endless love

'We all miss riding in the van...not that we want to go back to it.'   William King

'The Commodores have done what I tried to do.'   Kenny Rogers

'I was really pleased with it because it was one of the most beautiful songs I've ever recorded.'   Diana Ross, of her duet with Lionel Richie

The new year of 1979 began on a high note, when the Commodores won the Favourite Single in the pop/rock category at the sixth annual American Music Awards, staged before a star-studded audience at the Civic Auditorium in Santa Monica. They were also nominated for a trio of Grammy Awards – 'Three Times A Lady' in the Song of the Year and Best Performance by a Vocal Group categories, and the album *Natural High* in the Best R&B Vocal Performance section.

It was also the year when the beat was replaced by dance. Disco music gripped the industry, thanks to the phenomenal success of *Saturday Night Fever* and the Bee Gees, who many believed took disco/dance to the limit and were subsequently instrumental in its demise through huge overdoses of familiarity. Added to this was the glam-rock movement, where the music matched the colours of the artists' silks and sequins, jewellery and platform boots. Of course, Abba, the Swedish quartet who spoke limited English and won the Eurovision Song Contest with 'Waterloo', continued to surpass musical peaks, only to eventually disband in bewilderment. And 1979 was the year when the Commodores toured the world but not their home country, a move that failed to affect their selling power simply because of Lionel Richie's love of the ballad. To be fair, the guys were exhausted from months of touring without a break and their status in the US market was more or less established, as their record sales proved. Even so, there should have been a little cause for concern when, during their last tour, the performance at New York's Madison Square Garden was only two-thirds full. The soul/funk group L.T.D (Love, Togetherness, and Devotion) – with three hit singles to their credit – was the support act and had, according to critics, stolen the show. Benny Ashburn defended his group to David Nathan:

> L.T.D. are more of a boogey-ing band. Because of the hits we've had with our ballads – we now do five slow numbers in the show. People used to think of us as strictly a high-energy band so there is some readjustment. There were problems with getting some of our black audiences back. After 'Three Times A Lady' we definitely lost some of our black base and we started playing places where our audiences were eighty per cent white.

William King also conceded that the US stadium tours were getting more impersonal because of the vastness of the audiences, where the smallest crowd could be 12,000! On the other hand, overseas venues were generally much smaller, and audiences were 'right on top of you all the time', a more pleasing experience. He confessed they often pined for the old days, when they were a fledgling group, because the demands on them then were less.

> All we wanted was a hit record, to stay in the best hotels and drive the best cars. They were the highs, but it's only when you get there that you can appreciate where you came from. There is always further to go and we are constantly moving forward…We all miss riding in the van…not that we want to go back to it! And waking up in the middle of the night not knowing where you are on the road. I miss falling asleep in the van and getting cramps in my legs and Richie falling asleep with his head on my stomach…but you couldn't move him off because Tommy [McClary] was asleep on him! They were great days and we wouldn't have made it without them.

During July 1979 details of a mammoth world tour were announced to the media. It was planned to release their new album *Midnight Magic* and (as yet untitled) extracted single simultaneously in the USA and Britain on 29 July. This was to be the group's most extensive tour to date, incorporating appearances in Holland, Sweden, Switzerland, France, Belgium, Germany, South America, Hawaii, Japan, Australasia and, of course, their second home, Britain. In August they planned performances in Glasgow, Stafford and two nights at London's Wembley Arena, where tickets were priced at £6.00 and £4.40! The European performances, their first since the success of 'Three Times A Lady', showcased material from the new album and selected songs from their previous *Natural High* set, which had now passed treble platinum sales in the USA. The concert in Stockholm stuck in Lionel Richie's mind not because of its musical excellence but because 'It was a scandalous show! It was horrible…those women on the front row. We played "Brick House" and they just had no sense of shame whatsoever.'

'Sail On' was that first extracted single, born from Richie's exhaustion after years of touring and recording, and showed a frank insight into his state of mind at the time. Being a country and western slanted song, it wasn't intended for the Commodores. Richie had actually logged it away with others he'd composed, considering it more suitable for third-party artists. However, when James Carmichael heard the song during a chance visit to the composer's house, he insisted the Commodores record it. Yet another ballad, moaned R&B fans, leaving it to be snatched up by mainstream/pop buyers who quickly pushed it into the top ten on both sides of the Atlantic. Within two short months, its follow-up was issued. Titled 'Still', it shot to the US pole position and the British top four. Again penned by Richie, it was, he remarked, the direct result of his schoolfriend William Smith's divorce.

> They both sat down and said, 'Listen, we want to be friends, we said some things wrong…Let's get a divorce and that way [we] can still be in love and still love [each other] as friends'…I was very upset with what was happening to them. They felt they'd actually messed up a great friendship by getting married.

William Smith then told Roberta Plutzik for *Billboard* that he and Lionel had talked from nine one evening until the sunrise. 'We cried…I knew he was the old Skeet [his nickname for Richie] and that he cared. Six months later he sent me the song with the message that he'd written it with me in mind, and every line in "Sail On" refers to something we talked over.'

The song had other, more profitable, connotations for its composer. Country and western star Kenny Rogers was greatly impressed with it and contacted Richie's publishing house with a view to recording one of his compositions. Meantime, Commodores fans loved the interaction between piano and voice at the record's start and finish; the highly charged smooth melody contributed towards it being voted one of Richie's most poignant songs to date. William King believed fans would treat it as the official follow-up to 'Three Times A Lady' despite it being on another level. 'Last year he was nominated for Best Song of the Year, and I believe he's gone a step further with this song. It's a beautiful ballad but shouldn't be compared to "Three Times A Lady" because it's a whole 'nother thing.' Factually speaking, the ballad was Motown's forty-fifth single to hit the top spot in the USA (in 1979), and the Commodores' second. Only a handful of acts in Motown's history have had more number-one titles. The Supremes still led with twelve, followed by Stevie Wonder's six. The Temptations, the Jackson 5 and Diana Ross all had four, while Marvin Gaye had three. Tied with the Commodores, with two chart-toppers, were the Four Tops and the Miracles, with one each for Mary Wells, Edwin Starr, Michael Jackson, Thelma Houston, Eddie Kendricks and the Marvelettes.

With Lionel Richie as lead singer and composer, the Commodores could do little wrong, and during the past two years they had been ranked as the biggest black group earners. William King explained to David Nathan:

> Our plan has always been to surpass the Beatles; they came as close as anyone has ever done to reaching everyone but they missed out on a couple of things purely by timing. For example, the R&B crowd would never touch them – even if they liked them! They came during an era of conflict between black and white. You didn't see any Beatles' records on the floor of an average black home, like you might to some extent see that now with the Bee Gees. Times have changed. Now it doesn't matter much what colour you are. When we did a tour of the Midwest, eighty per cent of the audiences were white. We did a show in Seattle, Washington, that was ninety-nine per cent white. The world is getting better. It may not always look like it, but it is improving. (*Lionel Richie: An Illustrated Biography*)

Ironically, the black fraternity may not have supported the Beatles, yet without that group's public support and that of other British acts like Dusty Springfield, Motown artists would certainly have taken much longer to break down the barriers of the UK music industry, which up to the 1960s was ruled by white acts, companies and money. Lionel Richie took this issue one step further.

> I get so insulted when every artist in the world, like rockers, say 'Oh my God, I was inspired by Muddy Waters and Chuck Berry,' and that rock group made a hundred million dollars, stayed together for four years, broke up and went on to something else. Here's Muddy Waters and Chuck Berry, [and] they still haven't made a hundred million dollars and they work every day! ...Here's our big problem [and] I'm talking about America now. Who made B. B. King famous?

The guys fool about on the photo shoot for the *Midnight Magic* album (Lionel Richie, second/left).

48   Lionel Richie

White or black? Who made Chuck Berry the Godfather of all the Beatles and stuff? Who made Ella Fitzgerald, Ella Fitzgerald? White folks!

The age-old dispute would never be resolved but happily black and white artists worked hand in hand, recording in unity and with respect. It was the radio stations, particularly in Britain, which needed educating, and that was a much longer process!

The *Midnight Magic* album, on whose cover the Commodores' logo burst skywards from a horizontal terrain, was criticized in black quarters because the funk was lacking; the musical force was missing. Others felt it was one of the best to date; my own review is probably typical of the general feeling.

> As a complete album it's a veritable gem. Each member contributes material and there's a wealth of imagination on display. Side one gets right down to things with 'Gettin' It', a raunchy item penned by David Cochrane and William Orange. The McClary/Richie title track follows and motors along with more than a glance at the orthodox disco market. 'You're Special' slows things right down, but the production retains a gutsy approach with rich, deep bass lines and crisp brass work. 'Still'…is a touching ballad, more mature than 'Three Times A Lady' both as a song and in its treatment. Side two opens with the Milan Williams song 'Wonderland', a light intriguing floater which builds cleverly. McClary's 'Sexy Lady' follows and, whilst it's good dancefloor material, it's rather lacking in distinction. Then comes 'Lovin' You', a medium tempo smoothie written by bassman Ronald LaPread and showing a lot of class. Lionel Richie's 'Sail On' is positively one of the album's high spots…an altogether excellent all-round production and very classy vocal arrangement. The finale '12.01 A.M.' is merely a miniscule reprise of the title track. Perhaps a less ballsy album than might be expected from the band, but one that carries a great deal of substance.

William King said, at the time, 'The album is really a natural follow-up to everything we've done before. We feel the cover is strong. It's simple and we like simplicity. The music content comes from all angles.' A strong album indeed – it passed triple platinum sales in the USA, and peaked in the British top twenty. It was also richly sweet because it was the first to fall under the Commodores' new exclusive recording contract with Motown, which King described as 'beautiful'. For the next seven years, the deal required a new album every nine months, instead of the previous one album per year.

> I don't think Motown is above or below a whole lot of record companies. I think they have done the basics that a record company should do…their contribution to our success has been that of a record company. But, there are people within Motown who have done things for the Commodores that are above and beyond what was asked of them.

This was also true for another group, because four months later the Temptations, who had left Motown for a four-year spell with Atlantic Records, also re-signed with the company. Currently, in the studio the group was again working with Berry Gordy, in an attempt to recapture their past Motown glory. The result was the 'Power' single and album, which, although memorable, captured few sales. Nonetheless, the Temptations were back where they belonged.

The mighty Commodores arrived in Britain on 24 August 1979 on the first leg of their world tour, to meet the media and rehearse for their forthcoming performances. With support act, the Emotions, the sold-out Wembley Arena audiences welcomed the six Tuskegeeans like long-lost friends. Reviewer Gof Abbey wrote,

> If you're in earshot of the Commodores' dressing room all you can hear is 'the tape's running' being repeated. [Then] out they come, a couple at a time, and make their way to a darkened stage that has a hugo logo spelling out their name in lights. By the time the name is complete they are all on stage ready to burst into 'Flying High', which set the audience well and truly in motion. Following this with 'Brick House', one wonders if this pace can possibly be kept up. That is rapidly answered by the intro of 'Easy' after which the crowd erupted. Taking the pace up again with 'I Like What You Do' and slowing it again with 'Zoom' it has become obvious that they know just how to entertain an audience. Out of the bank of speakers booms the voice of Lionel Richie, who sets about convincing the audience – as if it needed convincing – just how grateful the group were for them making 'Three Times A Lady' a number one hit last year. Just as he winds up his speech, a white piano is raised behind the drum kits with Mr Richie seated to begin the intro to 'Still'. As the dry ice receded, the song came to an end and the roof was almost lifted from the rafters by the deafening applause. Then Richie dedicated 'Three Times A Lady' to everyone there...Keeping the tempo slow they continued with the current single 'Sail On' [before] bursting into 'Too Hot Ta Trot' which immediately set the crowd in motion again. After seventy-five exhausting minutes the group left the stage with the crowd howling for more. Back they came to close the show with the current album title 'Midnight Magic'. Drained, they returned to the comparative calm of their dressing room while...everyone left more than happy although probably asking themselves why 'Just To Be Close To You' had been omitted, or 'Machine Gun' or 'I Feel Sanctified', but then no-one is ever satisfied all of the time! (B&S)

Things went from a high to a low when, for some reason, Motown opted to extract a third single from *Midnight Magic*. Released in November 1979 in the USA, and during January 1980 in Britain, 'Wonderland' failed to sustain the hit status of its two precedessors. One reviewer groaned, 'It's a slow, melodic ballad that unfortunately lacks the elegance and beauty of both "Still" and "Sail On". In all honesty, the group may have fared better if they had varied their tempo and gone with one of the dance tracks from the album.' The release was not a wise move and certainly did the group no favours. While his group attracted criticism, Ronald LaPread's composition 'Daisy Lady', recorded by the group 7th Wonder, was the second single to be lifted from their *Climbing Higher* album. The single, also produced by LaPread, was distributed by Neil Bogart's Casablanca Records. The Commodore, who would later form Shaggy Dog Inc to handle his publishing and production interests, also planned to release his own work. However, another group member beat him to it. William King, on the other hand, disagreed with outside commitments, believing the membership should concentrate solely on their group to keep it stable and successful. Meanwhile, Kenny Rogers was still trying to speak to Lionel Richie.

Into a new decade, when Motown celebrated its twentieth anniversary, and with predictions that its favourite male group would rise even higher. The year started well as they were presented with the American Music Award for Favourite Soul/R&B Group. Unfortunately, it was not so for Lionel Richie, who saw in the 1980s in hospital, where he was being treated for a mild intestinal virus. He quickly recovered to return to Commodores duties, which included a trip to Japan, where in March they were honoured to be special guests at the 30th Tokyo Music Festival, one of the most prestigious events in Japan. During their stay they performed at Tokyo's Budokan and in Osaka. Like most Motown acts, the guys would enjoy years of loyal support (with and without Richie) from the Japanese nation.

Disco remained a potent force in the 1980s, as did romance and one-hit wonders. It was a changing decade, with mandatory 12-inch singles, costly promotional videos, jazz-funk, independent charts, theatrical glamour and a general feeling of 'anything goes'. International artists were safe in the knowledge they had paid their dues and would now reap the rewards and, to a certain extent, the Commodores fell into this category. They were highly paid and internationally known, but, apart from Lionel Richie, could any member of the public actually name another group member? It was this that would eventually push the group into turmoil. For the time being, at least, they beavered on to record their next album *Heroes*, from which 'Old-Fashioned Love' was the first taster. Both were issued in June 1980; the single hit the top twenty in the USA and bombed in Britain, prompting the rush release of the album's title, which also sold poorly. One reviewer called it

> a maudlin track [where] Lionel Richie adopts his big-production ballad voice, whilst the producer goes for the sensitive accompaniment of acoustic guitars and occasional strings; the pretentious lyrics only serve to increase the embarrassment quotient and make me wonder what happened to the band that made

'Machine Gun'…the quality of their releases has been steadily declining over the last four albums.

When 'Heroes' also failed, a third track, 'Jesus Is Love', was issued before the end of 1980. That, too, disappeared without trace. The group was struggling, as their selling power diminished (almost) overnight. Thankfully, the album itself held its own by peaking in the US top five, but without a hit single to promote it struggled into the British top fifty. A pity, because it was one of several heavyweight releases which spearheaded Motown's twentieth anniversary celebrations. Other albums included *Diana* from Diana Ross, her nineteenth for the company; Stevie Wonder's commercial *Hotter Than July*; and *The Motown 20th Anniversary Album*, a double release in a full-colour gatefold sleeve, containing forty of the company's 248 British chart entries.

Broadening their musical horizons by exposing new facets of their talent, *Heroes*, the Commodores' tenth album, which was two months behind schedule, introduced lyrics dealing with social issues, hints of jazz, pronounced gospel influences and an R&B flavour more suited to the Sam Cooke era. Reviews were mixed. John Abbey wrote,

> I am disappointed with it. Firstly because there's no ballad that can compare to 'Three Times A Lady', 'Still' or 'Sail On'. Much of the material is uptempo and there's a distinct lack of depth to the actual music. The last three cuts are all gospel tinged and inspirational, which I approve of from a musical viewpoint. Most likeable uptempo cuts are 'Old Fashioned Love', the funky 'Mighty Spirit', plus 'All The Way Down' and 'Got To Be Together'. But this isn't another *Natural High* or *Zoom*. (B&S)

Once again William King was elected spokesman, but this time to defend their work, as he told the reviewer,

> It's a little more intricate than anything we've tried before and that's another major step for us. It's not heavily slanted towards dancing because we have built up an association with the public whereby they want to listen to what we're saying. We selected these songs from a wide selection of material that we came in with. Some of the songs and arrangements would make Beethoven turn over in his grave. But from the twenty-five that we seriously considered, we chose a happy medium and a good balance of tunes.

Many felt that the group members were now pretentiously declaring themselves heroes, which prompted his quick retort that this was the furthest thing from their minds. 'That's why the picture on the cover has us looking towards heaven and with that glint in our eyes. What Richie is saying in the lyric is that everybody is a hero. In fact we went through five sets of lyrics before we settled on the ones that we used.' John Abbey, on the other hand, believed 'Heroes' had an interesting message but 'the slow, mesmeric track somehow never really grows on you in competition with [their] prior classics. This simply doesn't stand up in terms of commercial appeal.' He felt 'Jesus Is Love' to be a safer bet, yet when it was later issued as a single the Commodores dug a bigger hole for themselves. As a rule, religious-based songs rarely sell well in mainstream music, although titles like the Edwin Hawkins Singers' 'Oh Happy Day' in 1969 was an exception to the rule. King again took up the challenge.

> The spiritual songs have gone over really well. In fact, the [US] religious stations have created such a demand that the company is pressing up special 12-inch records with 'Jesus Is Love' on one side and 'Mighty Spirit' on the other…Putting 'Mighty Spirit' immediately before 'Jesus Is Love' [on the album] isn't such an abrupt introduction into 'Jesus Is Love' and it also meant an early musical exit for those listeners not interested in religious songs.

Interestingly, there were twenty-nine vocalists supporting the group on the last track, headed up by Merry Clayton, Yvonne Fair, Clydie King, Oren Waters and Venetta Fields. It took four hours in the studio to sort out the vocal balance of all these voices because they constantly blocked out the lead singers. 'I didn't sit down to write a gospel song. I guess it was because of my frustrations from listening to the news every night,' Richie pointed out.

> We've cluttered up our lives with money and wars…and the economy, and I just felt my inner frustration come out. And then I was in a conflict within myself as to whether I should use certain words and found myself intimidated. Should I use 'Jesus'? Should I use 'He'? Then I said 'Wait a minute, the full value of the song is Jesus, so let me give it the full value.'

While in the throes of finishing *Heroes*, the Commodores wrote and recorded the title track to the forthcoming Jay Weston film *Underground Aces*, and Platinum Hook, managed by the Commodores Entertainment Corporation, began working on their second album. As Lionel Richie was facing up to his current musical crisis, a young boy with whom he had worked during the early 1970s collected a double platinum award for sales of his latest album. Although still a member of the CBS Records signing the Jacksons (the name Jackson 5 was owned and therefore retained by Motown when the brothers switched record company), Michael branched out to record a solo album. *Off The Wall* was his first and at this point (1980) it had sold a staggering four million copies in the USA alone. It went on to spawn four top-ten singles and be listed in the top ten albums of all time in terms of actual sales. Of course, young Jackson would go on to release *Thriller* in 1982 – the top-selling album of all time!

When asked if he was disappointed that *Heroes* had attracted so much criticism and subsequent poor sales, Lionel Richie was indecisive. He realized that it was extremely risky not including a big ballad, yet believed they had to move into gospel because the time felt right, 'and the only way to do that is by making the song the main feature. So, we decided we'd take a gamble and do it that way. Realizing we were going to sacrifice the commercial airplay.' In retrospect, they sacrificed more than airplay, but when Richie quipped that hit records were no longer important to the group, he probably made one of the biggest mistakes in his career. He argued personalities were important because 'people had something to hang on to. Hit records are one thing but they are a year-to-year thing,' he told John Abbey. 'Personalities are forever. Our logo is a personality, we have to develop personalities so that when we write and sing a specific song people will say "I know why they wrote that".' Sadly, the Commodores lacked individual personalities because, of course, Richie was stealing the limelight. This was something he said he wanted to change, although in this interview with Abbey it appeared to be the last thing on his mind, preferring to promote himself:

> What I am trying to do for Lionel Richie is to build up a reputation that can be linked with the Commodores. Like Michael Jackson, he has a great personality by himself and then he enhances it all by linking up with the Jacksons and giving people twice their money's worth, so to speak.

The Commodores' 1980 nationwide tour of the USA was their first for two years and was their best-planned – no criss-crossing from state to state this time. However, two weeks before they were due to hit the road, Kenny Rogers personally contacted Lionel Richie with a view to recording with him. The request was turned down, but fate played its hand, as Richie, who was in Tuskegee at the time, recalled. 'Clyde was involved in a motorcycle accident and we had to postpone the tour until he was fully recovered, which took about three weeks…After fourteen years of constantly working with the Commodores I had three weeks off!' Benny Ashburn contacted Ken Kragen, Rogers's manager, to see if they were still interested, thrashed out a deal, and that same night Richie flew to Las Vegas. At the ensuing meeting he played two demo recordings, one untitled, so he had written 'baby I'm your knight in shining armour and I love you blah blah', and 'Goin' Back To Alabama', which he'd written two years previously. Richie recalled,

> I've never pitched a song before to an artist. [Kenny] spent a good half-hour saying, 'I've just got married to a lady named Marianne. She's such a lady. And me a country boy, I have no business being with a lady. By the way, Lionel, what's the name of the song?' I said, 'Er, "Lady"! Do you like it?' Kenny said, 'I love it, when can I record it?'

He further told *Billboard*'s Paul Grein that they cut both songs in the same night in an 8½-hour session. 'We kept it simple. There are only four rhythm musicians plus string and horn players. There are no gimmicks with Kenny, so the last thing you'd ever want to do is put an arp or a synthesizer behind him. He doesn't need that. Kenny sells lyrics.'

For his part, Rogers explained,

> The idea was that Lionel would come from R&B and I'd come from country, and we'd meet somewhere in pop. I hate to get stagnant. I was about to explode. I needed new input and that's where Lionel came in. I went to the very best in that field. The Commodores have done what I tried to do. They haven't limited themselves to any one area.

For Richie,

> Kenny was so genuine. I see why he is where he is. Forget about this superstar stuff, he rolled up his sleeves and said, 'Whatever it needs to get what you want, just tell me.' I produced Kenny standing side by side with him in the booth because I've always felt that as an artist there are days when I would like the whole world to be in there with me.

According to Ken Kragen, this working practice wasn't what Kenny was used to, because generally speaking he would walk into a studio, sing a song all the way through twice and walk out again. 'On "Lady", and the other stuff he did with him, Lionel stopped him on almost every word and Kenny just couldn't believe it. It was a totally different way of recording.'

'Lady', Richie's first production work outside the Commodores, soared to the top of the US singles chart in November 1980, where it stayed for six weeks, earning him two Grammy nominations, $1 million in royalties and a part-share in a cosmetic range of the same name. Despite his later bravado, Richie had found it difficult to give away a song he'd planned to record with the Commodores, who, of course, were in need of a hit single at this time. However, it was a challenge he needed, and it also enabled him to get involved with Kenny Rogers's *Share Your Love* album, on which his wife Brenda was also acknowledged as the album's co-ordinator.

> My wife had been peeping over my shoulder and watching people like Suzee Ikeda, Suzanne De Passe and James Carmichael for the last seven years or so. I thought she was playing about when she'd come into the studio with us. When she said she wanted to be my production assistant, I really didn't take her seriously. But I agreed to try her out on Kenny's album and she was so organized and so much on top of everything that it scared me. Not only did she do what a production assistant should do, but she organized my entire day – and my meals!

Released during March 1981, *Share Your Love* hit the US top ten and spawned the top-three hit 'I Don't Need You'.

It was natural that Lionel Richie's outside work provoked rumblings of him leaving the Commodores, a position augmented by Kenny Rogers because he constantly referred to his 'dear friend Lionel' and thanked him for his renewed international status. Sighed Richie,

> Every time Kenny made a personal appearance, and when I made a personal appearance, it caused a strain within the group. I would join the group and the press would be in the room, and as I walked in, the interviewers and cameramen would knock the other band members over just to start interviewing me...I'd say, 'I'd be glad to do an interview, but first would you pick up that guy off the floor because that's my drummer.' I started apologizing because I felt badly about what was happening.

Even though all rumours were strenuously denied at this time, Richie continued to milk the Kenny Rogers association. 'Working with [him] has given me a great opportunity to meet people in the business. He'll call me and say, "Come up to the house, I want you to meet somebody." We've developed a great relationship that will probably last a lifetime.' Not only did that last, but Richie later asked Ken Kragen to look after his solo projects, while Benny Ashburn continued to represent him as a member of the Commodores. Meanwhile, Ashburn was officially appointed an advisory commissioner for the 1984 Olympics scheduled to be held in Los Angeles, which would, ironically, benefit Richie but not his buddies.

With the Kenny Rogers project completed, the Commodores hit the road. They performed for four days in a week, whereupon they were free to relax or return home. By arranging the dates close together, they never had to travel more than four hours by bus, their preferred means of transport, because, apart from Milan Williams, who had a pilot's licence, they loathed flying. (In fact, Williams was involved in a scare during late 1980 when a single-engined plane piloted by him collided with a truck while attempting to make an emergency landing, as a result of engine trouble, on a Phoenix, Arizona, freeway. The plane burst into flames but neither Williams nor his passenger, the group's press agent Lester Morney, was seriously hurt. The truck driver also sustained minor injuries.) It was reported that Lionel Richie no longer travelled with the group but in a limousine with his wife, a move that further fuelled speculation of his imminent departure from the group that reared him. On a lighter point, the tour was staged by the company responsible for the Bee Gees' last trek, which included 360 stage lights. William King said, 'At first we had more but it got too hot, it was like a pressure cooker out there. And the stage costumes [were] the best we've ever had.' Although not sold out, the tour was a huge success, with no hitches except for the Madison Square Garden concert, where Bob Marley & the Wailers were second on the bill, with Kurtis Blow opening the proceedings. A more diverse handful of acts would be hard to find

– R&B/pop mixing with reggae mixing with rap – and the consequences were felt, as David Nathan wrote,

> Now Bob has played the Garden before – as a headliner – so what we got on this occasion was a seriously mixed audience, made up of rastas, the sophisticated cult-followers [mostly white] who have been into reggae for some completely mysterious reason and the black faithful fans of the Commodores. A few members of the audience were there too for opening act Kurtis Blow with his famous rappin' show, but a motley crew it was and the concert seemed to flow pretty well. (*B&S*)

He added that the Commodores had vastly improved since their last New York gig two years earlier but 'the current gospel segment at the close of the show was tedious'.

While Lionel Richie was working with Kenny Rogers, he was also beavering away on the Commodores' next album and, once the US tour was completed, intended to finish it for early 1981 release. However, another third-party request shot his schedule to pieces and, in doing so, caused immense problems. The result was the spectacular 'Endless Love', the title song from the Franco Zeffirelli film of the same name, starring Brooke Shields. Explaining what happened in 1980, Richie recalled a most exciting period of his life:

> Polygram called me and asked did I have a song for their new movie. I didn't have, so I went to see the movie although I really didn't want anything else to do at that time. Then Polygram said all they wanted was an instrumental and I could do that on a weekend; that would have been easy, no problem. Next thing I know, I get told they want lyrics and wanted me to sing them. So I agreed, still a weekend thing – no problem. Then I hear them say, 'We've got Diana Ross to sing it with you' – now I have a problem! This was turning into a bigger project by the minute but it turned out to be a wonderful weekend.

As an aside, the executives at Polygram were familiar with the singer's practice of composing in the bathroom ('It has been my experience that people will follow you all over the house but won't follow you into the bathroom') so sent him a box of toilet tissue and a bottle of champagne, with a note reading 'This should help you with your writing!'

> One major aspect, though, had to be sorted out, namely, where the two of us would record the track. Y'see, Diana was in Atlantic City doing some concerts and I was in New York, and neither of us had the time to visit each other. So, we decided to meet midway. She finished her concert at one in the morning and drove down, and I flew in. (Diana had already been given the song's melody but no lyrics – they hadn't been written yet.) We started around three, three-thirty, and finished around six, six-thirty, or so. Diana, once she showed, was a real professional. Diana Ross knows how to be Diana Ross. She kills a song! Let me

tell you something, I was amazed at one thing that happened. She was singing her piece and once she'd done it and I didn't realize, she waited for me to come in with my bit. Oh, my goodness, I thought, 'Diana Ross waiting on me!' We thought about doing a follow-up but 'Endless Love' can't really be followed. It was a great duet but these aren't recordings that come by easily. Just think of all the wonderful duets there have been before, like Marvin Gaye and Tammi Terrell, or Marvin and Diana, and so on, so it's pointless trying to outdo a good one. It has to be a project you come back to every now and again.

Diana Ross told J. Randy Taraborrelli, 'At first it wasn't a Motown single...Lionel's agreement was with Polygram [Records and Pictures]. When I got into the picture, Lionel and I agreed that it was only fair that Motown get [it].* I was really pleased with it because it was one of the most beautiful songs I've ever recorded' (*Call Her Miss Ross*).

It was later admitted that the Commodores had already rejected 'Endless Love', a song which, when released by Richie and Ross, catapulted to the US top position in August 1981, where it stayed for nine long weeks. The singers' relationship may have been idyllic on record but within months they would cross egos. When the Commodores performed in Las Vegas, Motown's diva saw the show and visited them backstage, whereupon she accepted an invitation from a delighted Lionel Richie to see them again in concert at Radio City Music Hall. Taraborrelli reported,

> Shortly after that, she came storming into her Manhattan office with a rolled-up copy of the New York *Daily News* in her hand. She slapped it down on the desk of one of her aides. 'Look at this!' Underneath her picture was the announcement – 'the special guest on the opening night of the Commodores' show will be none other than Diana Ross.'

It transpired the Commodores had advertised that Ms Ross would be performing and tickets were selling on her name. One of the star's assistants further told the author, '[Ms Ross] started swearing and screaming, saying she felt exploited and how could Lionel do this terrible thing. I'm sure she was more hurt than angry because she likes Richie a lot, but Miss Ross often lets her emotions run away with her.' Needless to say, Diana Ross's name was instantly removed from the billing and Radio City Music Hall publicly apologized.

It was not generally known but Diana Ross was planning to leave Motown and now, thanks to Lionel Richie, she was in a powerful bargaining position because 'Endless Love' was her biggest selling single to date. (Luther Vandross and Mariah Carey updated the song in 1994 to enjoy a top-five hit on both sides of the Atlantic.) She later signed with RCA/Capitol Records

---

* Taraborrelli noted that Motown boss, Berry Gordy, had insisted upon it.

for a reputed $20 million, leaving a devastated Berry Gordy to pick up the pieces, not knowing that within another two years, he would be forced to release another Motown megastar. Marvin Gaye had vowed he would never record for the company again following the release of his *In Our Lifetime* album, which he declared wasn't completed. 'I disavow publicly this being my work...they released it to make money.' Unfortunately, it didn't. The album was the unhappy singer's final release from the company that had supported him through troubled and barren times, and promoted him into international stardom. CBS Records took a huge chance when they signed Gaye in 1982, but, as it later transpired, he enjoyed one of his biggest hits there with 'Sexual Healing'.

'Endless Love' soared into the British top ten, where it became the last single to be released under Motown's licensing deal with EMI Records. Nominated for five Grammy Awards and a host of others, including an Oscar, the American Movie Award and one from the American Music Association, it was the most successful Motown single of all time (1981). The company had already enjoyed 53 number-one singles, and 'Endless Love' dominated the American singles chart longer than any of them. (Marvin Gaye's 'I Heard It Through The Grapevine' stayed seven weeks, and the Jackson 5's 'I'll Be There', five weeks.) It was also the most successful soundtrack single of all time and certainly remained more popular than the film! According to *Billboard*, 'Endless Love' was the most successful duet of all time. Paul McCartney and Stevie Wonder's 'Ebony & Ivory' and McCartney's duet with Michael Jackson, 'Say Say Say', were runners-up, with seven and six weeks respectively. While public and industry accolades were piled on Lionel Richie, little mention was made of Ronald LaPread's involvement with the disco quartet A Taste Of Honey, who had opened for the Commodores on their first US national tour.

With the duet now behind him, Richie was grilled at interviews about his pending departure from the group; he remained focused in his denial and his reply to John Abbey was typical.

> I've had that question thrown at me so many times. Right back to 'Three Times A Lady'. Later on down the line, you don't know what life will bring but right now I'm having such a good time with those crazy guys. And I'm not confined to being just a Commodore. I can do my outside work and then come back to the group when it's necessary. I'm getting the best of both worlds. By my returning to the Commodores each time I believe that I can only enhance [their] reputation. I don't think I need to put dynamite under the base of 13 years of togetherness [to] launch Lionel Richie. There is also a certain loyalty that I feel to these guys...so the idea of blowing up this house to build another isn't necessary. (*B&S*)

Picture taken from the 1981 album *In The Pocket* (Lionel Richie, middle row/right).

When Abbey asked if he planned a solo album, Richie diverted his answer to the forthcoming Commodores album on which he was currently working, was evasive about his future plans, but added the media were actually damaging his relationship with the group because 'people who are not aware of what it takes to keep a group together don't realize that they are helping out in adding to the paranoia of keeping a group intact. That's when the rift starts happening.'

Meanwhile the remaining Commodores held their silence in public, while in private they debated the viability of Richie staying with them. Clyde Orange no longer reaped the credit he deserved; not only was he the only trained musician in the group but he was the one with his finger on their musical pulse. He knew what their fans wanted, and it wasn't Richie's full-blown ballads, which is why 'Lady' and 'Endless Love' had been rejected so easily. Richie's commitments had started to clash with those of the Commodores, and when the group was booked, he had to be with them, so unfortunately it was a no-win situation for all of them.

Released at the same time as 'Endless Love' was 'Lady (You Bring Me Up)', a taster from the Commodores' next album titled, *In The Pocket*. Top British DJ, Mick Clark, said this about the single,

> I have been less than complimentary about the Commodores over the past year or two. To be honest, I have found their recent output ordinary at best, and in particular I have found their cloying, sentimental ballads too 'Terry Wogan' to be true. Well, now is the time for the band to hit back as this single must be their best in years. A bright, brassy, punchy dance tune right in keeping with what today's audience wants. The writer's credit indicates the absence of Lionel Richie (too busy with Kenny Rogers?) and maybe this is the key to their new approach. Either way, it's nice to see the Commodores making good funk records again. (*B&S*)

The single was a top-ten US hit but sold badly in Britain. A bitter blow to both the group and Motown/UK because the company was still celebrating the unprecedented success of two consecutive chart-topping titles, 'Being With You' by Smokey Robinson and 'One Day In My Life', a reissued 1975 track from Michael Jackson. It was the only time in Motown/UK's history that one artist followed another to the top.

In eight years the Commodores had released ten albums, all of which struck gold in the USA; two albums had passed platinum, one double platinum, and two triple platinum. Some reviewers felt their eleventh album, *In The Pocket*, lacked strength and had too many heavy-handed arrangements. However, Pete Tong believed it held the magic ingredient called success.

> The musical content won't change the course of black music history, but you have to be a 'vegetable' to be excused not noticing the changes. Since when has a Commodores' album included tracks like 'Lady (You Bring Me Up)'? The guys want to sell records. The rest of the set has its ups and downs, but the form of the LP is generally that of a modernized one, leaning away from those corny country influences of the late seventies – they've done that and now it's time to move on. 'Keep On Taking Me Higher' incorporates a very formal 'disco break', but one that totally suits the image of the Commodores. 'Oh No' and 'This Love' are the album's ballads, either of which might eventually become a single. The Commodores move on at a safe inoffensive pace – they play it safe! For some reason they stumbled during 'Heroes', but like a dignified old gentleman they quickly picked themselves up, and carried on regardless. (*B&S*)

*In The Pocket* peaked in the US top twenty and the British top seventy. It would be the last to feature Lionel Richie.

As Pete Tong predicted in his review, 'Oh No' was the second extracted single, an unremarkable release except perhaps for the sliding guitar solo, which carried it into the US top ten and British top fifty. Not so saleable, though, was Richie's last single with the Commodores. Titled 'Why You

Wanna Try Me', it stepped up the tempo into a gritty, funky rhythm riff that was similarly slanted to 'Lady (You Bring Me Up)'. Unpredictably, it died without a trace. However, at the close of 1981 Richie was represented in the US top one hundred with six singles: namely, 'Endless Love', 'Oh No' (which he wrote and co-produced), and 'Lady (You Bring Me Up)' (co-produced by him); Kenny Rogers's 'I Don't Need You' and follow-up 'Share Your Love'; and 'Still' recorded by John Schneider.

In one of his interviews after the release of *In The Pocket*, Lionel Richie went to great lengths to publicize the fact that Clyde Orange was the group's greatest talent. In effect, he was lining up his replacement. 'Before the Commodores made it in terms of records, Clyde was the lead vocalist. I was the horn holder and shoop-shoop guy. For the past few years because I wrote the songs I came to the front as being the lead singer. On this album he's now coming to light as the great performer he is'.

Meantime, behind closed doors, Motown executives told Lionel Richie, 'If you're gonna leave, now is the time.'

# 5 truly

'I wanted to play around and not be part of a self-contained group.'   Lionel Richie

'The separation wasn't hostile.'   Milan Williams

'He's an artist of quality.'   Suzanne De Passe

'I wasn't thinking of the word "solo" as a solo artist, I was only thinking of solo album,' said a bewildered Lionel Richie in 1981. 'What Motown asked me to do was to put out a solo album after the success of "Lady" and "Endless Love" because it was perfect timing. So, the word "solo" just meant record.' This certainly was a dilemma; he was at the crossroads of his career and knew his chance to grab a slice of solo stardom was now. With indecision plaguing him, he did what he always did in times of crisis; he consulted his grandmother in Tuskegee. Although Richie and his wife had made their home there, they had temporarily relocated to Los Angeles to be nearer his work. ('We love the California scene but it's just a wonderful playground, something you enjoy as a novelty. Our roots will always be in Alabama.') Following the visit, Richie took the easy option and decided to stay with the group but also to record a solo album.

Meanwhile, although the Commodores maintained a high profile with US fans, their British success went off the boil. Ballads, of course, were always their strongest songs, and best suited to Richie's voice, but how many high-calibre tracks was he capable of composing? Certainly of late the group's material had suffered from lack of creative imagination, and with Richie ploughing his energies into his own work, the future looked bleak for the remaining membership.

While still a group member, Richie worked on his first solo project. James Carmichael agreed to work with him ('He's been my backbone and I know I can count on him') alongside handpicked Los Angeles session musicians. The list was inspiring and costly, including Nathan Watts, Paulinho da Costa, Michael Boddicker, Joe Walsh and Greg Phillinganes, who composed one track with Richie, 'Serves You Right'. Tennis star Jimmy Connors, who had recently called upon the singer to partner him in a Las Vegas tennis tournament, assisted on support vocals on 'Tell Me', while Kenny Rogers sang second lead and backing vocals on 'My Love'. It was a star-studded recording, all right, where the inspiring Gene Page worked closely with Carmichael, under the control of the singer. There wasn't a Commodore in sight! In explaining this away, Richie was far from convincing:

> I wanted to play around and not be part of a self-contained group. It makes things easier that way. Working with a group can become hard work because each of us knows what part we have to play in the recording and we rely on each other to play that part. I didn't want a cast of thousands either in the production. The challenge was to find musicians who were willing to sweat and pull off precisely what I was looking for.

To all intents and purposes, the combination was perfect.

> I wanted to begin the album with a straight-to-the-gut approach so I chose 'It Serves You Right'. For me, R&B lyrics and country lyrics are the most direct in the world. They go straight from one person's mouth to another's ears. 'Wandering Stranger' is a song that sums up my inner feelings, and deals with my search and I think the search of a lot of people right now who are wandering around the streets without a clue as to what's going on.

As an aside, Richie often mentioned 'the brown beat-up' piano in interviews. This was the one used by singer/composer Carole King on her timeless *Tapestry* album released in 1970. A US number one for 15 weeks, it stayed on the chart for 302 weeks, the longest-charting album by a female. *Tapestry* also won Grammy Awards for Best Female Vocalist, Best Record and Best Song.

During the nine months it took to record his album, Richie performed 'Endless Love' at the 55th Academy Awards ceremony in Los Angeles during March 1982. The song had scooped the Favourite Single in both the Soul/R&B and Pop/Rock categories. He later sang it live with Diana Ross at the Oscars gala before a worldwide TV audience of 361 million. 'After that evening my life changed,' he said. Indeed it did, but first he was hit by tragedy in August 1982, when the group's mentor and manager Benny Ashburn died in New Jersey from a heart attack brought on by high blood pressure. He was only fifty-four years old. Richie and the Commodores were devastated. 'Losing Benny was more of a blow to the Commodores than if Richie had quit twenty times,' a saddened William King said at the time. Known as a lover of life and an ordinary guy, Ashburn possessed tough negotiation skills and protected the group as he would his own family. He had been greatly concerned about Richie's possible defection and, reputedly, was miffed when he hired Ken Kragen and an independent lawyer to look after his interests. Accepting that Richie's new life wouldn't include him or his expertise had hurt Ashburn, as a

Commodores source confided to David Nathan: 'You could tell he was uneasy about Lionel's moves but, on the other hand, he knew it was inevitable. He just wasn't the same guy. He seemed to get tired easily and he just didn't have the enthusiasm any more.'

Without Benny Ashburn, the singer later pointed out to journalists, the Commodores would never have become international stars.

> We came through this thing together. After all the hard and terrible days of struggling to make a living we wanted to enjoy our success together, and with Benny to share it all, the acclaim, the Oscars and all the success with us. He was like a father to us. For the five years we were on a big scale, the group didn't live next door to each other. We couldn't call each other daily, so we'd all phone Benny and he told us what was going on and where to meet up. He was the middle man who kept us all together. Benny kept his family, for that was exactly what it was, together and happy.

In the same interview, Richie explained that he now felt responsible for the group: 'Even with my work outside them, I am more concerned that I don't disrupt their organization. It must remain intact. I've always been a Commodore and we must keep our heritage alive above all else.' Former ABC television executive Charles Smiley became the group's new manager. Of course, nobody could fill the huge gap left by Ashburn, but right now they needed someone with a positive direction, a keen eye on the market and the knack of co-ordinating six individuals, as Richie emphasized.

> Trying to find that someone who cares is making it a really tense time right now. The Commodores are a package that took masterminding and as soon as I've finished my album I'm returning to Tuskegee to see the rest of the guys to decide what to do. We're like six crazy brothers; we've been too close for too long and the group is based on a lot of love. Nothing will change that. We have to make decisions together and make them work because it affects their lives and mine...I can't expect [them] to wait on me; it's hard to ask them to wait until I've finished my stuff before getting together and working together.

'Lucy' was released as a single in Britain in tribute to their late manager. Included on the recent *Love Songs* compilation, released in Britain only during July 1982, and of course on the group's final album with Lionel Richie, *In The Pocket*, it sold badly. On the other hand, *Love Songs* was a top-five album, licensed by Motown to K-Tel Records (the television marketing record company) to become their biggest selling British album to date.

Three months later, the *Lionel Richie* album hit the shops and was accompanied by an exhaustive promotional circus which had the singer criss-crossing the USA and taking foreign phone interviews during meal breaks. Other Motown albums issued at the same time were Jermaine

A solo artist at last! A promotional photograph for his 1982 debut album *Lionel Richie*.

Jackson's *Let Me Tickle Your Fancy*, the Dazz Band's *Keep It Live*, Billy Preston's *Pressin' On* and Rick James's *Throwin' Down*, which was the only one to do serious business. Interestingly, the Commodores' first album without Richie was put on hold to avoid clashing with the debut. After hearing the album, reviewers immediately predicted that the Commodores' future was doomed. With his funky roots a thing of the past, Richie presented himself as a sophisticated balladeer with all the polish and pizzazz of an established crooner. John Abbey noted that his song writing style was built around the distinctive piano dominated approach he uses on slower material — you'll note that he doesn't even play on the uptempo material on this album. So, if you liked 'Still', 'Sail On' and 'Endless Love' you'll end up approving whole-heartedly of similar ballads like 'Truly', the first single to be lifted from the album; 'You Mean More To Me' with its haunting 'Just To Be Close To You' type melody; the lyrically strong 'Wandering Stranger' and the song that is perhaps the most likely to emerge as a standard for the 80s, 'My Love'. My favourite is 'Tell Me', which is a little like 'Lady (You Bring Me Up)', the last Commodores uptempo hit, but both 'Round And Round' and 'Serves You Right' are bright and breezy enough. The stage is set for a triumphant solo debut by Lionel, and his fans won't be disappointed with this first offering. (B&S)

The double-gate album carried a dedication from the singer that included '...the man who brought six guys called the Commodores from the ground floor to the top of the world...Benny, you were loved and you will be missed, but your words will never be forgotten. To my brothers, the Commodores, thank you for 15 years of big fun, you are my second family and I love you.' In the first batch of interviews, he explained how he tackled the album.

> It was a strange feeling and it was only when we were finishing it off that I realized there was only me on it because my picture was on the front cover. It was different for me, for y'see, I was only used to submitting one song for a Commodores' album and when we thought about cutting something on me I realized I'd have to have nine to ten songs ready. Over the years I've written eighty to a hundred songs and I still had those so we had to decide which ones were the best. It was so hard that I asked James [Carmichael] to help me. He's one of the Commodores anyway. I also felt he was the right person, and he really wanted to give it a go. The whole experience was fun. I really enjoyed myself.

When asked whether he felt he should have given some of the material to the group to perhaps help them through this lean period, Richie pulled on his public, easy manner, saying,

> That's difficult to answer. You see everyone in the group writes songs and a lot of them are used on our albums. I'm lucky if I get two of my compositions on an album. There's six guys with a song each, so there isn't too much room for me anymore! If I said I was the group's writer, they'd kill me. I was never the writer for the Commodores, it was just that some of my songs became singles and were hits, and everyone assumed that the role was mine. I think a lot of the Commodores' non-success is lack of communication and co-ordination. There's also a lot of competition, and getting six guys in a studio isn't easy when we're all doing different projects.

It later transpired that James Carmichael wasn't in fact Richie's first choice, because of his history with the group, and he knew trying to prise the two apart wouldn't work. 'I wanted Quincy Jones but at the time he was tied up with Michael Jackson,' Richie divulged to Steven Ivory. 'He suggested I go to Maurice White who was also busy. At that point, Carmichael told me the Commodores were interested in producing themselves and that freed him up' (*Can't Slow Down*, CD notes). He also explained the way they worked together.

> I tape my idea with just the piano. Then Carmichael takes the tape and says, 'I hear it, meet me at the studio.' He puts the rhythm and the music around that piano. His job is to make it sound like a 'record' without destroying the innocence or sensitivity of the original thought.

Carmichael's view was, 'My mission is to help him reach his destination.' Without question the two were totally compatible and in tune with each other's talents, yet once Richie had left Motown, Carmichael did not appear to be an obvious choice.

As expected, 'Truly' was the first single, a title inspired by demand.

> I was performing in either Philadelphia or New York and there was a little girl in the audience who kept saying 'Endless Love' was her favourite song. She came backstage after the show with her mother, father and grandmother. They all said 'Endless Love' was their favourite song. The little girl asked me to write a song for her which resulted in 'Truly'.

Yet, in another interview, he stated he wrote the song for Barbra Streisand. 'It was one of those songs. The notes and words were written for [her] but then a couple of years later I was singing them myself. So I guess it's supposed to be.' The single topped the US chart for two weeks and soared into the British top ten. Not so the Commodores, who issued 'Painted Picture' (featuring lead vocals from Mean Machine member and co-writer Harold Hudson) as their first title without Richie, which struggled for any chart placings. Meanwhile, *Lionel Richie* became a top-three US album, and British top-ten entrant, and was the first from a black act to pass the one-million sales figure in 1982, on its way to platinum sales. While the momentum was building on his unprecedented solo success, a Commodores compilation, *All The Great Hits*, peaked in the US top forty, cashing in on the group's past successes before Richie announced his future plans.

> The success I've been fortunate enough to enjoy with my first album is tremendous and a lot of fun, but I experienced enough success with the Commodores to last me a lifetime. I'm past the glitter part and the money part of it, although money is always good, but I still get a bigger thrill out of recording and touring.

Admitting he never expected 'Lady' and 'Endless Love' to be the hits they were, he added, 'I merely did a job that I enjoyed. But don't get me wrong. I'm very happy it all happened.'

Now a CBS Records artist, Marvin Gaye was enjoying his most successful period in years following his defection from Motown. The erotically slanted single 'Sexual Healing' was an international million-seller, while its mother album *Midnight Love* would sell in excess of two million copies. However, it was Lionel Richie's friend, Michael Jackson, who would single-handedly haul the record business out of one of the worst slumps in its history with *Thriller* (1982). This album became the top-selling album of all time. With this and Richie's solo success on his mind, Marvin Gaye felt his popularity being eclipsed, as reported by David Ritz.

> In Marvin's mind, Richie was achieving the very thing that always eluded Gaye – stardom based on middle-of-the-road ballads. Though he admired Lionel's songwriting talent, it troubled Marvin to hear Richie referred to as the new Nat Cole, a title Gaye himself had long coveted. Doubly distressing was the fact that Richie's success was on the very label Marvin continued to claim never gave him the pop push he needed to crack the Johnny Mathis market. (*Divided Soul: The Life of Marvin Gaye*)

Tragically, Marvin never had a second stab at that market because his father shot him dead on 1 April 1984.

During December 1982 Charles 'Chuck' Smiley, in his role as the Commodores' manager, publicly contradicted rumours that Lionel Richie had left the group: 'There are several projects slated for the original six members.' He then announced a forthcoming British tour but wasn't clear about the actual group membership. In retrospect, perhaps Smiley should have spoken to Richie first, because with the 1983 release of 'You Are', his second single, he confirmed his intention to leave the Commodores, saying that he had already called a group meeting in Tuskegee. It had been an emotional gathering, reducing some to tears, and signified the break-up of lifelong friends, not just a professional unit. William King said, 'It hurt me because that's my brother…A lot of crazy stuff went on but that was one of the brothers deciding they wanted to leave.' And for Milan Williams,

> It was heartbreaking because I missed him as a friend and as a group member. It was hard to take but at the same time I knew that we had to move on because he had moved on…Lionel was always different and I don't mean that it's wrong to be different. Some people thrive when the spotlight is on them and others prefer a simpler kind of situation. His personality isn't the same as the rest of us, that's all.

Suzanne de Passe felt he had an extremely bright future. 'He's very talented. If he puts his mind to writing a Broadway show or scoring motion pictures or producing other artists or whatever, I think we'll see another kind of excellence from him…He's an artist of quality.'

truly

It's true to say the five other Commodores were tired of waiting in the wings while Richie concentrated on his solo career; in fact, he confessed in a *Playboy* interview that he was asked to leave because the others believed he had become bigger than the group itself. However, what he failed to say was that they were upset with his personal behaviour towards them, particularly when he walked off stage in the middle of a concert, claiming his throat hurt when that wasn't the case, and not riding with them in the tour bus, preferring to travel in a separate limousine with his wife. It is reported that if Benny Ashburn had lived, Richie probably would have stayed with the group, because Benny did not think the move a wise one. It would alienate Richie from the group, he had apparently said. But, when Motown then applied pressure on Richie to release solo work, he agreed. Besides, hadn't some of his best material already been rejected by the Commodores? The group believed their true niche was in R&B/funk, not with his love ballads that constantly drew them away from their black roots. With this in mind, Richie's departure allowed them to return to their original audience. Ken Kragen later told BBC Radio 2 that the singer and his wife had already discussed at length the possibility of a solo career. 'I was very friendly with Benny and I didn't want to take him away from the group or anything. But he made the decision to leave at that point, and the next thing I know, we have another client.'

Early in 1983 Lionel scooped several major US awards but none as important as a Grammy for the Best Pop Vocal Performance for 'Truly'. After seventeen previous nominations, he was finally honoured at the 25th annual ceremony. He was riding high on his second runaway single success, 'You Are', a top-five US hit; top fifty in Britain, the crisp, punchy, mid-tempo number was competing against Stevie Wonder's 'Frontline' and Bobby M's 'Let's Stay Together', also Motown hits. The company celebrated its twenty-fifth anniversary in 1983, promising it would introduce new signings and the dedicated promotion of acts like DeBarge, Mary Jane Girls and the mighty Dazz Band, while Gary Byrd's 12-inch single 'The Crown', featuring Stevie Wonder, promised to be the dance hit of the year. Charles Smiley's tour reached fruition but without Lionel Richie, when two dates were announced at London's Hammersmith Odeon in February 1983, as part of the Commodores' European tour. The visit was their first since 1979 and marked the debut of drummer Walter Orange as the group's recognized lead vocalist. Smiley did add that a Lionel Richie tour was in the pipeline.

The Commodores' London concerts were sell-outs and the reviews were excitable because, as one reviewer wrote,

> Anyone who feared the Commodores would be a spent force without Lionel Richie had their doubts discarded right from the start of what turned out to be

a highly energetic and equally enjoyable show...With the lights down, strange synthesizer sounds filled the Odeon and then wham! On came the lights and the band of twelve – five Commodores, five Mean Machine and two support vocalists – who launched themselves with such an energy that if you hadn't known that Lionel had left you wouldn't have noticed his absence amidst all the movement on stage. Without drawing breath, the guys took us through almost the entire group repertoire, and as they went into the ballads you could feel the expectant mood of the crowd waiting to see how they would handle songs so readily associated with Lionel. In the event, the vocals were shared by Walter Orange, Ronald LaPread, Thomas McClary and percussionist Kevin Smith, although the prominent voice was Walter's who, despite a throat infection, did a commendable job...There's no doubt that without Lionel the Commodores will possibly not be the same, but if they retain the sparkle, energy, and commitment shown here, then they look certain to retain their former position as one of the most successful music machines in the business.

To coincide with the visit, Motown/UK released 'Reach High', the theme from the US television sitcom *Teachers Only*, starring Lynn Redgrave and Tim Reid, and also included on the *All The Great Hits* compilation. Uptempo, featuring catchy but simple brass lines and subtle synthesizer support, the single was sadly predictable in its structure. John Abbey wrote, 'I defy anyone to recognize the Commodores by their vocals. And that's going to be the hard part – rebuilding a new image that will once again make them instantly recognizable.' In his liner notes for *The Best Of The Commodores*, A. Scott Galloway wrote that Kevin Smith was the lead vocalist. The media reported that after a successful audition Smith, born in Montgomery, Alabama, had been chosen to replace Richie. However, further investigation revealed that singer/composer Jeffrey Singleton was also successfully auditioned at the same time as Smith at Web 4 Studios in Atlanta and he was actually given a contract to join the group. 'Reach High' was his only recording with them.

By this time, Lionel Richie had released 'My Love', the first 30,000 of which were UK-released in a wraparound colour poster; it was the third to be taken from his debut album. The singer also won a Grand Prize at the Tokyo Music Festival, which he shared with Joe Cocker and Jennifer Warnes for their single 'Up Where We Belong'. On this first solo tour of Japan, Richie told the Festival's audience that his share of the award would go towards establishing a Japanese music scholarship fund. 'I feel proud to be able to put this money back into the young talent of Japan. If I hadn't had the help and the breaks early in my career, I would never be in a position to do this.'

To tie in with their twenty-fifth anniversary celebrations this year, new Motown/UK releases included *Anthology* projects from Diana Ross and the Commodores, plus a special *25 Number One Hits From 25 Years* compilation. A five-record set titled *The Motown Story* was also planned, together with *Motown Superstars Sing Motown Superstars*, an album of company artists singing other acts' songs, which remained unreleased for one reason or another. The Commodores' contribution was their version of the hit by Diana Ross and the Supremes, 'Forever Came Today'. Recorded in 1974 with James Carmichael producing, the vocals shifted from Lionel Richie to William King against a rock-and-roll backdrop that included a heavy guitar break and an 'I Heard It Through The Grapevine' lick towards the end. Obviously recorded when the Commodores were searching for their musical direction, but not a track to be proud of!

The highlight of this anniversary year was the five-hour spectacular 'Motown 25: Yesterday, Today, Forever', staged at Los Angeles' Pasadena Civic Auditorium with the proceeds donated to the National Association for Sickle Cell Disease. Suzanne de Passe co-ordinated the evening's spectacular entertainment, which included past and present Motown acts who flocked to honour Berry Gordy's achievement. As Smokey Robinson announced early on in the show, 'Once a Motowner, always a Motowner.' Yes, indeed, the artists returned with style, irrespective of hit record status, to relive Motown memories, even though many were allocated only a few minutes' stage time to do so. And, as is inevitable with this type of gala, some artists weren't even invited to perform. The highlights were released on video and included the opening moments, which featured a film of the front of 'Hitsville USA' and glimpsed the Miracles and the Supremes in the studio. Performing artists included Smokey Robinson (obviously!), the Miracles, Stevie Wonder, who paid tribute 'to all of you who have made it possible for a man from a black culture to have a dream fulfilled. The moments of magic that I've experienced because of you, the artists, management and staff of Motown, encouraged me to create music.' The Four Tops and the Temptations traded hits during a performance where the groups lightheartedly challenged each other with vocals and dance routines, after which Marvin Gaye reflected quietly at his piano to recall the roots of black music before his moving oration climaxed with 'What's Going On'. Returning to its glitzy showbusiness theme, guest DJs introduced high-speed performances from Martha Reeves, Mary Wells and Junior Walker, before introducing the Commodores, who, minus Richie, performed a thirty-second version of 'Brick House'. Richie was in Japan and was seen on film in a recording studio singing 'You Mean More To Me' to six-year-old Lanette Butler, who was featured in the sickle cell association's advertising campaign. The Jacksons followed, complete with Michael, who performed both with his brothers and alone, then Berry Gordy's younger generation of artists with DeBarge and High Inergy. An embarrassing performance from Britain's Adam Ant led into the gala's finale of the Supremes – Mary Wilson and Cindy Birdsong being reunited with their lead singer Diana Ross. It was not a performance of any note, due to onstage squabbling between Ross and Wilson, which was thankfully edited from the commercial video. Nonetheless, the evening was a huge success and a fitting tribute to Berry Gordy.

During September 1983, Motown finally released the Commodores' *13*, their first album without Lionel Richie, to coincide with a further British tour with support act Gary Byrd and the GB Experience, and two robotic dancers; clips from *Motown 25* were shown, before Gary performed an extended version of 'The Crown'. As earlier reported, unlike their previous releases, James Carmichael was not involved in *13*; instead, he worked on a second album for Lionel Richie, who said,

> The Commodores made the decision that they wanted to produce themselves. There's five producers in the group, so it wasn't James's decision. I reckoned that if you find something that's worked for eight or more years on hit records, why change it. So James works with me now. I don't know why the group made the decision they did. It seems strange.

Also this year, the group celebrated their fifteenth anniversary in the music business, and *13* was a fitting tribute to their remarkable talent, as one reviewer noted,

> This will come as a pleasant surprise to those critics who felt the group could not survive without Lionel. There's a far wider versatility and musical diversification because the focus is no longer on one member of the group. In fact, of the eight songs, three are performed by Harold Hudson who isn't a fully-fledged member of the group! Four cuts have particularly impressed me – two solid, uptempo items and a brace of ballads. Of the latter, 'Only You' is the cut that is recognisably the Commodores and heavily influenced by the Lionel Richie sound. However, the far more soulful 'Captured' features a sparkling Walter Orange vocal, leaning more towards the mainstream R&B sound. Uptempo items include the rousing and highly infectious 'I'm In Love' and the similarly slanted but perhaps more commercial 'Touchdown'. Of the remaining quartet 'Ooo, Woman You' is highly enterprising, with a heavy rock-pop feel to it, heightened by McClary's dominating guitar control over the rocking rhythm. 'Welcome Home' is a pleasant enough ballad; 'Nothing Like A Woman' is nicely orchestrated but not a great song, and 'Turn Off The Lights' catchy, without being devastating. All in all, a very impressive, industrious and enterprising album. (*B&S*)

Thomas McClary's view was,

> We have one ingredient missing – Lionel Richie – but we feel we can make up for that by adding quite a few new ingredients. We are no longer a group with one focal point...We have incorporated some innovative sounds, and we've dug

back and got back into our 'Brick House' groove, but we've also put something in there for the ladies...Our attitude has always been that the album we're working on can either make us or break us and so our attitude for this one was no different.

As for Lionel Richie,

> I like *13* but they need an identity, a focal point, they need a face. When I was with them, I was the lead singer and mine was the face of the group, like Mick Jagger and the Stones, or Michael Jackson and the Jacksons. I think Clyde should be that face for them. He's a prominent singer and seems to be the strongest. The album as a whole is, I think, geared towards the US. It's not a set for outside, although I do think it's a very good beginning for them.

Indeed, although on stage Clyde Orange had replaced Richie and in time intended to be the group's new lead singer, he said of Milan Williams, 'he was the group's original lead singer...Milan was largely responsible for the major input for our first two albums. And the guys in our group and in the Mean Machine will then become more involved in the back-up. Ultimately, though, it'll be the product that will determine the future.'

The gentle ballad 'Only You', written and produced by Milan Williams, was issued to coincide with the tour in September 1983. Interestingly, the Commodores weren't the only Motown stars due in Britain; Smokey Robinson had dates in October, while Junior Walker's tour kicked off in November, starting in London and taking in US air bases, before his final date at Maxims in Wigan, where, no doubt, he would be worshipped by followers on the northern soul circuit. While in London, the Commodores met the media, and the question most often asked was, of course, about Lionel Richie's departure. Milan Williams's response was typical, as he told John Abbey,

> The actual split was very emotional and for the first few dates we did without him, we missed him. However, we knew in advance what was going to happen and were able to adapt so that made it easier...We're financially secure, we're making good albums and giving good shows and they're the important things to us. We live simple lives in Alabama and Florida and we're just regular, everyday people. And it isn't a bad thing to be that way. The separation wasn't hostile. We have remained and will always be good friends. (*B&S*)

Once again the Commodores performed with zest and enthusiasm. They stomped and sang until the Hammersmith Odeon rocked with the relentless beat. Blending funk and ballad, the balanced show proved they were still an above-average band, but obviously it was impossible to replicate Lionel Richie's vocals on the tender love songs. This would continue to dog them throughout their remaining career, yet for their funk attitude they had no equal. A couple of unexpected highlights delighted the London audience – one was a version of Michael Jackson's 'Beat It', with Vesta Williams as support vocalist, while the other featured a 'Donna Summer' Commodore, resplendent in wig and dress, singing 'She Works Hard For The Money'. And so did the group.

Before 1983 ended, reviewer Justin Lubbock wrote, 'Whilst trying desperately to lay the ghost of Lionel Richie to rest, the Commodores have had undeserved problems in trying to hit home in their own right. Now with "Turn Off The Lights", a storming, no-holds belter, they appear to have their best chance to date.' Unfortunately, their best wasn't good enough.

Their luck would, however, change when they called upon their deceased friends for help.

# 6 hello

'I am ten times more famous since being assumed dead.'   Lionel Richie

'I thought going with a blind person was the worse suggestion ever on the planet.'   Lionel Richie

'I knew I could put out damn near everything but the hole in the middle.'   Skip Miller, of 'Can't Slow Down'

In September 1983 Lionel Richie embarked upon his first solo tour across the world, comprising 48 dates including three weeks in the Far East. He opened at Lake Tahoe in Nevada. The four Pointer Sisters were his support act, who won audiences over with performances that covered their nostalgic 1940s songs like 'Yes We Can Can' through to dance numbers that included 'I'm So Excited'. A perfect musical complement to the headliner. The tour was months in the planning; it had to be a vehicle to launch Richie as a solo superstar and one that would outshine anything that had gone before. To this end, Joe Layton, the respected Broadway director and choreographer, who had worked with Diana Ross, staged the show from the first song 'Truly', with the star seated at his piano, through to 'Endless Love', his duet with Diana Ross. 'She comes out of the darkness and you'd think it was the Oscar ceremony all over again. For a minute the audience really think she's there.' In actual fact, Diana appeared life-size on a video screen and the stage lighting gave a three-dimensional illusion. At the song's close, Richie, much to his audiences' amazement, held her hand! (Apparently Diana was not available for the tour because she considered the ticket prices at $20 too low. Whether this was true or not is conjecture; a more likely reason for her absence was her own touring commitments.) *Blues & Soul*'s gossip columnist jibed, 'Showing not the slightest flicker of amusement, Lionel gloats over her enlarged image, making eyes at the video. Motown/UK pray that he won't bring the idea to this country!' Choosing suitable musicians was also an awesome task, but with the help of Ken Kragen Richie hired those with the heaviest credentials.

There's Greg Phillinganes, he's the musical director, and he played with Stevie Wonder on 'Talking Book' and others. Then, Henry Davis, he's bass guitarist and comes from L.T.D. Carlos Rios, guitarist, has played on many Quincy Jones sessions. Drummer Gerry Brown has played a lot with Stanley Clarke, and my percussionist is a lady, Sheila Escovedo, and she's wonderful. Finally, there's Randy Stern, the keyboardist, who's done sessions with Cameo. I must tell you about Sheila. She's just great with the audiences. She entices them and gets them going. We spoil her rotten, though, being the only woman in the band. Brenda first saw her work and suggested to me that she'd be an asset to the band. I didn't have time to see her myself because I was tied up in the studios, but now I'm just as hooked. All the musicians are good to work with. When we all go out on stage, we're all glad to be there and we all enjoy it so much. It's not working, it's a real pleasure. And that makes the difference to the whole performance and it's a relief for me not to have to worry about how the musicians are doing, will they turn up on time, will they work OK, and things like that.

It's true to say Richie was extremely apprehensive about performing alone, as Greg Phillinganes explained on BBC Radio 2: 'He was in trepidations about the whole solo thing because he was so used to the band, and I think it was more evident when he was preparing for the first solo tour. That's when it became pretty apparent because in the studio he was pretty cool.' The first dates in Nevada were used to knock the show into shape before an estimated 3,000 people each date, as Richie explained. 'This was the very first time I'd appeared on stage without the Commodores and I was a little uptight. I walked out on stage and the crowd gave me a standing ovation. I couldn't believe it. I felt like I was home and it was wonderful.' His performance spanned the Commodores' ballads and his own work, including songs like 'All Night Long (All Night)' from his forthcoming album, at first titled *Positive Force* but renamed *Can't Slow Down* for release. The first major performance was staged in Toledo, Ohio, where 10,000 people flocked to see him; likewise, the four shows at New York's Radio City Music Hall, where on the last night Richie agreed to add a midnight performance to benefit three New York organizations, Symphony Space, The Actors Fund and the Dance Theatre of Harlem. Pupils at a local junior high school were extremely grateful for his donation of $10,000 but stunned when he delivered the cheque personally prior to singing a selection of his material at the school's piano. When the Richie touring circus reached Tuskegee on 29 October 1983 the mayor declared it to be 'Lionel Richie Day'. 'The town accorded me the ultimate honour, and put me on the front page of the local newspaper, and that has always been reserved for the mayor!' His family attended his performance but it was his beloved grandmother who showed the most enthusiasm about his career. 'It's really funny because she seems almost more concerned than I do about the way the records have been going and, when I'm home, she'll turn to me and say, "We've moved up a couple of places this week on the charts!" It's great to have that kind of support behind you.' His mother, on the other hand, told journalists, 'He's just my son, not somebody famous!'

Travelling from state to state, Richie noticed how different his audiences were because, he admitted, he just didn't know what to expect now that he was a solo entertainer with a group history.

> There's eight-year-olds, their mums and dads, grandmas, granddads, there's kids with red hair and orange hair, guys dressed in leather and chains, Rastafarians, all colours. Man, it's breathtaking. It's more like the United Nations than the United States – but I like it that way. And, another thing, I never know who's going to sing the songs. Me or them! I never get to finish a song. People are crying, some are fainting, screaming and shouting. It's real weird. It's like I'm just the cheerleader. And when we sing 'All Night Long' the stage is crowded because everyone gets up there with me.

Michael Jackson attended the Los Angeles performance. To avoid being recognized he wore an Afro wig and an oversized baseball jacket, and laughed as he watched Richie performing a 'Billie Jean' rap before telling the audience how he had taught the young Jackson to dance! Then, in November, Richie narrowly escaped death when the plane in which he was travelling from Tucson crashed on landing in Phoenix, Arizona. The plane's wheels collapsed, the tail section was damaged and the runway was so chewed up that it was closed for two hours. Newsflashes were networked across America claiming Lionel Richie had died in the crash. Later, greatly relieved, he quipped, 'I am ten times more famous since being assumed dead!'

Recorded at Ocean Way Studios, on Sunset Boulevard, in Hollywood, and based on swaying percussion laden with a Latin groove, 'All Night Long (All Night)' possessed so many great qualities – melody, style, a craftsmanship that was easily recognizable as the trademark of one of the world's most enterprising performers. The song was different from 'All Night Long', recently released by Rick James's protégés, the Mary Jane Girls. Their song went on to become a UK top-twenty hit in June 1983, while Richie's single catapulted to the top in 18 countries except Britain, where it stalled at number two, held off the top spot by Billy Joel's 'Uptown Girl'. It outsold 'Endless Love' to become Motown's biggest-selling single throughout the world. In Britain it also raced into the dance chart at number four, but record stores were unable to order the 12-inch version of the single because Motown/UK abided by its US parent's instruction not to release an extended version, as copies of this would flood the US market, disrupting the progress of the 7-inch single there. When the title topped the British dance chart, copies of the US 12-inch became available in specialist outlets. The US version differed from the late arrival of its British equivalent in that it featured the re-mixed album track, with the instrumental on the B-side, whereas the UK single featured the 7-inch version. Had the British 12-inch version been available earlier, Richie could well have enjoyed a UK number one. Nonetheless, it was the ninth best-selling single of 1983, one rung below Michael Jackson's 'Billie Jean'. The British outfit Culture Club, with Boy George at the helm, held the pole position with 'Karma Chameleon'. 'All Night Long (All Night)' was the only Motown song in the top ten, although Phil Collins's version of Diana Ross and the Supremes' 1966 hit 'You Can't Hurry Love' might warrant a mention!

Prior to the single being released, a meeting was held at Berry Gordy's house with his immediate A&R staff to discuss the whole *Can't Slow Down* project. Included were Willie Hutch and Raynoma Gordy-Singleton, who wrote in her book *Berry, Me and Motown*,

> A staff member believed the album's first single 'All Night Long' would bomb. He insisted that the public would bear him out, going on and on, until he glanced over to the chairman for what he expected would be some kind of salute. All Berry gave him was a trademark look of disgusted incomprehension. 'What the hell are you talking about? Man, I haven't even heard the damned record. But if Lionel Richie did it, as hot as he is, it's got to be a smash!'

It's not known whether the unnamed A&R staffer held onto his job!

Still backtracking on the music front, Lionel Richie, recently nicknamed the black Barry Manilow because of his love of ballads, deliberately broke away from this market with this calypso-flavoured single. And he couldn't resist adding a musical gimmick either, as part of the song's verse included the phrase 'tom bo li de say moi ya, yeah, jambo jumbo', which he identified as one of Bob Marley's chants that had no real meaning. The record's credits included a Dr Byron Greig as dialect coach, which conjured up several explanations but none so inventive as the singer's when he explained,

> He's really a gynaecologist from Los Angeles. My wife's gynaecologist and he's Jamaican. He would come by and visit us and I started listening to his accent. We got talking a lot, and when I was in the studios working on the single, I kept phoning him up, saying talk to me because I wanted to imitate him. I wanted to do something different with this record, and when I found myself saying some of his phrases, I knew I wanted to use his accent on the record. So, I'd stop my musicians in the middle of a session to phone him. I must have worried him to death. I suppose in the end I talked to him for two days on the phone.

James Carmichael remembered that 'All Night Long (All Night)' was not meant to be the song's title. 'He had what he called God's words [which] to him are the words he sets down. And he just sings along without thinking…he may mumble even…Listening back he kept hearing "all night long". So he decided the song's name was that. Now all he had to do was write it!' Richie later told Steven Ivory (for the CD album's notes) a slightly different version of the song's history, admitting it was the toughest he had composed and he was haunted by the fact that he couldn't finish it. All he had was the chorus and a section of the first verse, so it was constantly pushed aside. However, that changed by pure chance when Richie was leaving a pal's house and said, 'Listen, I gotta go 'cos I've been working all night long.' It was the hook he needed, but the problems weren't over yet, as he divulged, 'Bob Rafelson, who was going to direct the video, had breakdancers in one room listening to the track. We had a choir learning their background vocals in another room, and I was across the street rehearsing the song for a concert in Lake Tahoe that was the warm-up date for my tour.' Testing it as the show's finale, where the audience reacted wildly, he returned to Los Angeles to re-mix it before declaring it and the album to be finished. As there were only nine songs on it – when most albums held at least twelve – a nervous artist handed the masters to Berry Gordy, who in turn alerted Skip Miller, then Motown's label president, 'Radio was going to be all over it. It was like an instant greatest hits album. I knew I could put out damn near everything but the hole in the middle.' The project's overwhelming international appeal catapulted its creator into mainstream superstardom beyond his wildest dreams. He had created a musical masterpiece which needed regular promotional attention. In time, though, Lionel Richie would slow down but not through choice.

Supported by a powerful dance video produced by Mike Nesmith, former member of the Monkees, and directed by Bob Rafelson, who was also connected to the 1960s pop quartet, 'All Night Long (All Night)' just couldn't fail. Richie said, 'It's one thing to have a hit in America and Britain, but for the record to take off all over the world, well, that's something very hard for me to believe. I suppose you consider it as competing against "Three Times A Lady" and that was frightening enough for us as it was.' And he further remarked on BBC Radio 2, 'It was all night long for the rest of my life. In every country I became "Lionel Richie, all night long." They didn't know how to say anything else at the time. It used to be – "Lionel Richie, hello."...That's how powerful those songs became.' As an aside, when the single topped the US chart, Richie had secured six number-one singles in six years. His first was 'Three Times A Lady' with the Commodores in 1978, and 'Still' a year later. In 1980, Kenny Rogers took 'Lady' to the top, while 'Endless Love' followed a year later. 'Truly' was next in 1982. Only John Lennon, Paul McCartney and Barry Gibb have matched this achievement (all in 1983).

Released at the same time as Richie's international chart-topper, but only in the USA, was 'Only You' by the Commodores. The group was playing a dangerous game by performing a ballad that had all the hallmarks of a Lionel Richie composition, with the acoustic piano and strings dominating a very strong melody and a gripping chorus. 'Typical Richie maybe, but more importantly, it's typical Commodores and quite superb at that,' wrote critic Justin Lubbock. 'Walter Orange has always been a great vocalist.' Not great enough, unfortunately; the single stalled in the US top sixty.

Fellow Motown artist Stevie Wonder was also touring the USA, taking in dates in Atlantic City, Boston, New York and San Carlos, California. At the Radio City Music Hall, New York, he performed two new songs, 'Overjoyed' and 'Go Home', from his forthcoming album before paying tribute to Lionel Richie by singing a verse from 'All Night Long (All Night)', claiming it was his favourite record at the time. 'Right in the middle of the show, he stopped everything to play it on tape!' gushed Richie when he later discovered what had happened. 'Unfortunately, I wasn't there to hear it, but I phoned Stevie afterwards and said he was real crazy to do that. I just couldn't believe it. It was the greatest compliment of my life.' During their conversation, he asked Wonder whether his long-overdue album was ready for release. No.

> Only Stevie knows when it'll be ready. He doesn't have a co-producer or co-writers, and people like that, not like I do, and when you write say 17 or 18 songs for an album which you know can only hold eight or nine, it's difficult to decide which tracks to include. Now with me, it's a joint decision but with Stevie he makes the decision. There's nobody around to encourage him to stick to a deadline.

Years later, Wonder would change his working practices to include third parties, while Richie adopted his friend's lead by failing to deliver product on time.

Early in 1984 promoters of the forthcoming Olympic Games to be staged in Los Angeles announced that the closing ceremony would feature a surprise guest artist/s. The original plan, already mooted by Benny Ashburn, was to invite Lionel Richie to perform with Diana Ross and Michael Jackson, but for some reason they dropped out. The Olympic Committee then had a new offer for the ex-Commodore – to sing 'All Night Long (All Night)' by himself. No artist could pass this up, but Richie hesitated because he didn't feel he was ready for such a huge leap onto an international platform. So he consulted his friend Kenny Rogers. 'Lionel's problem is like that of every person who is new to superstardom,' he told Roberta Plutznik in *Billboard*. 'They think fans and producers are going to hate them if they say "no". It's just not true. People understand. I said to Lionel, "You have a tremendous responsibility to yourself".' Described by the event's producer David Wolper as an evening of 'majesty, inspiration and

Lionel, nicknamed the black Barry Manilow, released his second album *Can't Slow Down*, which sold in excess of four million copies during the first ten weeks of its release.

emotion', the closing ceremony was more like a sequence from *Close Encounters of the Third Kind* than the climax to an international sporting event. And Lionel Richie was the star who appeared from the spotlights! Ken Kragen said, 'There was just an image that I always think of – Lionel on the middle of the stadium at the Coliseum in Los Angeles. It was water and fire.' Once the performance was over, the star was deliriously happy, stating it was the greatest joy of his life!

As Motown prepared to issue Lionel Richie's second solo album, *Can't Slow Down*, in October 1983, Commodore Clyde Orange was working on his debut solo project. His history was so steeped in music, ranging from gospel and big bands through to funk, that the group wasn't the ideal vehicle with which to express himself. Meanwhile, Milan Williams worked with Dolly Parton's sister Stella; William King was recording a gospel album, while Thomas McClary had written and produced tracks for a Michael Hutton project. But everything was overshadowed by Lionel Richie's second album, a collection of newly written songs.

> I was looking for more uptempo songs this time that wouldn't sound like everyone else's. Michael Jackson seems to have that market sewn up for the next few years or so, and I wanted to create my own unique sound. I prefer to write new

songs for new projects, although I'm sure I must have some good songs in store by now that I've forgotten about.

Musician Michael Boddicker again worked with Richie, and told BBC Radio 2,

> There was a battle. Cal [Harris, engineer] liked this, James liked this, Lionel liked this. They didn't throw punches but they sure let each other know what they liked and what they didn't like, and what they thought should be there to make Lionel's record the best they could make. There'd be a James Carmichael mix, there'd be a Cal Harris mix, and there'd be a Lionel Richie mix, and then they'd duke it out, combining the three to get the end product. It was an amazing process.

He then recalled an incident highlighting James Carmichael's unusual recording techniques, one which could have ended in disaster.

> James is one of the most gifted acoustic arrangers in the record industry and he'd written this gorgeous string arrangement for 'Penny Lover'. 'Michael, I'd like to see how it sounds if it was a synthesized oboe instead of an oboe' and put the string tracks in record. I said, 'This is a slave track, right?' meaning this was a back-up of the original. And he said, 'No, it's the master' and erased the acoustic strings for the first verse and first chorus. I just about had a heart attack. I said, 'Don't you want to think about this or have it as a back-up?' He didn't care about it, it was the essence of what the song needed that he cared about.

*Can't Slow Down* spawned further hit singles, one being 'Running With The Night' (originally called 'Strangers In The Night'), which was supported by a promotional video directed by Bob Giraldi, who was responsible for Michael Jackson's 'Beat It' video, among others. Richie wrote this track with Cynthia Weil, whose work with her husband, Barry Mann, was extremely well respected and included the classics 'Walking In The Rain', 'Looking Through The Eyes Of Love' and 'You've Lost That Loving Feeling'.

> Lionel and I shared the same attorneys, and they knew he occasionally got stuck on lyrics. Music was always easier for him, so they suggested the two of us get together. Lionel had a melody which ended up being 'Running With The Night', and he was blocked on it, and he had so much to do, he just couldn't listen to it one more time. He wanted me to write something that would be very visual and would make a music video. So, that's what I tried to do.

She further explained, 'When we'd talk about a lyric we would talk about Lionel-izing it. And in that sense he makes everything his own.' She also believed he had effortlessly crossed from funk to country to pop music 'and I don't know how easy that was [for him]. I think radio tends to stereotype you and wants you to make those changes. There's a certain amount of courage that goes into that. [Lionel] had that, he never hesitated to follow his creative instincts.'

Three future singles – 'Hello', 'Stuck On You' and 'Penny Lover' – were all true Richie ballads and attracted middle-of-the-road buyers to the album, in addition to the remnants of the black music fans who had stuck with his music. He quite freely admitted he faced a musical dilemma with the new project because as much as he yearned to break free from the ballads, he knew to do so would lose him at least four million fans.

> And if 'All Night Long' hadn't been a hit and I dedicated the whole album to that sound I'm in trouble because that's it until the next time I go into the studios. Recording uptempo tracks is my way of brightening up things now and again because I don't want to fall into the trap of giving people what they expect, or have come to expect from me. I was also afraid of falling into the middle-of-the-road market with slow songs because that's not what I want to do right now.

Selling over four million copies during the first ten weeks of release, it passed the ten-million mark in the USA alone, with 15 million worldwide, tying with Bruce Springsteen's *Born In The USA*, one of the strongest-selling albums in the history of the charts. It was also the twelfth best-selling album in Britain during 1983; Michael Jackson's *Thriller* was number one.

Credited as writer and production assistant, Brenda Harvey's input was noticeable on the album because Richie emphasized her need to be a part of his working life. 'I try not to let it affect our personal life, though, but it's difficult to live with Lionel Richie because I tend to put my mark on everything. Everyone who comes through our front door is aware of me, the artist, which can be pretty boring at times.'

Out of eight tracks, five were top-ten singles, so Richie had got the balance just right. He also followed Michael Jackson's precedent by simultaneously securing the number one-position in the US pop and black album and singles charts with *Can't Slow Down* and 'All Night Long (All Night)'. Jackson's achievement was with the *Thriller* album and 'Billie Jean' single. Other Motown albums released at the same time were the Four Tops' *Back Where I Belong*, their first since returning to Motown; Junior Walker's *Blow The House Down*; the Stone City Band's *Out From The Shadow* and *The Mary Jane Girls*. All were strong releases but against *Can't Slow Down* they stood no chance, particularly when the album became Motown's first CD release, alongside a series of *Command Performances* from Diana Ross, Marvin Gaye, Smokey Robinson and the Miracles, Michael Jackson and the Jackson 5.

'Running With The Night' was the second extracted single, but it failed to reach the grade of its predecessor by hitting the US and British top ten. Shortly after this release, the singer hosted the American Music Awards special staged in Los Angeles, where he also received the Favourite Soul Single award for 'All Night Long (All Night)'. He smoothly co-ordinated the ceremony with his warm personality and was an integral part of the show's success. Dick Clark, executive producer of the ABC-TV annual broadcast, asked if he would be the solo host for the next Awards ceremony in 1985. When Richie agreed, he became the first artist to achieve this role two years running. Meantime, the 1984 ceremony was dominated by Michael Jackson – no surprise there! – when he won eight awards (Best Pop Album and Best Soul Album for *Thriller*; Best Pop Single for 'Billie Jean'; Favourite Pop and Soul Male Vocalist; Best Pop and Soul Video for 'Beat It') and a Merit Award presented to him by Diana Ross, who described him as a dream in motion. Jackson had also been nominated for a staggering twelve Grammy Awards, eleven for *Thriller* and one for his narration of the MCA Records *E.T.* album in the Best Recording for Children category. Lionel Richie fell behind him with only five nominations, but joined him to celebrate the talents of producer/composer Quincy Jones for a two-hour documentary due to be screened in March 1984. The programme was to feature Jones, with interviews from his associates, who also included Diana Ross, plus concert and studio footage. 'People said that [the Music Awards were] going to ruin my career,' reflected Richie. 'What happened was *Thriller* was the hip thing at the time. But sometimes being number two goes a long way.'

The track that screamed to be lifted from *Can't Slow Down* was the ripe, ready-to-pluck ballad 'Hello'. (As the marketing ploy with 'Three Times A Lady' and *Natural High* was so financially rewarding, Motown/UK had again decided to milk the album's sales by releasing the inferior 'Running With The Night' as the next single.) One review gushed, '"Hello" is simply a typically stunning Richie slowie that has become his trademark. Jam-packed full of the inimitable Richie qualities, this song will cause the hairs on the back of your neck to stand to attention in the same way as his other creations. A number one all the way!'

The prediction was spot on. The single became a worldwide number-one record, and, statistically speaking, became Motown's 302nd British hit (including reissues) since 1964, when Mary Wells's US single 'My Guy' reached number five. Richie's British sales were helped by the 12-inch version, which contained extended instrumental versions of 'All Night Long (All Night)' and 'Running With The Night' on the flipside. When 'Hello' and 'Can't Slow Down' became British chart-toppers simultaneously, the singer was holidaying in Hawaii prior to returning to Los Angeles to start work on his next album. Spending six weeks at the top of the British chart, 'Hello' sold in excess of 800,000 copies to beat the Commodores' 'Three Times A Lady' as the longest running number one with five weeks, following Diana

Ross's 'I'm Still Waiting' (four weeks). Additionally, when the single was UK-released in March 1984 – a month after its US outing, when it was Motown's first official picture disc – *Can't Slow Down* had sold over 600,000 copies to become one of Britain's top three best-selling albums, alongside George Benson's *In Your Eyes* and, of course, Michael Jackson's *Thriller*.

To promote this slice of Richie magic, he starred in a promotional video, directed again by Bob Giraldi, with 25-year-old Laura Carrington playing a blind girl. Perhaps, in hindsight, the shockingly bad video could have been changed. It was an emotional love story which certain quarters of the media criticized as being in extremely bad taste. For example, *Melody Maker's* Dessa Fox wrote,

> The leading lady has been given a white stick, told to flutter her eyes, look enigmatic and in general behave like a sugar-fed Bambi. What she is not doing is acting human, like the rest of us. The sleaziest section of 'Hello' comes at the end of the bed sequence. The telephone rings and – in an insult to blind people everywhere, who know exactly where familiar noise sources are – this 'actress' attempts to squeeze tears from us sentimental record buyers by groping around for the telephone.

Richie played a drama teacher, coaching a class of students in scenes which could have been swiped from *Fame*, who falls in love with a blind student. The video shows him 'haunting' her, which, some journalists suggested, could be interpreted as a trailer for a John Carpenter horror/thriller film. According to Laura Carrington, one scene was actually edited out: 'I did a naked shower scene, where the camera panned up my legs and back as I got out of the shower and groped for a towel. But neither Lionel nor Bob Giraldi thought it was suitable because they wanted the video to be wholesome.' Playing a blind girl was an enormous challenge, she said, and 'It took enormous concentration to block out everything that passed in front of me. But playing opposite Lionel was one of the biggest breaks an actress could wish for.' Her sculpting skills in the video left a lot to be desired, but the finished bust did bring tears to the teacher's eyes. According to Bob Giraldi, 'The lyrics say it all – "Is it me you're looking for?" She sculpts this oversized head of Lionel on just what she can imagine. So from afar he had admired her and loved her, and that basically is what the song was to me.' When asked its fate, Richie laughed, 'It fell off the table in the middle of the last take. I remember going to Giraldi and going "It doesn't look like me, Bob. It's kinda awful!" And he said, "Lionel...she's blind!" I remember that. I never did keep it.' (Today, there is a website devoted to building the Lionel Richie head!) He further told broadcaster Jeremy Vine, 'I thought going with a blind person was the worst suggestion ever on the planet', while Giraldi admitted that, in retrospect, he understood the criticism but pointed out that '"Hello" remains a piece of work that I'm proud of.'

Promotional videos were coming into their own, playing a vital role in the life of a single, and from the early 1980s artists relied on producers and directors like Bob Giraldi to present their music on film in the most innovative and memorable manner possible. The videos were not documentaries, rather mini-motion pictures, portraying little window-boxes of the song. 'I began to work with mostly black artists because I gravitated to their music,' Giraldi remembered on BBC Radio 2. 'They were hot and started to come after certain directors and I happened to be in the club. I had a great time.'

Finally, when 'Hello' topped the US chart, 1984 became the seventh consecutive year that a Lionel Richie composition occupied this position. Irving Berlin was the only sole composer in music's history to beat this, with nine songs. Richie tied with Cole Porter, also with seven. Paul McCartney was third with six. However, as the single's sales peaked, a New York housewife, Marjorie White, made an allegation of plagiarism, claiming she had written the song under its original title 'I'm Not Ready To Go'.

On the upside and also in March, the singer signed a major deal with the soft drinks company Pepsi Cola in what was described as the largest and most comprehensive agreement between a corporation and a recording artist. The two-year contract ensured that Pepsi Cola would sponsor his 1984/1985 concerts and fund a television spectacular and/or film. Richie, on the other hand, would endorse the soft drink via a series of commercials and compose a number of songs for the company's advertising campaigns. In negotiating the deal, Richie was promised that Pepsi would join him in contributing to charitable organizations. 'For a long time I have had an interest in talented kids with no opportunities. Unlike a lot of corporations that merely pay lip service, Pepsi has signed on the dotted line to do something about it.' The company also felt his public image was suited to their marketing strategies and paid an estimated $8 million for the privilege. Richie's agreement followed hotly on the heels of a similar deal Pepsi Cola had made with the Jacksons, whereby the company would sponsor the group's 'Victory' tour in return for television advertising endorsements. During the filming of one commercial, Michael suffered second-degree burns on his scalp after an accident involving a special effects smoke bomb. The young Jackson was hospitalized and continued to receive daily treatment upon his discharge. It cost Pepsi a cool $5.5 million to conclude the Jacksons' agreement. When the first commercials featuring the group were shown on US television, after being premiered at the Grammy Awards broadcast, they were shown free of charge because the television station considered them to be news stories! This saved Pepsi $3 million in airtime costs. Not to be beaten, Pepsi's biggest competitor, Coca-Cola, announced a three-year, $7 million contract with Spanish heart-throb Julio Iglesias, whose son would later record with Lionel Richie.

Tour sponsorship was big business during the 1980s because it meant the sponsor's product would be advertised extensively throughout the tour (on tickets, posters, merchandise, etc.), although the artist was not necessarily required to mention the sponsor from the stage. However, when Germany's Adidas sponsored Rod Stewart's European tour, he was required to kick their footballs – very carefully – into the audience! Touring costs soared drastically, particularly for international stars like Lionel Richie and the Jacksons, who both insisted on elaborate and expensive stage sets and lighting. For example, promoter Charles Sullivan paid approximately $45 million ($12 million in cash in advance) for the rights to promote the Jacksons' US 'Victory' tour, which was expected to generate $100 million. Prior to this the biggest gross figure generated by a US tour was $34 million by the Rolling Stones in 1983. The Jacksons also gave underprivileged children about $1 million worth of tickets, while Pepsi Cola gave away a further 24,000 tickets via a drinks campaign.

Before Lionel Richie could step foot on stage he was condemned by the Promoters Association (which represents prominent black promoters in the USA) for not involving local black promoters in the tour. The Association charged that, of the tour's forty-one dates, black promoters were responsible for only four. Jesse Boseman, founder of the Association, told *Billboard*, 'Richie's situation is gross. Blacks helped to make Richie when he was with the Commodores. He had a black manager and a black base. Now he has a booking agent, Howard Rose, who has stopped adequate black participation.' The singer's manager Ken Kragen retaliated by saying the Association was attempting to turn a business arrangement into a civil rights issue. 'Lionel doesn't hire on a basis of colour; he's only interested in who can do the best job. Lionel's attitude is not to buckle one inch to this kind of approach. He doesn't want to bow to unreasonable and unfair charges and pressure.' However, Kragen did admit that his client no longer had a strong black following, and explained that during his last US tour, black attendance was as low as two per cent. For this coming tour, however, black radio stations would be used substantially to advertise the show, he said, and confirmed that Richie's deal with Pepsi Cola included funnelling money into black communities. The Jacksons, too, were similarly criticized, but it was later proven that neither act was known to hire whites in preference to blacks. Richie subsequently met the Reverend Al Sharpton, who was intending to lead demonstrations at his concerts. Sharpton agreed to abandon his plans when the singer confirmed black promoters would co-promote thirteen to seventeen concerts, at least.

For his second nationwide tour, Lionel Richie asked Tina Turner to be his support act. A band was hastily organized to tour with her, as she had just released 'Let's Stay Together', her version of the Al Green classic, and her debut for a newly signed recording deal with Capitol Records. She was the ex-wife and singing partner of Ike Turner; together with the Ikettes they had recorded and toured as the Ike & Tina Turner Revue, where she perfected her (now-legendary) sexy stage antics and powerful vocal presence. Tina would ideally complement Richie's laid-back approach to entertaining. 'It was real hard being on stage by myself at first. Lionel's crowd wasn't my crowd and I was singing brand-new material and the only thing they wanted to hear was "Nutbush City Limits", "Let's Stay Together" and "Proud Mary".' However, she persevered with her new material, and when radio stations aired their support, audiences began to appreciate her explosive talent. Within months she would be touring again – as the headliner – but at this point in her career, the Lionel Richie tour was a windfall that went on to help launch her first album as a soloist, *Private Dancer*. The two artists apparently first met by chance at Los Angeles airport. Eddy Armani wrote in *The Real T*,

> She spotted Lionel and his wife Brenda. Tina had never met Lionel before, and at that time he was the hottest solo recording artist in the world, topping global charts with slow melodies and romantic tunes. With absolutely nothing to lose, Tina marched straight up to him and introduced herself....'I know we've never met before but I have to let you know that I love these ballads you're writing, particularly "Still". I use it in my new show. I know how busy you are, but I'd love for you to write something for me.'

The response wasn't what Tina expected as the Richies excitedly declared they were great admirers.

> 'My wife and I are big fans of yours.' Cutting Lionel off, Brenda excitedly piped in, 'I just love your music. We have all your recordings.' Between Lionel and Brenda, Tina suddenly felt as she had introduced herself to two star-struck fans. Lionel and his wife were the sweetest people on earth and weren't shy about letting [her] know how much they idolized her...Lionel didn't let Tina go without changing phone numbers and he told her he would love to write a special song for her.

The fifty-city US tour was a huge success, as David Nathan reported:

> Lionel Richie is one of today's performers who knows how to give his audience exactly what they want. Interspersing his music with warm, friendly comments to the audience, Lionel's show is well-paced and runs the gamut from the sensitive ballads to the obvious climax with 'All Night Long'. Opening the show was Tina Turner...As always clad in the most mini of mini-skirts, long blonde hair thrown from side to side, she demonstrated why she's been called the hardest-working

woman in show business, dashing from one side of the stage to another, everything done at high energy level. Tina's closing was in contrast to Lionel's opening. To the strains of 'Truly', Lionel hit the stage to tumultuous applause from the capacity crowd. Special effects – such as a tilting grand piano – added to the excitement on stage as Lionel went straight into 'Serves You Right'.

The singer's performance spanned his work with the Commodores, including, of course, 'Three Times A Lady', for which Tina rejoined him on stage. Nothing was left to chance; it was a highly charged, emotional, audience-participating monster of a show which eventually burnt itself out, prompting Nathan to close his review with 'Lionel has established himself at the very top, and the professional, exciting way in which he performs marks him as an entertainer who will be around for a very long time.'

While Richie was touring his home country, the Commodores announced British club and concert dates for September 1984, including London's Hammersmith Odeon. It was unclear whether any new material would be available for the tour because, Motown/UK explained, it was not known whether the group had any plans to record in the near future. And within a month another Commodore embarked upon a solo career. Thomas McClary, who had recently been working with Klique, signed to MCA Records. He said the deciding factor in leaving the group was the increasing difficulty in satisfying his own creative needs. 'I had fifteen great years with the Commodores and I love those guys. I think we accomplished all the goals we set out to and we'll certainly go down in history for what we achieved. The Commodores has become an international household word.' He further told John Abbey,

> For me there has always been a dream inside to attain new goals. Things that couldn't really be implemented from inside of the group. And they require time to devote to them and being part of a group such as the Commodores made it impossible. Sure, I was able to get off a little to write and produce but that just made the desire even greater.

Lionel Richie was a background vocalist on McClary's first solo single 'Thin Walls', taken from his eponymous album, about which he said, 'I'm really perfectly satisfied with the album and working with Lionel again was very satisfying. We always had a great time working together, and Lionel's own success has served as an inspiration to me.' One reviewer noted, 'Not the most instant of albums...instead of following Lionel Richie's steps after leaving the Commodores, this debut solo album isn't blatantly commercial.' Unfortunately, Richie's success didn't rub off on McClary, which left him no option but to plough his creative energies into working with other acts. Of the Commodores at this time, he divulged, they were completing their next album but he wasn't included on it. 'I offered my services as a writer but the guys felt it best that I make a clean split if I intended to leave the group, and I understand and respect their decision.' What wasn't publicly known, however, was they had, in fact, recently recruited session singer J. D. Nicholas as their lead singer and together they were working on a new album with producer Dennis Lambert.

Also at this time, *Billboard* announced an all-time record in that black artists currently accounted for six of the top-ten pop albums in the USA. Prince's *Purple Rain* topped the chart for the fourth consecutive week, while Tina Turner's *Private Dancer* had jumped to the number four spot. Ray Parker Jr's soundtrack album for *Ghostbusters* was steady at six; the Jacksons' *Victory* album was at seven, Lionel Richie's *Can't Slow Down* at eight, and the Pointer Sisters' *Break Out* at ten.

Before the close of 1984, two further tracks were extracted as singles from *Can't Slow Down*, namely, the familiar-sounding 'Stuck On You', which hit the US top three and British top twenty, and 'Penny Lover', co-written with his wife Brenda, which was a US top-ten and British top-twenty hit. Producer/writer and Richie mentor Norman Whitfield could be seen as a nightclub bouncer on the video for 'Penny Lover', which, by the way, had already been re-recorded by Katie Kissoon as her second single for Jive Records. 'The title I came up with was really a working title. I was going to change it to "Oh My Lover", but "Penny Lover" just sounded right.' *Blues & Soul* printed the title as 'Penny Loser', which, compared to his other successes, it was! Richie commented, 'We finally got to the point…where the album was becoming a "greatest hits" package and that's when the company stopped putting out singles and just sold the rest of the album…The only song that didn't get played that much was [the album's] title…it was the quietest song.' Subsequently, it was the only track not lifted for single release. 'I could not turn on the radio without hearing either "All Night Long" or something else off the album,' James Carmichael said on BBC Radio 2. 'Every station you turned to, there it was. I knew we had struck off on something special.' The album has stood the test of time; twenty years later the arrangements remain freshly melodic, the musicians' energy is still vital and the songs timeless. It was an interesting musical document of the era and was, many believed, Lionel Richie and James Carmichael taking on Michael Jackson and Quincy Jones with *Thriller*.

It was indeed a glorious period, as noted by Nelson George:

> *Thriller* sold twenty million copies in the US and Lionel Richie's *All Night Long* and *Can't Slow Down* sold over ten million, confirming the feast-or-famine cycle in popular music. A black who crossed over could sell a humongous number of records. And the fact that so few succeeded didn't stifle the dream. (*The Death of Rhythm & Blues*)

Luckily, Lionel Richie's dream lasted for a while yet.

# 7 we are the world

'It's good enough as it is. Just put it out there.'   Diana Ross, talking about 'Missing You'

'I will admit that when Lionel left, it was a real downer.'   William King

'Being famous is like being put in a little capsule that isolates you from being a normal human.'   Lionel Richie

Tragedy struck the music world on 1 April 1984 when Marvin Gaye was shot dead by his father in their family home in Los Angeles. Fans, friends, the media and business acquaintances joined recording artists to pay tribute to a troubled star who was such a huge influence on Lionel Richie and the way he approached his songwriting. Gaye's work had inspired so many fellow artists and young acts, while his music was loved by millions more. Motown artists were among the first to remember his magic, including the Temptations, who dedicated their *Truly For You* album to him. Smokey Robinson recalled one of his greatest pleasures was working with Gaye in the studio, and Michael Jackson's brother Jermaine felt his death had left a big void in his life because he influenced the way he worked. Certain artists took their tributes one step further by recording their feelings. Stevie Wonder wrote 'Lighting Up The Candles', which he sang at Gaye's funeral and later included in his *Jungle Fever* album, and Teena Marie composed and recorded 'My Dear Mr Gaye' with Leon Ware, who had composed 'I Want You' with Marvin. However, it was Gaye's colleague Edwin Starr who released one of the first singles, in May 1984, titled 'Marvin: From A Friend To A Friend' and penned by British DJ Mick Collins.

> The minute I heard it I knew that I had to record it. It said everything about the tragedy and the man. I could have started from scratch but Mick's demo had such honesty and feeling that I considered it would be wrong to ignore it. In fact, I don't suppose I'd have been interested in the project had it been written by a Lionel Richie or a Stevie Wonder. (Edwin Starr)

Nonetheless, someone *was* interested in a Lionel Richie composition – Diana Ross. Bearing in mind how Marvin Gaye had viewed her as a competitor at Motown and the clashes that occurred while they were recording the one-off *Diana & Marvin* album in 1973, it seemed to the public a strange move for her to make. The song 'Missing You' was the perfect loving tribute, containing all the heartfelt emotions expected from Richie's pen complemented by Ross's wistful vocals against a moody, low-key arrangement. Richie also played piano and, with James Carmichael, arranged and produced the song. Diana said the song was born from a conversation she'd had with Smokey Robinson. 'We were talking about how we were missing Marvin and what he meant to us as well as to music. Then Lionel and I got to talking about how we need to tell people that we love them while they're still alive. Lionel used all this to write that beautiful and special song.' According to J. Randy Taraborrelli, the recording session was far from amicable despite the two artists having previously worked together: 'Diana and Lionel apparently had their share of problems in the recording studio, because the song was released before it was even finished – the vocals were incomplete at the end. "It's good enough as it is," Diana declared. "Just put it out there"' (*Call Her Miss Ross*).

The poignant single soared into the US top ten late in 1984, peaking at number one in the R&B listing; sadly, the uninhibited sentiments in the song were lost on the British public as it disappeared without a trace, surprisingly for a Richie ballad, and for a single accompanied by one of the most thoughtfully compiled promotional videos. Diana's own company Anaid [Diana reversed] Film Productions produced it, and she took second place in order to devote most of the viewing time to sequences of two other Motown casualties, Florence Ballard (Supremes) and Paul Williams (Temptations), her own late mother, and extensive footage of Marvin Gaye. It transpired that the video was played more than the single, despite extensive re-promotion activities by Ross's record company Capitol. 'Missing You' was later included on Ross's *Swept Away*, her fourth album for RCA Records.

By now *Can't Slow Down* wasn't; in fact, it had passed five million sales in the USA alone, and was Motown's first to do so, although Stevie Wonder's 1976 '*Songs In The Key Of Life* generated more income because it was a double set. It also logged 52 consecutive weeks in the US top ten – only the third album in pop history to complete a full year in the top ten and produce four top-ten singles. The other acts to have achieved this are Fleetwood Mac with *Rumours* and, inevitably, Michael Jackson with *Thriller*. On the downside, Lionel Richie was once more being sued for plagiarism. This time, songwriter Gene Thompson accused the singer of copying extracts from his composition 'Somebody's Got To Love' on both 'Stuck On You' and 'Hello'. Other defendants in the case were James Carmichael, Brockman Music (Richie's publishing house) and Motown Records. The suit, filed in Los Angeles' Federal District Court, alleged that Thompson gave an agent for the singer a copy of the song in June 1980, and a second copy a month later. Nothing further was reported on the case.

Following the television coverage of horrendous scenes of starving and dying people in Ethiopia, the Boomtown Rats' lead singer Bob Geldof was moved to approach the cream of British recording artists, including Boy George, George Michael, Sting, Paul Weller, Phil Collins, Simon Le Bon, Martin Kemp, Rick Parfitt and Francis Rossi, to record a single about the tragedy and donate all the royalties to Ethiopia. The single 'Do They Know It's Christmas?', written by Geldof and Midge Ure, was recorded at London's Sarm Studios and released by Mercury/Phonogram Records under the collective name of Band Aid. The British public flocked to buy the single, sending it to the top of the chart, an achievement that was repeated on an international scale.

The British project prompted singer Harry Belafonte to organize a similar event in the USA. He contacted Lionel Richie's manager Ken Kragen at Christmas 1984 about a concert to raise funds to fight starvation in Africa. Kragen felt a concert would not raise enough money, so they discussed the possibility of recording a US Band Aid single. Kragen recalled, 'I was heading over to Lionel Richie's house to take him to ...an awards ceremony with his wife Brenda. When I got there I told him about the conversation with Harry and that I thought we'd better do a record. Lionel said, "I'm in".' Kragen then spoke to Kenny Rogers, before contacting Quincy Jones. 'He said let me get hold of "Stinky", that's what they called Michael Jackson 'cos he was so squeaky clean. A few hours later he called back and said Michael not only wants to participate, he wants to write the song with Lionel.' The following day, while Brenda Richie was shopping, she chanced to meet Stevie Wonder, whom she persuaded to contact her husband. 'When I said I was gonna do the song, I wasn't aware that Ken was working on it then,' Lionel Richie told BBC Radio 2. 'So I'm sitting there with Michael, just talking it out, not realizing the pressure. We just thought it was going to be Quincy, Michael, Stevie and myself.' Ken Kragen had other ideas; while the two were working together at Jackson's home, Hayvenhurst, he recruited forty-five of the most important recording artists in America, and possibly the world, to join him in song: artists like Tina Turner, Ray Charles, Diana Ross, Smokey Robinson, Bob Dylan, Dionne Warwick, Cyndi Lauper, the Pointer Sisters, Billy Joel, Bruce Springsteen, with another fifty waiting in the wings. But no Commodores. 'I can't really say how the song came about. Neither one of us saw the other put his hands on the keyboard. That's how we write,' Lionel Richie told *Billboard*. 'He brought in an idea, I brought in an idea. We went back, we listened, and then we smashed both ideas together. The music came first.' Latoya Jackson stayed with her brother and Richie for the week it took to compose the song, and she claims that Richie contributed only two lines, leaving Michael to write the rest. Whatever the percentage, the song 'We Are The World' was completed on 21 January 1985. The instrumental tracks were recorded first and were distributed to all participants by Federal Express, which, in the spirit of the event, footed the bill. Enclosed with the cassette was a note from Quincy Jones saying 'Leave your ego at the door'.

> Deciding to do the recording on the night of the American Music Awards, 28th January, was perhaps the key decision that I made. It was the perfect way to make sure I could get the maximum number of artists to take part. I knew that a number of key artists would be at the Awards [like] I knew there were certain artists who would attract the others. (Ken Kragen)

> We had twelve hours to do one song because voices are not like instruments or rhythm sections. Voices give out and we had the greatest singers on the planet. God was with us, that's the main thing…[The artists] came in with the right spirit to try to do something…everybody was outside of themselves which was great, and they wanted to do something collective that would be good for us and other people. (Quincy Jones)

> Quincy came in and locked in all the voices. Who would sing what. It was just an interesting blend of cultures and music. We wanted to save lives. That was all that mattered. (Lionel Richie)

> I think 'We Are The World' is a very spiritual song but spiritual in a very special sense. I was proud to be a part of that song and to be one of the musicians there that night. We were united by our desire to make a difference. (Michael Jackson)

Michael Jackson arrived at the A&M Studios in Hollywood early in the day to record his vocal segment, and stayed after the actual recording session to film his performance, which was to be slotted into the finished video. Participating artists began arriving at the studios from 10 p.m. onwards: Bruce Springsteen arrived with no bodyguards or entourage; Diana Ross made a grand entrance, hugging Quincy Jones before jumping onto Bob Dylan's lap; Stevie Wonder was led in; and when Lionel Richie arrived at 10.30 p.m., having just hosted the American Music Awards ceremony, where he also scooped six trophies, he first acknowledged Bette Midler by saying how good she looked. Each soloist found his/her name taped on the floor, and six microphones stood in a semi-circle. The song's chorus, which featured all the artists, was recorded first, after which the soloists added their parts. By 8 a.m. Lionel Richie and Quincy Jones were the only musicians left in the studio. Jones had, by the way, taken time out from composing the soundtrack to *The Color Purple* movie to oversee this project. That soundtrack contained input from several artists like Andrea Crouch, Tata

Vega and Lionel Richie, who, with Jones and Rod Temperton, had written 'Miss Celie's Blues (Sister)'.

'We Are The World', credited to USA For Africa, was released in March 1985 and three weeks later it hit the US singles chart at the top. It was the eighth consecutive year that Lionel Richie had written a number-one song there. The charting pattern spread across the world including Britain, where it stayed on the listing for nine weeks. Following its release, Richie said he was inundated with letters from Americans who were also in need, 'People told me about losing their farms, people who are losing their way and can't quite figure out what to do about their lives, and people losing everything their families were built on.' He was also deeply concerned about the dreadful state of the world, particularly his home country. In a press release he said,

> I look at the desperate world we are creating. We're wiping out the people who are the foundation of what America is about. The guys who don't have an IQ of 150, who never wanted to be anything but a shoemaker and now have no work. All you have to do is say 'America's in trouble' and they're the first ones who will fight your wars for you. But don't use them and abuse them. These are the people who lost their sons in Vietnam. These are the people who, when there's a tax increase, will be hit by it. I don't mind growth and progress but in this thing called change we are losing the most important thing there is – people. Awareness is what I'm concerned about now. Your responsibility to yourself and the world, your contribution. I'm at the point and at the world's point where there's no more time for dreaming about pie in the sky. People are losing their jobs. People are starving. They can't wait for some brave new world that's going to happen tomorrow. Some of them are about to lose everything today.

A later benefit event, Hands Across America, in which approximately seven million people across the USA held hands in a human chain for fifteen minutes, raised money to fight hunger and homelessness in America. USA For Africa's single, album and worldwide sales of related products, like T-shirts, sweatshirts, videos and posters, went on to earn an estimated $63 million for African famine relief, funding 500 projects in eighteen countries. 'We collected some Grammy awards and began to hear easy-listening versions of "We Are The World" in elevators along with "Billie Jean",' Michael Jackson wrote in *Moon Walk*. 'Since first writing it, I had thought that song should be sung by children. When I finally heard children singing it on producer George Duke's version, I almost cried. It's the best version I've heard.' Jackson then retired from the business for nearly three years to record the *Bad* album, the follow-up to *Thriller*.

In July 1985 Bob Geldof and concert promoter Harvey Goldsmith staged Live Aid at Wembley Stadium. It was the world's largest-ever concert and was transmitted worldwide live by the BBC. The marathon included Queen, Sade, Sting, Phil Collins, Dire Straits, David Bowie, Status Quo, Elton John and Kiki Dee. Following the British spectacular during the day, the US contribution took over the nighttime, and was also transmitted live by satellite for worldwide viewing. The US gala featured Tina Turner, Mick Jagger, Patti LaBelle, Madonna, Bob Dylan, Hall & Oates, (ex-Temptations) David Ruffin and Eddie Kendricks, and Lionel Richie.

> I arrived at the place for the concert during the afternoon, and was rushed to a trailer. Every legendary guitarist was in that trailer, talking about what key they should play in and other things. One of those guys was Eric Clapton. When I was introduced to him, Eric said, 'I've been studying your music' and I couldn't have been more delighted when he followed that with 'Maybe we can get together to record in the future'.

During this musical marathon, countries including Australia, Japan, Norway, Russia, Austria and Yugoslavia presented their own acts. The British leg of the event was criticized for being white-dominated, and prior to the trans-Atlantic link-up, several black acts complained to the US promoter that black music was not sufficiently represented. Prior to the Live Aid concerts, Mick Jagger and David Bowie secretly teamed up to record and video their version of Martha and the Vandellas' 'Dancing In The Street'. The single obviously became an international chart-topper and all royalties went to the Ethiopian Fund. Various other Live Aid fund-raising activities took place in the ensuing months on both sides of the Atlantic, including Sports Aid and Disco Aid.

At the 1985 Grammy Awards ceremony in March, Lionel Richie won the Album of the Year category with *Can't Slow Down* and Producer of the Year, with James Carmichael and David Foster. Michael Jackson, who had won eight awards in 1984, scooped one Grammy for his 'Making Michael Jackson's *Thriller*' video, while Tina Turner collected three. After Diana Ross had made the presentation to her, Ross sang 'I Just Called To Say I Love You', a sultry version of Stevie Wonder's 1984 international chart-topper. During the year Richie was the recipient of numerous awards like ASCAP's Song of the Year for 'All Night Long (All Night)', Writer of the Year, and Best Publisher of the Year (Brockman Music); six American Music Awards, and the one that probably thrilled him most – an Honorary Doctor of Music degree from Tuskegee University. He said, 'When fame first strikes it's kinda overwhelming because you automatically realize that one day you wake up and you're not invisible anymore. Now that works really well for the first couple of years, but there are days that you want to be invisible and you realize that you can't. That's a trying period of time.'

Diana Ross's 'Missing You' was replaced at the top of the US R&B chart by the Commodores no less, with their first hit single since the defections of Lionel Richie and Thomas McClary. Titled 'Nightshift', it was penned by Clyde Orange, Dennis Lambert and Franne Golde, and, like its predecessor, paid tribute to the late Marvin Gaye. Golde told *Billboard* that she pictured singers on a nightshift in heaven

> coming out and giving their concert. And when I explained that, Dennis said, 'Gonna be some sweet sounds coming down on the nightshift.' The song wrote itself from then on. It took two mornings in the studio, while Dennis was with the Commodores. We got the *Billboard Book of Top 40 Hits* and looked up Marvin Gaye and Jackie Wilson. I wrote down all the titles of their songs, and we incorporated that into the lyric.

By now the Commodores were desperate for hit material and had approached writer/producer Dennis Lambert to work with them. It wasn't general knowledge yet, but the group had recruited newcomer J. D. (James Dean) Nicholas, an ex-member of the British soul combo, Heatwave ('Always And Forever', 'Boogie Nights', 'Grooveline'), who had more recently worked as a session singer with Ray Parker, Jr, and Diana Ross, among others. The two groups had originally met at a television station and had kept in touch. When Heatwave disbanded, Nicholas pursued solo work before being approached to replace Lionel Richie in the Commodores. 'They didn't want a Lionel Richie soundalike or lookalike, but they needed someone to fill the space. I joined them in November 1983...about the same time as Thomas McClary left the group. My first big project with them was the album *Nightshift*.'

This delightful, stylish, mid-tempo 'Nightshift' single soared into the top three on both sides of the Atlantic, returning the Commodores to their rightful place as A-list performers. 'I think a lot of people have been wondering what happened to us. Even Motown,' William King told John Abbey. 'But we always planned to do solo projects, even way back when we started...However, I will admit that when Lionel left, it was a real downer. It was as if everyone had deserted us. I think a lot of people expected the group to break up.' His departure was, he added, more traumatic than that of Thomas McClary, because he and Richie had been roommates for the ten years they had spent travelling. 'On stage, Lionel was missed because he's such a strong personality. However, the four original members who are left are all totally dedicated to the group...and getting the group right back on top again.' 'Nightshift' was the third-biggest hit for the Commodores, a Grammy Award winner in the Best R&B Performance by a Duo or Group category, and was the title track on their new album, also produced by Dennis Lambert. William King said,

> The album is a team effort. We always listened to outside material but we always felt we could come up with better songs ourselves, but this album is different in

that respect, because three of the songs on it were written by people outside of the group...Working with Dennis was really great. It was like having Carmichael back with us again.

Album reviewer Ralph Tee called it 'contemporary black music, falling in the direction of rock/soul rather than electro/funk'. Comparing the album to recordings by British singer Paul Young, Tee felt that apart from 'Nightshift' the only other worthy track was 'Janet', a dreamy mid-tempo item with a superbly infectious chorus.

> Following behind are the ballads 'A Woman In My Life' and 'Lay Back', [and] the rock numbers like 'Slip Of The Tongue' I'd rather not comment on. While this album is being regarded as a return-to-form album, it's basically three tracks which have made it so. It also makes me wonder, considering the disaster the *13* album was, why they should continue to churn out tracks like 'Animal Instinct' and others I haven't talked about.

On the strength of the single's success, the album went straight into the British soul chart at number four, while *Can't Slow Down* dropped from 13 to 21 in the listing.

Following the cancellation of the previously announced British tour, the Commodores rescheduled dates for February and March 1985, when fans raved that J. D. Nicholas had easily stepped into the gap left by Lionel Richie. Once the tour was over, the group had US dates stretching from New York to Hawaii, and were elected into the Alabama Hall of Fame for their services to music. 'Animal Instinct' was issued as the follow-up to 'Nightshift', an 'afternoon shuffler' which did just that into the US top fifty and British top eighty. Before the end of 1985, the tuneful, mid-paced 'Janet' was extracted for single release to coincide with the group's second British visit of the year. Like its predecessor it failed. And Motown/UK issued a further television-advertised compilation, *The Very Best Of The Commodores*, a top-thirty hit, to mark the fact they were planning to leave the company!

Meanwhile, Lionel Richie, who had been supervising the extensive construction and expansion of his palatial Bel Air mansion, was beavering away on his next solo project, but in October 1985 he deviated from his schedule to promote 'Say You, Say Me'. The song was the main title from Taylor Hackford's *White Nights* movie, the stories of two dancers trying to escape from the Soviet Union – Mikhail Baryshnikov, the world's greatest ballet star, and Gregory Hines, an American soldier and tap dancer who had defected to the Soviet Union. Gary LeMel, then head of the music department at Columbia Pictures recalled, 'We showed [Lionel] the film and he loved it. He definitely wanted to write a title song. A couple of weeks later I heard back from Ken Kragen, who said, "Look, he can't seem to write anything called 'White Nights' but he's written something that he thinks is one of the better things he's written and it fits the picture perfectly".' He listened to a demo of the song and agreed it was perfect for the film. Meanwhile, there was another problem brewing.

> Lionel was supposed to deliver his new solo album to Motown on a certain date. Motown would not allow us to have 'Say You, Say Me' on the soundtrack but they agreed to release it as a single in time to promote the picture. As things turned out, Lionel didn't finish his album for almost a year. The movie didn't suffer but the soundtrack album would have sold more had the song been on it.

In December 1985 'Say You, Say Me' became Richie's ninth self-penned US chart-topper three weeks after Phil Collins and Marilyn Martin's 'Separate Lives' (also included in *White Nights*) had topped the chart. It also won an American Academy Award for Best Song, the Golden Globe Award for Best Song in 1986, and was his ninth solo British hit, at number eight.

> You think I'm talking about a boy and girl [in the song] but there's something else whispering at you under the surface. It could be about a romance, about white and black, American and Russian, Baryshnikov and Hines, but it's about the awakening of the inner person to stand and be strong. It's about the *White Nights* movie but if you never see the movie, it'll still apply to the barriers that you run into in a love affair. The line 'behind the walls of doubt' applies to what we go through falling in and out of love, or discovering a loved one. Yet it also deals with capitalism and communism and civil rights, the complete spectrum of barriers. Why isn't the world the way it should be? I'm the songwriter, and it's my job to sprinkle the message, even if subliminally, on the airwaves.

Considered to be his most simplistic, the straightforward melody of 'Say You, Say Me' was blemished by the sudden change of musical pace towards the song's close. A movement that was innovative for Richie, but not one that everyone agreed with, including James Carmichael. 'It was a song that I thought should have remained in one given tempo. Lionel heard the song with this switch in tempo and nothing would satisfy him but to leave that tempo change in.' Richie's response was, 'I love that bridge! But I did get hell from DJs and my record company!' The song – with the offending bridge – later went on to win the singer an Oscar for the Best Original Song. 'And that was a very big moment,' reflected Ken Kragen. 'An exciting moment. That may have been one of the true thrills for Lionel of all time.' It was also a thrill for Motown because the single was its fourth top-selling item of all time, following the Jackson 5's 'I'll Be There', Marvin Gaye's 'I Heard It Through The Grapevine' and 'Endless Love'.

Alongside his good fortune with 'Say You, Say Me', Richie was publicly forced to defend the 'We Are The World' project because, of the several million dollars raised, only $10 million had been spent. 'We made a promise that we would make payments direct to the people in need, bypassing governments if need be,' he argued. 'We wanted to avoid all of the usual obstacles. The bottom line is that we have been feeding and helping people.' He then spoke of his wish to be an everyday person, which was, quite frankly, something he'd never be again, and laughed,

> You spend your whole life saying 'I want to be famous'. But being famous is like being put in a little capsule that isolates you from being a normal human. You're offered a delicious world with everything you could want, yet you're separated from normal people by limousines and bodyguards. So you have to struggle to get back to real human life.

Like many artists of his ilk, he said, he went to extraordinary lengths to experience some degree of normality, and he cited one example:

> Way past midnight when it's so dark that I won't be recognized, I sneak out and people tell me the story of their lives. And from these stories come the songs. Other times I go out and walk along the beach at three in the morning. One night there was moonlight and I saw what looked like a man huddled up like a bundle, sitting on the sand. I wondered what he could be all about. Then I heard a voice. It said, 'Lionel, I want to let you know how proud we are of what you've done.' I couldn't quite see his face but the voice sounded educated. The man stood up and came over to shake my hand. It turned out he was a bagman, but there was a dignity in his voice. He told me his story. He was a lawyer in Pittsburgh, calculating how much time he had to put in to buy a Porsche and pay for his house. To make it, he was working incredible hours. Suddenly, he realized he was labouring away his life like a slave, and the Porsche and his house were his master. So he cashed it in, sold his house and car, bought a plane ticket and flew to Los Angeles. Now he lives on the beach and once a year he buys a new sleeping-bag, and he enjoys life. He explained that every night when the restaurants close they throw out leftover food. And every morning the shops throw out yesterday's papers. So he eats gourmet meals and is always on top of what's going on in the world...It's a wonderful world we live in, but you have to be in communication with that kind of person to know it.

Behind his successful public persona, it appeared all was not well in the Richie camp, when *Billboard* reported that he had left not only Ken Kragen but also Motown, to sign with RCA Records. The record company quickly issued a denial, but not Kragen, who had come under criticism the previous year for employing a high percentage of whites on Richie's US tour. It was true Richie had caused Motown problems by the non-delivery of his third solo album in time for pre-Christmas release. This had affected the company's financial situation, as Berry Gordy explained, 'We had become dangerously dependent on the handful of our superstars... When we got a new album from one of them it meant an influx of millions; when we didn't, it meant trouble. And without developing successful new acts, it meant even bigger trouble.' Meantime, on the manager/client front, a later statement confirmed Ken Kragen and Richie had split in February 1986. 'The departure of Lionel was a friendly situation. I was still very close to Richie and continued to attempt to do whatever I could to help his career. I was always confident that things would work out fine.' The split was overseen by several advisers, and although no specific reason was given, it appeared Kragen's committed involvement with charity work played its part. He cited 'Hands Across America' 'as one of the most demanding projects I've ever undertaken. The event literally takes as much time as a dozen management clients and frankly it entails a responsibility to the American public.' Howard Bloom, an independent publicity agent, said, 'Every manager in the world has put their name on a list. Lionel's dance card is very full, but he isn't dancing.'

With a Motown press release declaring a new album was pending, Lionel Richie announced his intention to tour Britain for the first time as a soloist during the summer of 1986. Before the print had dried on this statement, the tour was postponed because, like other American artists including Patti LaBelle, Prince and 'Wimpo' Stallone, he was avoiding Europe, fearing terrorist retaliation to President Reagan's bombing of Libya. This stance prompted one magazine to write, 'C'mon, Yanks – what's going on? John Wayne must be turning in his grave.' However, three cheers for Diana Ross, who refused to join this 'chain reaction' by not only daring to visit Britain but intending to purchase property in London as well. To placate growing public impatience for new Richie product, Motown/UK released *Lionel Richie – The Composer: Great Love Songs With The Commodores And Diana Ross*, with great success.

News also hit the tabloids that Richie was to make his screen debut playing a business tycoon in the comedy film *Serving Time*, which prompted the comment, 'If shooting takes as long as his new album's taking, I doubt if you'll need to start queuing at your local flea pit till late 1989!'

# 8 dancing on the ceiling

'I will not be locked away behind walls, or be shut out of this world entirely.'   Lionel Richie

'I am actually learning about myself in public.'   Lionel Richie

'Lionel Richie is just one of the people I'm disappointed in.'   Frank Elson

As expected, the Commodores finally left Motown, following rumours that the two parties were at loggerheads, especially since the defection of Lionel Richie. The group negotiated with several record companies until they finally secured a deal with Polygram. When they went into the studio to cut their debut album, Lionel Richie delivered his third, titled *Dancing On The Ceiling*, in August 1986; its title track had been issued as a single in June. He said he was inspired to write the song after a late-night drive down Sunset Boulevard. 'I pulled up after hearing a load of noise coming from people inside a club. Sitting in the car listening to them, I heard a voice say, "What's been going on in there?" The reply was, "Man, we've been dancing on the ceiling." I wrote the title down and drove home. The excitement that could be generated from that one line was incredible.' Described by Nelson George as 'very gimmicky and very calculated but that was the turning point of his career in terms of perception in the market place... [a] far move away from his black base and one hopes the entire album is not as grooveless' (*The Death of Rhythm & Blues*). The same writer also observed how strange it was that 'so many English white singers want to be Otis Redding whilst so many black American singers want to be Barry Manilow.' True, Lionel Richie was catering for a much wider audience now than he had as a member of the Commodores; the gritty southern funk had certainly been replaced by slick rock/pop and, horror of horrors, mainstream commerciality. He had left his true soul fans way behind to concentrate on the more lucrative market, and there seemed little hope of any return. Frank Elson wrote,

> Success means that you get swallowed up into the hype that is 'showbiz'. Your music and commitment is watered down in the quest for sales. You wear the correct gear and appear on the correct shows...you also make some sickly

> videos...I'm not against success...I'm not against musical progression. Marvin Gaye and Stevie Wonder both moved away from the hit factory machine into thoughtful music, sold into the rock music market, and neither lost one iota of their soulful feeling...Lionel Richie is just one of the people I'm disappointed in. (B&S)

Australian fan Peter Antal rushed to the singer's defence:

> There seems to be a lot of talk these days as to what is and what isn't soul, but let's get one thing absolutely clear – Lionel Richie has not sold out. Ever since he left the Commodores he has given his fans an unbelievable amount of variety with [his] albums, and I consider the criticism of him to be confused with a determined effort by Lionel to experiment in an attempt to broaden his own unique talent for a wider audience...Lionel has supplied soul with some of its finest moments and despite his massive success on an international level will never lose his black roots.

The promotional video for 'Dancing On The Ceiling' was directed by Stanley Donen, who had previously worked with Fred Astaire and Gene Kelly. The idea came from the 1951 film *The Royal Wedding* (the British title was *Wedding Bells*), in which Astaire danced from the floor to the ceiling and upside-down. Richie and his dancers repeated this routine, which took six weeks to perfect, whereas the singer learned his routines in seven days. It was a spectacular video, as Ken Kragen explained at the time, 'Stanley Donen was a very famous director who had directed a lot of Fred Astaire movies...You see him in the room and he goes up the walls and now he's dancing on the ceiling. And Stanley brought that in and...Lionel got to duplicate Astaire and it was just a fabulous time.' The singer called it his outrageous video. 'If ever there was a word for "outrageous" this video is it. But how we danced on the walls and ceilings will remain a secret. All I will say is it was magical.' The single hit number two in the USA and number seven in Britain, proving his selling power had returned with a vengeance. Hot on its heels, the *Dancing On The Ceiling* album roared into the charts around the world after it had captured the pole position in the USA and a slot lower in Britain.

Among other tracks on the album was 'Ballerina Girl', which Richie wrote for his daughter Nicole, who had been living with him and Brenda since she was three and whom they formally adopted in 1990. 'There are people out there who want to hear me doing a love ballad and I wanted to make sure I didn't let those people down. This time I related those feelings to a child by portraying a child's innocence.' He spoke further about his daughter to Michael Parkinson during a 2004 interview.

> We ran into Nicole. A little girl on the stage at a Prince concert and the interesting thing about it is, her mother was part of the wardrobe group, and we

realized this little girl had no business being on the stage playing the tambourine in the middle of this concert. As time went on, we ran into her again and realized that the mother could not take care of this child. So we said we'd be her guardians. We just fell in love with the child.

As time passed, it became clear that Nicole could not return to her mother (who has never been named publicly), so the Richies began the process of legally adopting her. Michael Jackson was asked to be her godfather.

'Deep River Woman' began its life as a ballad before Richie decided he wanted to record a country and western tune. 'And I wanted to use Alabama. I was told they don't duet or do backing vocals for anyone, but when I phoned them they said they'd love to do it. I ran all the way to Nashville and took a day and half to cut the song. We ate southern-style food for breakfast, lunch and supper.' The reggae slice 'Sela' was an expression his wife's grandmother used, which meant 'listen', and was instant in its appeal, while 'Love Will Conquer All' represented emotional power.

> The power of the Olympics where I performed and the 2.6 billion people watching that, then to do the 'We Are The World' single followed by the Live Aid concert watched by something like 1.8 billion people. All those people turning on their TV sets and the whole world singing that song, well, I can't say I wasn't affected in some way. This track is where my insides come out, and I just had to write it down, to get all these feelings out of me. Cynthia Weil helped me with the lyrics, and the other female singers like Marva King just brought it all out.

The longest track, 'Don't Stop', flowed like a Marvin Gaye song with Richie's vocals emulating the late star, a strange experience held together by a continuous beat. Reviewers were adamant they were listening to a collection of future singles because each track stood on its own merits; it was a brilliant pop album, which left pure soul music lovers looking elsewhere.

This third album showed his growth and possibly revealed for the first time his inner thoughts. Richie explained he felt more at ease with this project.

> A lot of feelings have opened up here. When it comes down to the cross-section of songs, let's say I pulled out my musical resumé! This has been an interesting year and four months for me. It feels like I've crammed nine years into that time. I've grown a lot, learnt a lot, and had the opportunity to record some of my feelings. I'm just glad I finally could bring it all together.

The singer admitted he was under great pressure to record another *Can't Slow Down* in much the same way as Michael Jackson felt the strain with *Thriller*. Suzanne de Passe came to Richie's defence by saying, 'A record company puts on an artist to sell, sell, sell, more, more, more, bigger, bigger and there's the self-imposed pressure that is [like] I want to deliver for my fans. I want to deliver for my spirit. I want to deliver because I enjoy what happens when people love my music.' Adding his opinion during a BBC Radio 2 interview, James Carmichael said, 'There was a pressure when you have a great deal of success. You don't want to let yourself down because you know you can reach a certain level and [then] go beyond that level. Internally, there was a great deal of pressure.'

With its subtle, mellow mood, 'Love Will Conquer All' followed 'Dancing On The Ceiling' in September 1986 to hit the US top ten, although it faltered in the British top fifty. The US success was attributed to the start of Richie's 'Outrageous' tour, which had just kicked off with Sheila E (Escovedo) as support act. 'Deep River Woman'/'Ballerina Girl' was the next release in the USA, while Motown/UK put 'Ballerina Girl' on the topside. Motown (US) then followed suit when 'Deep River Woman' failed nationally. To help push the struggling record the company released a promotional 12-inch single titled 'A Special Service To Country Radio', featuring 'Deep River Woman', 'Stuck On You' and 'Sail On' with the Commodores. A commercial 12-inch single of 'Ballerina Girl' included a previously unavailable instrumental of 'Dancing On The Ceiling' on the flipside. Both were minor hits. This blip was definitely not in the Richie/Motown game plan.

As the ex-Commodore was flexing his dancing muscles on stage, the band he left behind released the first single under their Polygram deal. The dance track titled 'Goin' To The Bank', with newcomer J. D. Nicholas's gimmicky Cockney rap, scored better than their last Motown singles, to reach the top two in the US R&B listing, the top sixty mainstream, and the British top fifty, a position encouraged by the group touring the country. During an interview for *Blues & Soul*, Milan Williams explained why they had left Motown. 'It was something like a divorce, but it simply had to happen. Even though "Nightshift" was a big record for us, I think the move was on the cards back then. We always did our best for Motown and we've left some dear friends behind. But it was time to move on, time to get out from Richie's shadow.' He also confirmed that original member Ronald LaPread had also left the line-up (he moved, with his wife, to Auckland, New Zealand), reducing the Commodores to a quartet. Williams insisted the parting was amicable:

> Just the right move at the right time...I feel we have the group exactly the way we want it. Exactly the way we wish it had always been. The chemistry has never been better...Now we have a fresh start. There are no personality conflicts within the group and no ego problems. We realised we had to let go of the Richie sound [and] we left that behind at Motown. We now stand at the gateway to something that we expect to keep us established for the next four or five years.

The single was swiped from the *United* album, which combined several musical styles and which 'reunited' them, albeit briefly, with James Carmichael and Calvin Harris. One reviewer noted, 'The reconfigured line-up simply couldn't match the original band's intensity, versatility, or distinctiveness.' While another wrote,

> Having had some serious departure problems to get over, the Commodores have finally staggered back to re-enter the race and now look in pretty good shape as their current chart single 'Goin' To The Bank' would suggest. It's pleasing to report that the chaps endorse that success with a solid (if unspectacular) album which will go some considerable way in re-establishing their credibility and confidence.

With production credits shared among Dennis Lambert, Greg Mathieson, William King, Milan Williams and, of course, James Carmichael – and with Clyde Orange and J. D. Nicholas as joint lead vocalists – *United* was so crucial to the group's continuing career, because with its success would come tour bookings, vital to sustain the act's popularity on the live circuit and a source of regular income. But it wasn't to be this time round, because after the release of a handful of singles, the group, totally dissatisfied with the way Polygram had treated them, moved on. 'A lot of the album just wasn't in the pocket,' J. D. Nicholas told David Nathan.

> And the record company was disturbed about that. It was more of a producer's album and in that particular case the producer was very closed minded and didn't receive our input too well. The album didn't reflect the personalities of the people in the group…We didn't feel as if the company took as much interest in it as we'd have liked, and we still think the title cut could have been a big hit for us.

A year later, the Commodores recorded the *Rise Up* album for Blue Moon. Lionel Richie, meantime, had, with Stevie Wonder and Smokey Robinson, recently narrated *The Motown Story – The First Twenty-Five Years* for commercial release. In three CDs, the story started with the Miracles' 'Bad Girl' and closed with 'Say You, Say Me'.

Known for his charitable services, and to ensure there was no public showdown regarding his reluctance to work with black organizations this time around, Richie arranged with promoters for special benefits to be given to inner-city children in the areas he was booked to appear. Children who had maintained a B-average or higher at school, and who had avoided disciplinary action over a specified period of time, would be eligible to win free concert tickets, tour jackets, and to have the opportunity to meet him. 'Education is real important to me, and it's even more important to the future of this country,' he declared at the time. 'I grew up on a college campus. Most kids don't have that privilege. I loved school so much that I still hang on to my college apartment. I'd like to help kids feel a little of the fun of being a good student.' His campaign, supported by school superintendents in forty cities, was given a tremendous boost when Pepsi Cola donated 100,000 Lionel Richie Super Student T-shirts and 10,000 tour jackets and, with Richie, presented two college scholarships to the grand prize-winners.

We're looking forward to about five to six months on the road because I've decided I've been away for long enough. Only problem is I know people in each state and city and I intend to see everyone. Over the years I've met a lot of

The wonderful 'Outrageous Tour' sold over 400,000 tickets in a month. The singer later took London by storm!!

people, right back to when I started out in what I call the 'back of the van' days. And I want to see them again, and the new friends out there. I am only here because of these people, and some of them gave me the greatest advice in the world.

The Outrageous Tour sold in excess of 400,000 tickets in a month after the tour got under way during September 1986 in Phoenix, Arizona. In New York City, for example, fans snapped up 30,000 tickets for the Madison Square Garden concerts the first day they went on sale. During one of the shows he was joined on stage by his wife while he sang 'Lady' to her in celebration of their eleventh wedding anniversary. The ninety-minute, fifteen-song performance opened with 'Hello' and continued with the singer concentrating on hits like 'Say You, Say Me', 'Dancing On The Ceiling' and 'Deep River Woman', when Alabama was featured on video. By the close of the tour he had played before 1.5 million people, with the overwhelming hysteria of the tour generating thousands of record sales in its wake. Nelson George (surprisingly) pointed out in *Billboard* that no single black music act was actually dominating the marketplace at present. 'Lionel Richie and Tina Turner have current product, but the excitement level generated by their previous efforts is not there. Perhaps the answer or part thereof lies in the undeniable fact that both parties are guilty of straying from their black roots.' It was fair comment and the two artists were fair game, and they carried this stigma with them throughout their later careers. In interviews they did themselves no favours by reflecting upon their upbringing and early struggles, which, of course, were light years ago in terms of musical styles. These remarks only encouraged journalists like Frank Elson to rightly comment, 'For Lionel Richie and Tina Turner [I would offer] trips back to their roots so's they can see what a waste of their talents they're currently engaged in.'

The staging for this tour was designed to keep the special effects from upstaging the performers. So there was no stage as such; instead, the musicians and instruments stood on ten-foot-high modular hydraulic units that moved around during the show. Hanging immediately above these mobile islands were twenty tons of equipment, including 150 computerized, swivelling lights and 600 stationary lights. As a final touch, Richie's nine-foot-long Yamaha grand piano was motorized. The intention was then to take the tour to Britain, but due to the previously mentioned terrorist threats against US citizens flying there, Richie re-routed to Australia, where he opened at Melbourne's Entertainment Centre. His audience included a slew of tennis stars like Martina Navratilova, Pam Shriver, Ivan Lendl and Yannick Noah, and visiting star Elton John, who was recovering from an operation to remove nodules from his vocal chords to treat a recurring throat problem. Happily, the benign nodules were cauterized by surgical laser beam and Elton John made a full recovery but he was unable to talk or sing for some time. So, when he joined Lionel Richie on stage in Australia he confined himself to playing piano. Meanwhile, back home, Richie was one of the few black artists to appear in the country and western top-thirty chart with 'Deep River Woman'!

In January 1987 Motown launched its new male superstar – Bruce Willis, who was better known for his loud-mouthed character David Addison in the popular television detective series *Moonlighting*, in which his co-star Cybill Shepherd (Maddie Hayes) tolerated his off-beat and extremely irritating antics. He went on to become a box-office hit as the New York City detective John McClane in the *Die Hard* movies, plus other top starring roles. As it was considered imperative to portray him not as an actor crossing over into music but a singer first and foremost, the character 'Bruno Radolini' was invented, with a fictitious musical biography to match, an entertaining ploy and one that worked. *The Return Of Bruno* album spawned a handful of million-selling singles like 'Respect Yourself' (which was Motown's highest US chart entry by a white artist), 'Young Blood' and 'Under The Boardwalk' with the Temptations on support vocals.

Bruce Willis was exactly what Lionel Richie wasn't! He successfully mixed gritty funk and hard-hitting R&B with a touch of commerciality, as a backdrop to his coarse, weathered, soulful vocals. This accepted styling was an updated interpretation of early Commodores material and was possibly proof that, had the group stayed together, they could have been forerunners in producing this decade's new styling of black music. For some time, then, Bruce Willis – or Bruno Radolini – was a serious competitor for Motown's top male singer award.

A month after the US tour ended, British tour dates were announced as part of Lionel Richie's ongoing European trek. To publicize pending tours as much as possible, artists usually engaged in a continuous round of interviews, or allowed stories to leak to the media. (Probably one of the most famous of these was by his friend Michael Jackson when he announced his intention to sleep in a hyperbaric chamber to extend his life-span!) With a hot artist like Lionel Richie, there was no doubt his tour would sell out but nothing was left to chance, and a crazy story cropped up in an edition of *Blues & Soul* which told of a young couple from Kent who won flights to New York. The wife took some persuading to go because she wasn't keen on cities and certainly not the Big Apple and its high crime rate.

> Relaxing in the bar of their posh hotel after traipsing around the town, he tells her there's no fear of muggers in such a grand place and to see herself to their 14th floor room. She's alone in the lift and still a bit wary, when the door opens on the first floor and a rather large gent gets in with a big dog. She presses herself firmly against the lift wall when the pooch starts leaping about…when the gent shouts 'Get down!' (to the dog) she timidly sinks down on all fours. Now

the large gent thinks that this scenario is hilarious, and is still cracking up when he exits with his dog at his appointed floor.

The next morning, and every subsequent morning during their stay, a large bouquet of flowers arrives for his wife, and her husband wonders what's going on. When their trip is over and they go to check out of the hotel, they find that their bar bill has been paid and that there's another bouquet of flowers waiting...with a card reading 'Thanks for the best laugh I've ever had. Love, Lionel Richie'!

And it's all true.

'Lionel Richie's Outrageous Tour' hit Paris, West Germany, Sweden and Norway, after dates in Britain's National Exhibition Centre (NEC) in Birmingham during March 1987. The London concerts at Wembley Arena followed in May because 'I want to crank up the show so that by the time we get to London it will be ready, be ablaze. Also I wanted to take the show to a small venue first although performing in Birmingham scares me. You'd think I'd be confident as I've had plenty of years of practice.' The Birmingham shows were sold out in three hours. British Telecom's computer logged 90,000 calls an hour into the NEC box office, where fifty emergency lines were hastily installed with extra staff hired to answer the calls and cater for the lengthy queues wanting tickets. Richie then added an extra date to his London performances on 6 May, for a charity event in aid of the Prince's Trust. Both the Prince and Princess of Wales attended and all proceeds were donated to the Trust.

To capitalize on their star's visit, Motown/UK released a souvenir double package featuring 'Sela', with photographs from his current world tour on the sleeve. Each package also contained a competition form, with the first prize being a pair of tickets for the concert at Wembley Arena. The single was remixed by Steve Thompson and Michael Barbiero, Richie filmed its promotional video in New York, and the sales stopped in the top fifty.

The singer took London by storm! Wembley Arena was more than ablaze, it was a throbbing inferno from the show's opening notes. Prior to appearing on stage to sing 'Hello', his computerized piano spookily played the song's opening bars. Once on stage, he saw the audience rise as one to welcome him; the sight was awesome and emotional because he could never, in his wildest dreams, have expected such a thunderous show of love from a British audience. 'All Night Long' and 'Running With The Night' followed, where he and his band simultaneously danced together against a backdrop of exploding fireworks and a stage lighting display. The pace then slowed down and the response was deafening. The piano rose off the stage for 'Say You, Say Me' before disappearing through the stage at the close of the song, followed by Richie, whose exit was well disguised by pumping dry ice. Upon his return, he duetted with Vickie Randle on 'Love

Will Conquer All' and 'Endless Love' – thankfully the Diana Ross video had been dropped – whereupon he again remembered his time with the Commodores before singing his version of 'Lady' which he penned for Kenny Rogers. A second exit and return saw Richie funk to 'Don't Stop' with the band once again joining in the dance routines, utilizing the individuals' talents to the full. And none more so than when halfway through 'Dancing On The Ceiling' several musicians were suspended high in the air above the stage, while Richie remained with both feet firmly on the floor. And when the stage rose to meet the 'dancing' musicians, the audience was one hysterical voice. The finale was an impromptu version of 'We Are The World', when arms were raised high and thousands of voices sang along with the star in an emotional version of the USA For Africa original. Naturally, critics sharpened their pencils and were varied in their reviews: diehard soul fans loathed the hi-tech and showbiz flavour that US audiences loved so much, while mainstream reviewers praised the entire performance as the best in popular music.

Even though performing still scared Richie, he admitted his audiences helped overcome the nagging nervousness, especially the Europeans.

> They have always come forward to tell me their feelings and of course they have always played my music. It's only ironic that the tragedy of terrorism has marred so much travelling around for so many artists. It's a strange thing, but no matter how great you are in America, you never get the respect you get in England. You're only as big as your last hit single, yet in England artists who have been ice-cold in the States for years are always welcome. People like Chuck Berry, and all those wonderful blues and soul performers come any time because England treats them as legendary. And that's a wonderful feeling, I can tell you.

Being a world artist, Richie believed he was an obvious target for personal attack, which probably had influenced his decision to reschedule his British tour after the bombing of Libya. Now, he said, he refused to be intimidated.

> I could never get into the situation of not flying or not walking in the streets. Unfortunately, this problem is the nature of the world we live in. We have all been brought up with the idea that the bomb will go off at any time. So I live my life one day at a time. There's only one safe bet in this world and that is that death will always come as a surprise. Yes, I'm recognizable, but I do hang out with a lot of people and that is extremely important to me. I can't walk down the street anymore and I miss that, although there are certain times I can go out. Usually at night is the best time. During the day you don't see me for longer than a block. When I go shopping I tell myself, it's shopping and talking and entertaining at the same time. I just can't go out and shop, period. So, yes, that's one of the rough points.

> I will not be locked away behind walls, or be shut out of this world entirely. I can usually go out to watch baseball and tennis and, thanks to television coverage, I can always keep up. However, it makes it all the more fun to go to the game because I know so many of the players. Fame is hard to deal with. It's like a double-edged sword most of the time. Once I make up my mind what direction to go in I convince myself that that is what I am going to do. Thereafter, one side of me is the analyser, the nervous side, that's always saying is this the right thing to do, or is that the right move? What makes this business extremely difficult is there is no rehearsal time. I am actually learning about myself in public. Unfortunately, there's no school to learn to handle fame. Like, it's hard enough getting married but at least you can work out the problems in private. I'm lucky though, the analyser, or the nervous side of me, usually comes out calmly in public which is what people want to see and expect from me.

When 'Lionel Richie's Outrageous Tour' of Europe ended, the singer was invited to perform in Russia, a move he wanted to make despite the country's governmental restrictions, as he elaborated.

> If you take away the governments of the world, people are people, fans are fans. In isolated places of the world people are oppressed, but people get around any obstacle. Like they listen to their records – R&B, rock and so on – and they go to discos or something similar on weekends, just like everybody else. It's the ideas of the older generation that are making this oppression, but they're dying off now, leaving the newer generation to bring in what they want. I believe certain morals are good, and I'm sure the governments are going to change, and that Russia in particular already has a brand-new breed in there. They will get back into the race, into the competitive world. I mean, look at all the technology that exists now…that is a positive progression in itself. Music is bringing people together. Music is a medium and a strong force that has cut through areas where politicians, for example, can't. Attitudes and situations get changed with the least resistance. The key civil rights movement succeeded with non-violence and I'm convinced you can get through to anyone with music. A guy will listen to all kinds of music on his car radio. He leaves his house for his place of work, gets in the car and there's music. Even the biggest bigot in the world can be influenced in this way. Politicians listen to the radio via this means. I suppose it's like a form of brainwashing. And their kids bring music home. Their parents scream and shout the music is too loud, yet – whether they like it or not – they have been influenced by that music.

Michael Frenchick was one who was influenced by Richie's music – but wrongly so. He sued the singer for $50 million, alleging that 'Dancing On The Ceiling' was partly his composition. Once again, no more was heard of the claim. Ken Kragen said, 'When anybody writes a hit song, about five people come out of the woodwork and say "I wrote that".' Musician Michael Boddicker said, 'Lionel has the best attitude about having to endure the crap of being a successful artist. I've watched [him] be so strong, but there are certainly things that could break lesser human beings [like] break the spirit. His spirit seems to be pretty unstoppable.'

Without a doubt, 1987 was Lionel Richie's most successful year because he was at the very top of his profession. The black megastar; a world artist. His position was probably best summed up by Quincy Jones, when he said on BBC Radio 2, 'I think every artist has a particular time that they're in tune with what's happening. Even though they can have hits over more decades...I think there's a certain time [when] they're in tune with what the public wants to hear...There's some kind of instinct that's working and Lionel transcended the eighties [because] I think he was particularly in tune at that time.' In his relatively short career, Richie had spent 34 weeks at the top of the US chart, and his nine number-one singles gave him one more than the eight recorded by the Rolling Stones, who, of course, had been recording for twice as long as the ex-Commodore. Further, in 1987 *Can't Slow Down* had sold over ten million copies in the USA alone, 15 million worldwide. *Lionel Richie* passed the four-million sales mark, likewise his third album *Dancing On The Ceiling*. His presence was requested all over the world. The awards and honours flowed endlessly, each marking a particular remarkable achievement. The demands on his talent were endless and constant. There really was no end to what Lionel Richie could do. This certainly was his time.

But it wasn't his record company's time. Overall it was not a good year for record sales and, when the company announced its relatively poor achievement, Berry Gordy had no choice but to put Motown up for sale.

And there was more trouble brewing, because as Lionel Richie's star continued on its glittering ascent, his personal life would hit an all-time low.

# 9 don't wanna lose you

'Lionel Richie Runs Away As Outraged Wife Beats Up Girlfriend.'  *National Enquirer*

'I knew he was special and that was that.'   Diane Alexander

'It wasn't that I was disenchanted with Motown. I'd just been there enough.'   Lionel Richie

In June 1988 the Motown name, its record catalogues and artists' contracts were sold. Jobete, Stone Diamond, and the film and television operations were not part of the deal. Syreeta, who had been signed with the company since 1968, explained that

> for the past two years Berry Gordy had put his own personal money into Motown to try and save it because he felt a responsibility to us, to all the artists who were there. Nobody wants to put their baby out. It's like a father giving his daughter away in marriage, he knows he still has the connection but there's something there that's a little uncomfortable.

Clyde Orange said, 'It was saddening because a lot of black entertainers got their start, like us, at Motown and Berry Gordy wasn't just a figurehead to us. But time brings about a change and all we can do is hope that the company will come back together.'

The *New York Times* had reported that Motown's annual turnover had nosedived from $100 million to $20 million and that at least half of that revenue had been generated from repacking old material. Several artists had defected to other companies, leaving Stevie Wonder, Lionel Richie and Smokey Robinson as the company's prime sellers, even though their sales were erratic. And since returning to Motown, even the Four Tops and the Temptations had failed to recapture past successes. Berry Gordy had (reluctantly) juggled offers from companies including Virgin Records and, of course, the patient MCA Records, who had remained keen to conclude their original interest. However, by this time, MCA Records had teamed up with Boston Ventures, an investment conglomerate, who offered 80 per cent of the asking price of $61 million and had also agreed to Gordy's contractual demands. The sale sent shockwaves through the industry and marked the end of the fans' love affair with Berry Gordy, who symbolized black success in a white-dominated world, particularly Britain, Motown's second home and most significant selling market after the USA. Motown without Berry Gordy was unthinkable! MCA Records' Jheryl Busby, who stepped into Gordy's shoes, was one of several to subsequently take over the company's helm, but none came anywhere near Gordy, the ambitious young man, with fire in his heart, music in his bloodstream and a family loan in his pocket.

Also in June 1988 another story sent shockwaves through the media. The *National Enquirer* magazine led the way with front-page headlines ('Lionel Richie Runs Away As Outraged Wife Beats Up Girlfriend') reporting that a private detective, hired by Brenda Harvey-Richie, had advised her that her husband was in a Beverly Hills apartment owned by dancer Diane Alexander. Brenda had for quite a time suspected her husband of having an affair and, according to a source close to the couple, 'Brenda has done everything to stop Lionel's womanizing...She has hired private detectives to follow him and get information on women he was seeing, then she'd call the women and tell them to stay away from her man.' Apparently, the outraged wife immediately went to Alexander's home, and pushed her way in through the front door as her husband was leaving. She assaulted him with a kick in the groin, before charging into the apartment, where she kicked out a window. 'He went to his Porsche and waited there,' eyewitness Betty Kubinec told the *National Enquirer*. '[He] drove off as the police arrived. He didn't interfere at all as these two women were fighting over him.' Brenda was bleeding from a cut on her leg suffered when she smashed the window, reported the eyewitness. 'When I got there, Diane was writhing on the floor and Brenda was pulling Diane's hair with all her might and banging her head ruthlessly on the floor.' It was a dreadful altercation between the two women, only ending when six policemen pulled them apart. Paramedics treated the cut leg before transferring her to a nearby hospital to be checked out, on her way to the police station. Beverly Hills Police Lieutenant Robert Curtis confirmed that Richie's wife was booked on 29 June 1988 at 6.55 a.m. with charges of battery, vandalism, trespassing, resisting arrest, disturbing the peace and 'corporal injury to a spouse'. She stayed incarcerated until 9 a.m. and was released on $5000 bail. A day later Diane Alexander told the media she didn't want to press charges. 'I don't want to make this any bigger than it is. I just want to forget about it.' She further told *National Enquirer* reporters Alan Braham Smith and David Perel, 'She's psychotic. I feel this woman would kill me. The last time I spoke to her was on the phone a year ago and at that time she made threats. Since then I hadn't seen or heard of her until last night.'

In an interview with broadcaster Jeremy Vine years later, Lionel Richie said it was reported that he had been in bed with Diane Alexander.

> We weren't. We were standing out in the front yard. No bed. The news stories varied...slowly but surely we went from the front yard to the steps, to the doorway, to inside and now the bed. My wife was angry and there was an argument, but the thing that people forgot to mention was we were separated. Back then the tabloids didn't know [I] was separated. All they heard was – 'My god, he's been caught with this other woman.' But we'd been separated for four/five months already. The issue was we had a massive argument in the middle of Beverly Hills somewhere, and of course that went straight to the tabloids. From there that story has lived on forever in the history of love and marriage.

The singer also later told *Jet* magazine that he was called a 'wuss' for allowing a woman to get the better of him. A statement he angrily objected to because he was raised not to condone violence and certainly would not hit a woman.

> I said to one member of the press, 'Let me ask you a question – would you have liked it the other way if it was said "Lionel Richie Beat Up His Wife?" Does that sound better?' The guy said 'No.' Then I said when a couple has an argument and it gets physical, wouldn't most guys just not throw a punch at all? I didn't do anything to Brenda, and that sounds better than I knocked her out.

It was reported that this was not the first time the police had been called to an incident that involved the Richies. During October 1987, the couple became involved in a screaming match at their Beverly Hills home. It transpired that Richie ran outside and jumped into his car to leave, but his wife joined him, grabbed the steering wheel and rammed his Porsche into the wall of a neighbour's estate. A second visit that month occurred when neighbours complained that the couple were shouting at each other in their driveway. No charges were filed. Then on 3 July 1988 the Sunday tabloid, the *News of the World*, reported that the singer had fathered a baby by another girlfriend, Michelle Jordan. No further information was made public, thankfully, because to have this relentless invasion into his privacy, where his personal life was splashed across tabloid headlines before being dissected in print, was as devastating for Richie as it was hurtful.

On a more tasteful subject, in early 1989 the Commodores released the *Rock Solid* album in Britain via Polydor Records, to coincide with their lengthy tour of the country during April. Following these dates, the group performed in Japan, Korea, Mexico, Scandinavia and Canada. They then planned an eight-date 'fact-finding' tour of South Africa, highlighting the country's problems with attendant reporters and camera crew. The tour was unfortunately cancelled due to a lack of co-operation from anti-apartheid groups and the inability to find a charity willing to accept donations from the tour's proceeds.

In describing *Rock Solid*, Bob Killbourn believed it was

> an adequate enough offering that includes attention-grabbing ballads in the shape of 'Thank You', 'Right Here And Now' and 'So Nice' with J. D. Nicholas and Walter Orange sharing lead vocals. But overall the album is a little disappointing with the majority of the tracks following an unimaginative and unfulfilling course...The Commodores are veteran performers with an enviable track record. 'Tis a pity their recent releases have dropped somewhat below par. The current single 'Grrip', in comparison to many direct competitive outings for dance floor attention, still appears lightweight to these ears. (*B&S*)

To date, the Commodores had survived thanks to the success of 'Nightshift' and 'Goin' To The Bank' but to be brutally realistic, they needed future success, not past hits. 'We wanted a record that would be well-rounded,' J. D. Nicholas told David Nathan. 'We feel that we've come up with an album that will satisfy our faithful fans...We just wanted to make a good record.' The bulk of the group's income, Clyde Orange divulged, came from private parties: '[They] have kept us working even when the records weren't doing that well. It's easy to get caught up in doing them too. You can get more money than playing a stadium with 10,000 people sometimes.' With the release of this new album, it went without saying that the group longed to return to their 1978 high-ranking status when 'Three Times A Lady' peaked. 'There's not much we haven't accomplished through the years but we would like to re-attain that place we were at when we were at our peak. It's hard to have a platinum album like we did with *Nightshift* and then have nothing.' By the end of the year, the group was without a record deal, and Milan Williams opted to leave the line-up. It was said that Williams had refused to participate in the trip to South Africa, whereupon he had been ousted from the group. The remaining three members – Walter 'Clyde' Orange, William 'Wak' King and J. D. Nicholas – and the Mean Machine considered disbanding the Commodores but decided the time wasn't right. As long as they could perform, they would continue. And, of course, reissued material was another form of promotion, although not so instant in appeal as television advertising. When 'Easy' was used as the musical backdrop for a Halifax Building Society commercial, the single subsequently re-entered the British top-twenty chart.

On the recording front, the Commodores, now a trio, were dreadfully unhappy and disillusioned. So much so, they asked to be released from their recording contract with Polydor after a period of confusion and disappointment, They intended to begin the mammoth task of creating new digital recordings of their classic hits. With the best digital recording technology available, they produced sufficient material for four new albums –

*Commodores Hits, Vol. 1, Commodores Hits, Vol. 2, Commodores Christmas* and *Commodores XX – No Tricks*. Rather than suffer the same fate that befell them with Polydor, the group formed their own record company, and during August 1992 Commodores Records & Entertainment was born. Through this company, a series of international and domestic licensing and distribution deals were completed which ensured the release of the albums.

Lionel Richie's last major performances of the 1980s were at the Songwriters Hall of Fame's twentieth anniversary gala, and on America's *Top Ten* television show. His final British placing was the 'Sela' single in March 1987. Although this decade was definitely his time, his turbulent personal life slowly overshadowed the success he had so dedicatedly achieved. 'I realized I had missed twelve family reunions in a row. I had to slow down,' Richie also told journalists. 'I didn't know how to stop. Also, there was this fear factor that the motivation to keep on wasn't there.' He intended to place his career on hold for one year, and on his return would celebrate with a new album and a world tour. 'I found myself standing there one evening with that Oscar in my hand for "Say You, Say Me". "We Are The World" is playing, and I'm hanging upside-down off the ceiling, saying, "I think I need a vacation,"' he divulged to Sue Russell of *Hello*. 'I think I stopped in order to slide back down the mountain a little bit because I found something very terrifying about the top. Do you know what's up there? Nothing! No one to box. No one to go against. So I think I created this kind of self-imposed exile.'

Admitting he had worked for seventeen years without a serious break, Richie was tired beyond words and in need of a lengthy rest away from the music business. Since 1982, when he issued his *Lionel Richie* album, his life had been a whirlwind of work, with little time for a personal life. When he wasn't in the studio, he was touring or on promotional trips anywhere in the world, or was engrossed in some project or other. Many, like Ken Kragen, believed his inability to decline work – whether it be hosting a show or guesting at a benefit concert – added to his enormous workload, and knowing he rarely turned down a request only led to more! Motown, too, requested new material be always delivered on time, as stipulated in their recording contract with him. But sometimes this didn't happen. Kragen said,

> You are basically fielding [execs] from the record company saying 'We need the album. You told us we were going to have it a month ago.'...He's a perfectionist and he wants everything perfect, and that takes him a great deal of time. I think that putting stuff off, or taking a long time to do things, or worrying about a decision, are probably the only negatives I could ever think of with Lionel Richie. (BBC Radio 2)

Suzanne de Passe also aired her reservations on BBC Radio 2: 'Lionel as a person is very special. He is very amiable and very easy to talk to and approach. But he's also able to use that charm as a weapon to keep him from doing anything he doesn't want to do.'

The first few months he felt he was going through a withdrawal process.

> God help anyone who was around me at nine o'clock at night when I normally would go on stage. And I realized that I spoke to my mother and father like 'Man, how you doin'? Good to see you, dad.' Total showbiz. Mr Hollywood. I literally had to just calm down. So I detoxed and…I started liking it. I really started getting into my feelings.

And he used the time wisely. For instance, he was able to deal with his divorce without the glare of the public spotlight. 'It was quite an experience dealing with the press and all the kinds of stuff people were saying.' He further told *Hello!*

> It frightened me a little that I was supposed to be this guy with the perfect marriage, the perfect songs, the perfect house. I felt I was setting myself up for something. I kept waiting for something to go wrong. I just didn't have any idea the loss was going to come in my house. It was all personal. It was something I had to deal with, and it was the best and worst of times. It was almost like – the family's tight, then the kids go off to college and the two people break up because they don't know how to deal with each other any more. Suddenly, we found ourselves with no more showbiz, just in the home together. And nothing in common!

Richie was then dealt a double blow. Shortly into his self-imposed holiday, his father Lyonel told him he had emphysema, and when he died in 1990 his son was devastated. 'You could see that he was failing, so I was not about to go back on the road. It ended up being three years of going back and forth to Tuskegee.'

With his emotions raw and feeling extremely vulnerable, Lionel Richie was diagnosed with polyps on his larynx. His surgeon told him he might never sing again. 'It was the worst thing…I've never heard anything so terrible.' Julie Andrews had suffered from the same condition but, unlike Richie, she lost her singing voice altogether. After two operations to rectify the problem, his left vocal chord haemorrhaged in October 1991.

The music world trundled on without him, and perhaps the most innovative and lasting form introduced was rap, where chanted or shouted words replaced melodic lyrics. MC Hammer and Vanilla Ice were forerunners in this new kind of street music that now exploded on the market, although it was acknowledged that the first rap exponents were young blacks from New York known as the Sugarhill Gang, with their 15-minute epic 'Rapper's Delight' of 1979. This was a styling Lionel Richie would later adopt. Meanwhile, Nicole's godfather, Michael Jackson, published his autobiography *Moonwalk* and was the subject of adverse media attention following plastic surgery on his face – which he categorically denied. During 1991 he released his *Dangerous* album, but within two years a lawsuit was filed against him for seducing the thirteen-year-old actor Jordy Chandler. Jackson immediately claimed he was innocent of the charges, later settling the case by paying the teenager a reputed $20 million. This was one of several charges to be brought against the singer during the next few years. 'I know Mike very well...here's a guy who missed everything,' Richie said, 'who came from a very complex family, trying his best to hold onto something called childhood. The older he gets the more trouble he gets into.' Indeed he did; in November 2003 Jackson was taken into custody by the Santa Barbara County Sheriff's Department on charges of child molestation, to which he pleaded not guilty. In 2005, charged with further child offences, he went to trial before a grand jury, in a highly publicized legal battle, and was found not guilty in June 2005. 'I hope Michael survives, but he's been trying forever to hold on to this childlike thing, and forever we've been trying to tell him "Michael, you're an old guy now!"' Richie told Jeremy Vine.

> He built Disneyland [Neverland] because he loves children. 'I love them so much I'll bring them out to the house and they can stay for the weekend.' Wrong answer; it just doesn't work. And at that point you have to stop and say, 'This is not the way it works.' I think Michael has to grow up and face the facts, or it's going to hurt you. He's the one that has to make it work. I've been there with him many times and I understand when he says 'bed'. We think of 'bed'. He has what we call therapeutic beds, they roll up into futon-type things so the kids that are handicapped can either lie back, [or] lie over to see a movie. He got into trouble with [that] but maybe the time has come when he's got to stop.

As an aside, Michael Jackson was now the father of three and had married and divorced twice.

On the entertainment front, the Beatles, Bob Dylan, Diana Ross and the Supremes, the Beach Boys and the Drifters were inducted into the Rock and Roll Hall of Fame, and Richie missed participating in Nelson Mandela's 70th Birthday Party in 1988 at London's Wembley Stadium. When the massive event was screened in the USA it was billed as 'Freedom Fest – A Concert for the Freedom of the World', but with most of the references to South Africa, the anti-apartheid movement and Mandela himself edited out due to pressure from advertisers like Coca-Cola! Contributing artists included American stars Whitney Houston, Natalie Cole, Al Green and Stevie Wonder, alongside British artists such as George Michael and Eurythmics.

The early 1990s represented his valley in the shadow of death, Lionel Richie told journalist Marianne Macdonald. 'All these things were happening to me at the same time. I was going through a divorce and Nicole kept saying "Dad, why don't you come home?", and my dad was dying.' By comparison, at a more minor level, the singer had to contend with music-industry rumour and innuendo that he had literally dried up, was no longer capable of writing a song, let alone performing on stage. He had lost his confidence, was burned out. The patient singer bade his time and allowed the remarks to run their course, before telling the press that he was aware of all the adverse comments surrounding his absence.

> ...People saying I was afraid to put out a new record and so on. People saying 'You'll never be able to top that' or 'You've peaked.' I've stopped letting that stuff bother me. You can't fear failure in this business, you must constantly challenge yourself and take it one song at a time. As long as you're enjoying yourself making music, it's never a chore.

He also told reporter Sue Russell,

> People looked at me to write earthy songs that are of a timeless, lyrical quality. When you're about 19 to 30 you can write about 'I touched her hand'. But when you get to be 35 or more, that's not going to do it. So it was a very interesting growing-up period. I just needed a little bit more character...the cub scout days were just about over. (*Hello!*)

Before his sabbatical drew to an end, Richie was told a dear friend was dying from AIDS.

> Loss was something new for me. I couldn't shrug it off or whistle it away. I had to look loss in the face and ask myself, 'Can I survive these blows? Am I strong enough?' I'm glad to say I am...I've lived through an incredible period of growth. A period of pain and introspection and change. A period different than anything I've ever encountered, but ultimately a wonderful period of creative expression. I'm thankful for the struggle.

In all the misery there was a joyous event, the birth of his son Miles B. Richie on 27 May 1994, his first with Diane Alexander. They would also have a daughter Sofia, born on 24 August 1998. A delighted Richie told Pete Lewis, 'Miles showed up on the planet and amazingly just pumped me right up. I realized here's a kid who's on the planet who has no early concept of what I've done for a living. So I [needed] to do something to say "Hey, this is dad".'

In May 1991, speculation circulated within the music industry that Lionel Richie was actually planning to record an album with the Commodores, followed by a US tour later in the year. It was a false tale, and one of many that would dog their careers during the years. However, they were meanwhile inducted into the Brick Hall of Fame during the second annual National Association of Brick Distributors gala in New York, in recognition of services, of all things, to the brick industry! 'Tis absolutely true!

When Richie's absence from the public spotlight become increasingly noticeable, Motown's publicity office stated that he was recording new material which would not be issued until his divorce was finalized, presumably because any immediate record sales would form part of the divorce settlement. Richie later told David Nathan that he and Brenda were friends. 'And I'd say she's been the best ally I could have had. We both had a laugh at some of the things people said about what happened between us in the last few years but I'm glad to say that we survived all that as friends' (*Lionel Richie: An Illustrated Biography*). He admitted that it had been difficult sustaining his 'nice guy' image in the public arena and the experience was not one he intended to repeat.

The next album, planned in 1990, contained only three new tracks – a huge disappointment for patient fans. He explained what happened:

> I took some songs in to Jheryl Busby and he heard the first three and said 'Stop right there!' Jheryl's known for his great ears and I had been putting together other songs prior to meeting with him and I was going crazy trying to figure out which three to play for him. Since he stopped me after the first three that made it a whole lot easier.

The singer had been in discussions with the new Motown president about compiling a 'greatest hits' package which would portray his career to date,

> ...but I got into a bit of a panic mode about it, trying to figure out which ten songs to put on the album. If I'd had my way and we were deciding what to put on there from an artistic standpoint, it would have been a triple CD. I'd have included 'Zoom', which is one of my all-time favourite Commodores songs and 'Wandering Stranger', which summed up my feelings after leaving the group. As it was, we decided to go for the eleven number-one singles in order of popularity.

Titled *Back To Front* and released in May 1992, the compilation shot to the top of the British album chart, where it stayed for a staggering six weeks; US sales pushed it into the top twenty, which was possibly an indication that US fans were not as loyal as British ones – a trait that has, of course, helped 'forgotten' black artists. Ben E. King is a prime example, with 'Stand By Me'; when this was used in a Levi Jeans advertisement, it was reissued for the third time, to give him his first-ever British chart-topper. The single also rejuvenated his career and won him a new recording contract. With Lionel Richie's compilation, reviews reflected on his career to date, like that printed in *Blues & Soul*:

Returning to public life after a journey through what he called 'his valley of the shadow of death', Lionel Richie promoted his 1992 album *Back To Front*.

His track record is stunning, his sales potential [still] heavy, and his innate ability to compose hits practically unbeatable. Sure, he's been knocked for sugary sweet sentiments, tacky videos and soppy love songs, yet he's proved his critics wrong time and again when thanks to public devotion he's smiled all the way to the bank. Lionel is a walking, talking music machine, but being a sensitive human being takes precedence, outshining all the mechanics involved in being a hit maker. He writes from the heart and he is all heart. So, here we have what is basically a 'greatest hits' package, celebrating his time with the Commodores ('Sail On', 'Three Times A Lady', 'Easy' and 'Still'), his solitary duet with Diana Ross ('Endless Love'), and a selection of his most exciting solo tracks which have been tried, tested and sold ('Dancing On The Ceiling', 'Hello', 'All Night Long [All Night]', 'Truly', 'Penny Lover', 'Stuck On You', 'Say You, Say Me', 'Running With The Night'). And for someone who prides himself with a huge catalogue of compositions waiting to be released, we've waited five years for a measly three new tracks!

It was difficult for him to return to public life. There was never any doubt that he was a gifted composer but the music world had changed during his absence and after a while he wasn't missed. His music as a soloist and as a Commodore was played regularly on 'golden oldie' radio slots, and fans, however faithful, believed they had been abandoned. So, it is probably true to say that upon his return his input was less valued – the R&B crowd had long since dismissed him, and mainstream record-buyers had moved on. Lionel Richie needed to be reinvented and presented in a way that would easily be accepted.

> It's very hard to come back and be a big pop star after such a hiatus. (Nelson George)

> He made a choice to step back for a while because of his own personal life and things that were going on. And then he came back. I think he had to make an effort. He'd been away to find out where his place was in the current musical landscape and he's talented enough that he can do that. (Cynthia Weil)

> People go through the death (of their father), people go through divorces and separations in their family, but not in the famous world. So it was quite an education and quite painful too because, try to write a love song in the middle of a divorce. It's not the same as being blissfully in love. Or try to get to grips with the next wonderful tour when your father's in hospital dying. It was really the growing up of Lionel Richie, the passage of life I had to go through. (Lionel Richie)

The truth of the matter was, Richie was used to being in control, but he could not stop his father dying. His marriage was doomed and he was powerless to stop that happening as well. 'It becomes this juggling act of opinions and what you should do,' he sighed. It was also a learning process, which James Carmichael believed the singer had to experience. 'This really knocked him. It made him shut down. But he's always looking at life – what does this situation mean...which is the better road to take. So, there was no way in which he wouldn't have been influenced by the situations that occurred in his life.'

'Do It To Me' was the first extracted single, released prior to the album's release, with disappointing results. It stalled in the US top thirty, and the British top forty. '[The song] was to remind my fans that I was a Commodore. It's like going back to my foundation, to my R&B side and this seems like the perfect time to do a song like that since I haven't had a record out in years.' The second new track, 'My Destiny', was also the next single, which fared better than its predecessor in Britain by soaring into the top ten. 'I wanted to do a tune that would be reminiscent of those great old Motown songs, with the flavour and guts of those songs. I looked back at the Motown catalogue and came up with this song and we put a street vibe underneath it.' Finally, 'Love, Oh Love', which he explained was a song with a message.

> Every twenty years or so, you have a 'window' where you can write a song that speaks of the times you live in. Bob Dylan's 'Blowin' In The Wind' is just that perfect window. As he said, times are a-changin' and now we have new problems to deal with – the changes in Europe, South Africa, the homeless situation – everything is upside down. I wrote 'Love, Oh Love' because love truly is the answer.

The singer produced the new trio with Stewart Levine, best known for his work with Boy George, Simply Red and B. B. King, and gushed, 'I really enjoyed being back in the studio again. I can remember times in the past when I was recording albums and I'd get bored in the middle and lose interest. I felt motivated and really focused as a result of being away.' The album was dedicated in particular to his first wife – 'You've been an incredible force and inspiration for me from the beginning. I could not have done it without you!' – and to his late father – 'I loved him and admired him. And I was very blessed and fortunate to have him as my father.'

To support the album's release, Lionel Richie flew to London for a surprise one-off performance at the Town and Country Club in Camden Town, on 27 May 1992. The visit was deliberately low-key and within a smaller venue at Richie's express request because he considered this to be the best response to the questions raised about his quiet recording career of late and his absence from the live stage for the last five years. A smaller venue was a more comfortable way to mark his return to the public arena, and was, of course, less of a financial risk than an arena tour, which might have been impossible to fill. With low ticket prices, stalwart fans couldn't believe they would see Richie perform in such a vastly inadequate venue as the Town and Country Club. Supported by an eight-piece American band that included keyboardist Greg Phillanganes, the ninety-minute show treated the audience to a selection of Commodores material, interspliced with Richie's own solo work, for which he sat at the piano. The Club was packed to the rafters with a frenzied audience who couldn't believe their good fortune. When Courtney Pine and his saxophone was introduced on stage to join in 'Do It To Me', the excitement escalated to fever pitch! 'All Night Long (All Night)' and 'Dancing On The Ceiling' closed the show, which saw the very welcome return of a conquering hero. Similar intimate shows were repeated in Paris, Hamburg and Amsterdam as part of his comeback campaign, ending with an appearance at New York's Ritz Club, where he performed to a packed house.

His other significant performance this year was in October, when he joined Elton John, George Michael, Whoopi Goldberg, Bruce Hornsby and others at Madison Square Garden. The sell-out occasion was the 'To Give Is To Love' concert, benefiting the Elizabeth Taylor AIDS Foundation.

It was not realized at the time, but the platinum-selling *Back To Front* was Lionel Richie's last album under his deal with Motown Records. When he announced he had signed a five-album deal with Mercury Records, worth at least $30 million, the industry and fans reeled from disbelief. He had been with Motown for twenty years, both as a member of the Commodores and as a soloist, and now, more than ever before, the company needed him to help it survive. One consolation was that it held on to his and the group's back catalogue (including unreleased titles), which, naturally, would be issued at regular intervals, particularly as the specialist Motown market grew during the new millennium. Richie told the media he had joined Mercury Records 'because they're in the process of building and growing. I like that better than being with a fat cat.' He also told *Blues & Soul*'s Pete Lewis,

> It wasn't that I was disenchanted with Motown, I'd just been there enough... I call Motown 'Motown University'. I've been going to school there for twenty-odd years and sooner or later you must graduate. So, with Berry Gordy having left and the machine that had been there becoming kind of dissipated, I figured it was the perfect time to make a move. With Mercury I am for the first time part of a huge worldwide distribution arm, particularly because they just didn't have anyone like me and I like being a unique facet of a company.

Compared with the heady, frenetic 1980s, Lionel Richie's new decade was tame and more in tune with what he wanted to do. During 1993 he confined himself to recording and enjoying his life with his family, although Richie and Diane Alexander decided not to marry immediately his divorce was settled because they both needed a time of readjustment. Richie was adamant he wouldn't make the same mistake twice with a relationship. 'I was very close to Diane and I found myself coming back and forth into this wonderful friendship. What I liked most was she wanted nothing to do with show business,' he told *Hello!* In the same interview Diane continued, 'I knew he was special but he was married and that was that. I just figured we had a connection from that first day we saw each other. I tried, in those first five years, to date other guys and it was really hard.' When later asked if Richie had changed since their first meeting, she smiled, 'He's a little slower. He used to be up in the morning and work out, play tennis, then go do a show. Then go to a club and have dinner, go to bed at four. Forget it! Those days are over. He's home by midnight and he sleeps.'

The music never stopped for the group he left behind. The Commodores joined forces with the former ladies of the Supremes (Lynda Laurence, Scherrie Payne and Sundray Tucker) early in 1994 to tour Britain as double headliners. Both acts were dazzling; the visual and vocal excitement never let up. While the Commodores worked up a heavy sweat during their frenetic funky show, the Supremes were elegant and sophisticated, authentically representing the world-famous trio.

The death of his father, the divorce and the loss of a friend through AIDS took their toll, and Richie incorporated his feelings into the material he was preparing for his first album since leaving Motown. In 1996 Lionel Richie was ready to resurface with *Louder Than Words* on Mercury Records. He explained at the time,

> There was a lot of growth, a lot of introspection during that time. Although I may have been out of the public eye, I never stopped going into the studio, putting down ideas and listening to what else was out there. I've always found that there are two stages to writing; the first involves actually living your life in order to gain the experiences, digest them and write about them, and the second phase is actually recording them. I was on the road or in a recording studio for over seventeen years non-stop and I needed to step back and actually digest some of my life before I could go back to writing about it again. People have asked me [throughout] my whole career 'Where do the songs originate?' There is no formula, but I readily admit there is nothing quite as humbling as a microphone hanging in the middle of a room, while you are sitting there in front of a blank piece of paper trying to get the next song done.

He readily admitted that he's more relaxed in writing love songs, and confessed luck played a huge role in his song-writing achievements.

> Of all the topics in the world to write about, I got lucky and chose love. And it's the only thing that doesn't go out of style. I don't care if you're twenty, fifty or one hundred. I don't care if you like grunge, metal, country, pop. Gangsta rap or R&B. It doesn't matter because sooner or later you're going to say those three

corny words to someone. And when you use those three words you've just stepped into my arena.

During a conversation with journalist Robert E. Johnson, the star remarked, 'I can say some lyrics on a record and the whole world sings them back to me in six months. And I ask, "Why me, God?...Why not the guy next to me?"...There is no answer I can come up with...I give credit to my co-writer because all I did was write down what He told me to write down.' Working irregular hours was the key, Richie continued. 'From about eleven to about seven in the morning is a very wonderful time because, as they say, God ain't worried with too many other folks. I know He's very busy during the day, so I wait for late night, and it works for me!'

Motown label-mate Smokey Robinson, also an accredited composer and like Richie an ex-lead singer of a group (the Miracles), was also humbled at the power he wielded with his lyrics.

> I like to write and I'm very critical and I think the quality of a song has to do with whether it can stand the test of time...There are a lot of songs that are written that cannot stand that kind of test...They're just like my children to me and that makes them all very special. If I liked a song enough to record it, then it fulfilled my ambitions for it. I never imagined the impact my music would have. Not in my wildest dreams did it occur to me. I almost never dared to dream that I'd have the kind of career that I've had so far. It's an awesome experience and one that I feel very blessed to have had.

If Smokey Robinson had any failings at all with his songwriting it would be the uncommercial slant of his music. Lionel Richie, on the other hand, enjoyed his chart success because he aimed his music at mainstream audiences, whereas Robinson maintained his wonderful distinctive R&B edge, without gimmickry. And, as a result, he was less successful.

> I'm the guy who finds the words that people find it hard to say. I say it for them and it makes it sound like it's supposed to be coming out of their mouths. Guys don't say that much [but] women will tell me 'I met my boyfriend to this' and 'I went on a date and we did this on this song'. Guys only say one word – 'thanks'.

Having nothing but praise for Lionel's composing talent, Greg Phillinganes agreed. 'It's his unique ability to take very basic feelings and make them simple declarations of them...people realize that these are really good songs and they sound as well today as they did 20 years ago. So he's very blessed to have that quality in his writing.'

During January 1996 he presented a taster from his forthcoming album to the audience at the American Music Awards. The song 'Don't Wanna Lose You' was to be the first single lifted from his first new album for ten years, and one that his public waited for with bated breath. With

'I'm the guy who finds the words that people find it hard to say.'

hints of the Commodores' 'Just To Be Close To You', the title went on to become a disappointing top-forty US hit, while in Britain fans welcomed their musical hero with a united front, elevating the song into the top twenty. Regarded as Richie's 'comeback' album, *Louder Than Words* probably came under more critical attack than his previous 'safe' albums. 'A lot is riding on the back of [this] and make no mistake about it,' wrote reviewer Jeff Lorez.

   It's probably why the likes of Babyface, Jimmy Jam and Terry Lewis and David Foster have been called in to help out. More for moral support and credibility rather than for contributing ground-breaking tracks. Probably a masterstroke with this album was the reuniting Lionel with James Carmichael for the bulk of the songs. Thus, many of the cuts are vintage Commodores. (*B&S*)

Richie responded by telling Lorez,

> When I first got to Jam & Lewis' studio, the joke of it was I walked in through the door thinking I was gonna do something airy and off into the left field, and they just said 'We're not trying to be disrespectful, Lionel, but can you say "*awww*" like you did in "Brick House"?' Then the next thing they say is 'We're not going five steps forward, we're going a few steps back. There's a lot of people who loved your work with the Commodores, so why don't we return to that flavour?' And of course once I started writing I fell in love again with the idea of what I used to do.

The trio of tracks, 'Don't Wanna Lose You', 'Say I Do' and 'I Wanna Take You Down', was the result. The late Marvin Gaye's music springs to mind with 'Change', where Richie admitted the singer's influence:

> I'd go by Marvin's studio and marvel at how, stretched out on a couch, he'd construct his vocals, one track on top of another. I loved Marvin for the complexity of his creations. Every time you'd hear a Marvin song, you'd discover something new. That's what I was going for with 'Change'. It's the one song where Carmichael had to pull me back and say 'Enough, Rich'. Man, I was deep into it.

Known for his successful compositions for Madonna and Whitney Houston, Richie collaborated with Babyface on 'Ordinary Girl', a gentle and pleasant track without being outstanding. 'Our collaboration was smooth as silk,' Richie recalled. 'We spoke awhile about the story, this notion of a natural woman anchoring a restless man. Then Face played me a great track. I started putting on melody and suggesting lyrics, and he did the same. The rest is history.'

'Babyface in a way became Lionel Richie to some degree,' Nelson George noted.

> Maybe not as a performer totally, but certainly as a songwriter whose way was ballads and love songs. And so it could have been an incredible collaboration but it didn't really come off. Part of the song was Babyface and part was Lionel Richie. It wasn't one song…Lionel became one of the artists who hip hop rebelled against because he seemed to be the soft, bland music that hip hop came to take out.

Richie defended his work by insisting

> The turning point came at a rap concert. I wanted to hear what the hip street was saying. Backstage, I told some of the cats that I was considering using rap on my next record. 'Why do that?' they asked. 'You're the man with the melodies.

We're looking to you to tell us where to go. We're the ones sampling you. You don't need to sample us. Just be you.'

Some of Richie's best were included on *Louder Than Words*, like 'Still In Love', with its deep Alabama soul influences; the sombre laments of 'Can't Get Over You'; and 'Piece Of Love', bringing back memories of the haunting 'Hello'. The easy, relaxed 'Nothing Else Matters' and the subtlety found in 'Say I Do' were also classed as his finest work since the Commodores.

> As a songwriter I never wanted to be the best R&B or country composer, I just wanted to be the best. I wanted to be classed with Stevie Wonder, Lennon and McCartney, Elton John and Bernie Taupin. That meant universal messages. I hope songs like 'Can't Get Over You' fit into that category. I don't see myself as a virtuoso vocalist in the Streisand or Sinatra class, but I do think I'm a credible storyteller.

Closing the album were the vocal jazz cut 'Lovers At First Sight', featuring Richie's tenor sax playing, and 'Climbing', with its anthemic, classical arrangement and about which the singer had this to say:

> I went home to Alabama...to my childhood home on the campus of Tuskegee University where my grandmother taught classical piano and my mom taught elementary school. I needed to sit and meditate and be still. Seeing me in this introspective mode, a homeboy came by and said, 'I've got some inspirational tapes for you.' They turned out to be a complete retrospective of all my recorded work. Homeboy was saying 'Hey, man, the answer is within.' I tried to put that feeling into 'Climbing', a song I see as my 'Sergeant Pepper'. It's my classical fantasy and my way of saying 'Have the courage to face the changes you're going through.' I'm talking to the people but I'm also talking to myself.

In the same promotional release, Richie confessed he'd lived songs like 'Lovers At First Sight' and it had taken immense courage to put his feelings into music,

> not only because of the character of the story, but because it challenged my jazz technique. The truth is jazz predates my passion for R&B. Before joining the Commodores, I was a saxophonist hooked on John Coltrane, Sonny Rollins and Stan Getz. After laying down the vocals on 'Lovers' I was going to call in a tenor saxophonist but Carmichael wouldn't hear of it. 'You're going to play that solo, Rich,' he said. Well, it took a few minutes to warm up but once I started blowing that bad boy I was back in a space of freedom and poetry I hadn't felt in twenty-five years.

Working again with James Carmichael was an obvious move for Richie because although he wanted to involve third-party writers and producers, he also needed a steadying hand, a friendly face and a comfort zone within which to work. And who knew him better than Carmichael? '[He's] my musical integrity, my arranging integrity,' the singer told journalist Pete Lewis.

> What I like is that he has a common ear. Even though he's in the business he hears music as a lay person would hear it. Plus I love his sense of simplicity. He is from the school where you're supposed to hum everything through the album and nothing gets in the way of the vocal...In the great words of James Carmichael, 'It's not what you play, it's what you don't play that counts.'

Richie also relied on his criticism and straightforward attitude in the studio, which he said glued his productions together, and their work together is clearly bonded on tracks like 'Climbing' and 'Lovers At First Sight'. Carmichael said, 'We understand each other well enough that we can just pick right up, even though there are years in between, we can just proceed.'

Richie took full responsibility for the album's pot-pourri of music, and instead of hinting at, say, R&B, blues, classical, and country and western, he opted to record individual songs in those styles because he excelled in them all. He further told Pete Lewis:

> After a while you start thinking 'What [in] the world should I do? Should I hold this back for the next album or do I let it all fly now?' After being off for so long, I decided to let it fly and put it all out, but at the same time...I didn't want to divide my crowd up into too many different areas...So it was wonderful when I finally selected the songs to hear that common thread of Lionel Richie running through all of it and the title *Louder Than Words* reflects the fact that the songs themselves speak louder than anything I'll ever say in life. You just put the record on and each song in its own context will explain itself. (*B&S*)

In retrospect, the whole album was an explanation of his painful hiatus, although it is thought his deepest feelings may have been disguised to a certain extent.

> I took that blue period and put it on record. I didn't just bury it and go on with this happy-go-lucky life. It was important to me to document it. Every once in a while you have to stop being the artist and go 'I don't care whether it's sold around the world, I need to get this out of my soul.'

One reviewer felt that Richie had become disconnected musically from what 'is the mainstream of R&B, which is ironic since he was a great songwriter in that tradition, and is a great songwriter period. I don't think that invalidates the work he's done.'

On a happier note, Lionel Richie married Diane Alexander on 21 December 1996, after they had been living together for four years. The intimate ceremony, shared with immediate family and friends, was held at the Metropolitan Club in New York. During the ceremony, conducted by

Dr James Forbes, the couple were flanked by a maid of honour, a best man and their son Miles, who was the ring-bearer. At the candlelit reception that followed, the couple danced to 'Say I Do', which Richie had written for his new wife.

*Louder Than Words* paled in comparison to his previous solo albums, which had easily spawned a handful of runaway singles, yet it passed gold status in the USA, where it was a top-thirty hit. In Britain it soared to number eleven, whereupon a second track was released in November 1996, namely, 'Still In Love', which struggled into the top seventy. Nonetheless, it was a solid show of support for the returning ex-Commodore and led to him winning the Lifetime Achievement Award at the Music of Black Origin's first award ceremony, staged in Covent Garden, London. After collecting the honour, Richie performed before the packed audience in the New Connaught Rooms.

Now back in the public arena, so to speak, plans were being lined up for Lionel Richie to tour the world in 1998. However, before he hit the road, he would hit the big screen for his first serious acting debut alongside Whitney Houston and Denzel Washington.

# 10 angel

'She's still the greatest pair of legs in the business.'   Lionel Richie on Tina Turner

'Clyde is the funkiest little creature on the planet.'   Lionel Richie

'Lionel Richie could be regarded as black music's answer to Barry Manilow.'   Charles Waring

While Lionel Richie was promoting *Louder Than Words* in April 1996, he started filming the Penny Marshall movie *The Preacher's Wife*. Co-starring Whitney Houston (hot from her hit movies *The Bodyguard* and *Waiting to Exhale*) and international star Denzel Washington, the film was a revamp of a 1947 original titled *The Bishop's Wife*, which had earned Academy Award nominations for both Best Picture and Best Director. Starring Cary Grant as an angel who was sent to earth to help a struggling cleric, the film combined elements of Frank Capra's *It's a Wonderful Life* and Charles Dickens's *A Christmas Carol* and was a feel-good Christmas celebration. Penny Marshall updated the original story to bring the characters to life in the 1990s. Richie played a club-owner Britsloe, while Whitney Houston played Julia, wife of the Reverend Henry Biggs, played by Courtney B. Vance. Denzel Washington was the angel, named Dudley, whose arrival causes trouble when all his best intentions go haywire. Critic James Berardinelli wrote in his review that he felt the film was dated and

> beneath the warm sentiments and likable personalities, *The Preacher's Wife* is rather trite…It has better production values than its predecessor, but the intangibles aren't the same. An element of magic is missing…The uplifting moral here is that miracles can happen for those who believe. *The Preacher's Wife* is about reclaiming lost faith and spreading the message of love [and] these are themes common to almost every beloved holiday classic.

But for Richie, 'I enjoyed every minute of it…I have just a little vignette in the whole scheme of the movie. Denzel Washington, Whitney Houston, Gregory Hines and Courtney Vance are all part of the wonderful cast. I'm actually the freshman of the group and was way out of my league.' The movie soundtrack was released in early 1997, running the gospel theme throughout the entire album, where on occasion Whitney Houston was joined by the Georgia Mass Choir and her mother, gospel star Cissy, was a huge success.

Returning to the recording front, with no news of a studio follow-up to *Louder Than Words*, Motown/UK rifled its vaults for a Lionel Richie compilation titled *Truly – The Love Songs*, dedicated with love to Diane, Miles and Nicole. Inside the CD notes was the singer's inscription, 'I find love [is] difficult to explain, impossible to control, comes when you least expect it and is for each of us a unique experience. I hope you can identify with and enjoy some of [my] experiences.' Listeners were treated to his tried-and-tested 'experiences' like 'My Destiny', 'Hello', 'Say You, Say Me'; 'Endless Love' with Diana Ross; and a handful with the Commodores including 'Three Times A Lady', 'Sail On' and 'Still'. Despite being old material, the release, packaged in sepia pictures and gold lettering, shot into the British top five in January 1998, selling 300,000 on the way, yet again proving the popularity of this American musical combination.

From records to television and the four-hour documentary special for the ABC network to celebrate Motown's fortieth anniversary. Diana Ross hosted *Motown 40: The Music Is Forever*, which traced the company's rise to international success during the 1960s with clips from leading acts like the Temptations, the Supremes, Four Tops, and so on. An insight was given to company writers, producers and musicians, through to Motown's film/television achievements, and music was presented from a wide selection of artists including Lionel Richie and the Commodores; their songs were later released as a double CD package.

Three months later, Richie performed at the 'People's Party' of Birmingham Radio/Midlands Broadcasting, alongside contemporary acts like Mica Paris, B*Witched and All Saints, in Birmingham (England), and in June he joined a more spectacular 'Ultimate Dance Party' at the Hammerstein Ballroom in New York, where his co-stars this time included disco favourites the Village People. He then performed once more at the Prince's Trust's charity gala in London's Hyde Park, before telling the media he planned to tour: 'The world has grown since I left the industry. Places you'd never consider performing before – Poland, Hungary, China – are wide open now, saying "Come on in and play". So, it all makes for a very interesting second time around.'

He also promoted his new album, scheduled for British release in June 1998, by saying, '*Louder Than Words* cleared the air a lot. It got rid of a lot of baggage. *Time* is my healing record...The album actually scared me, but that it my yardstick. Anything that scares me to death or gets me nervous is usually a good thing. And it usually foretells the direction in which I should be going.' He also told the media,

> My first solo album was written at a time of uncertainty for me, having just left the Commodores, and there was a lot of anxiety and emotion in it. I've never liked touring with that sort of stuff. It's hard to go on stage and just put on a happy face when you don't feel it inside. With *Can't Slow Down*, I'd gotten rid of that baggage and the album was the freedom that came after.

He said he now drew parallels with that period, and *Time* was the result. Packaged in sepia (again!), the pictures showed the singer in serious and grimacing poses; none suggested a happy musical journey.

As an indication of the pending album's mood, 'Closest Thing To Heaven', written by Diane Warren, was issued as a single to struggle into the British top thirty. 'It was one of those tunes you hear and say to yourself, "I should have written that." Melodically, lyrically it just felt correct.' Diane Warren told BBC Radio 2, 'I loved his version…When a songwriter, especially one like Lionel who doesn't need to record other people's songs, does one of my songs, I'm deeply honoured – and very grateful!' The song was one of two penned by the highly respected Ms Warren; the haunting 'I Hear Your Voice' was the other, which Richie co-wrote with her and David Foster. 'The lyric line is basically saying that no matter how I try to remove myself…I can hear your voice inside my head,' said the singer of the track. 'The key to all songs that last is finding a subject that people live by every day. You find a phrase that people really say, like…"I hear your voice".'

Believing that *Time* was the right project to record at this point in his career, Richie said he was inspired by his grandmother's hundredth birthday, when his present was a copy of a newspaper from her birthdate in 1893, which carried the same headlines as 1998: the front-page issues were poverty, unemployment, the economy and race wars. 'That made me see clearly that nothing has changed.' His new album was also influenced by his family life, his homes in Los Angeles and Alabama, and his world travels, and showed, many felt, an enthusiasm that was lacking in *Louder Than Words*. Once again, Richie commented on several tracks, kicking in with the album's opener, 'Zoomin'', which, he insisted, reflected his then state of mind.

> It's not about leaving the planet but zoomin' away from the state of consciousness we find ourselves in today. We've gotten to the point where we're accepting tragedy as the norm, and the message we're sending our kids is horrible. For generations we've been sending the same messages about war and violence as the way to solve our problems. In the song, I'm observing what's going on.

One of the album's most endearing ballads, 'Forever', he wrote the night before he married Diane Alexander in December 1996. 'It's telling the one you love that you'll always be there…this song was expressing my thoughts at the time, the kind of bliss I was feeling.' In contrast, he used

'Everytime' as his confessional, admitting he was too weak to escape the power of the woman he loved.

> I've found out that the only way we learn is through our mistakes. As human beings, we usually get love wrong before we get it right. We'll have that jewel in front of us, and we won't show our appreciation for it until it's walking away or gone. Personally, I've found that relationships are not 'real' until there is conflict, and they only get stronger through that conflict.

The track 'Stay' expressed his passion, love and lust ('I haven't written like this since "Brick House" back in 1977'), while 'The Way I Feel' echoed the thoughts in 'Three Times A Lady', and 'Lady' was a song he never intended to record, believing Kenny Rogers's version was the perfect interpretation. 'I did it last year at a benefit and got this incredible reaction,' Richie explained. 'I recorded it afterwards and when the people at the record label heard it, they insisted that we included it on the album. In fact, I had to take a song off to put it on here, but I'm happy I did it.' Other tracks included the R&B-inspired 'Touch', 'To The Rhythm', where he worked with The Boogie Man from Showtime At The Apollo, and the album's title 'Time', where the message was simple, following the lines of his previous compositions 'This Is Your Life' and 'Zoom'. Richie enlarged,

> It's about coming to grips with our own morality…I've discovered the glorious side of things – death, tragedy, the ups and downs, and that life has a beginning, middle and end. What we do with that middle is our business…God is watching us, not in charge of us, and what we do with our lives is up to us. *Time* is a reflection on what's happening, where we are and where we're going.

Clearly a release of considerable personal soul-searching, *Time* was a confusing piece of work to present to mainstream record-buyers. This situation, of course, reflected that of his one-time fellow Motowner Marvin Gaye, who demanded Berry Gordy release his ground-breaking project *What's Going On* in 1971, otherwise he would never record for the company again. An extremely reluctant Gordy agreed, and *What's Going On*, crammed with the artist's opinions on world and US issues, humanity and environmental tragedies, became revered as one of the most significant releases of the modern world, and was, perhaps, responsible for the changing mood of black music. Interestingly, *What's Going On* was a runaway US hit but bombed in Britain; nonetheless, it has remained a regular seller on catalogue in re-mixed and extended versions. *Time*, on the other hand, peaked below the top one hundred in the USA, but fared better in Britain by hitting the top forty. Hardly representative of Lionel Richie's past selling power but a reflection, once more, of his loyal British fan base. But how long could it last?

Sixteen years previously the high-flying Lionel Richie had lent the struggling Tina Turner a hand by inviting her to be his support act for a cross-America tour. She returned that favour in 2000 by throwing Richie a lifeline to help him rebuild his career as a performer. Tagged the 'Twenty Four Seven Tour' after her current album, this was the sixty-year-old's final stadium tour; kicking off in Minneapolis during March and stretching through to mid-June, the trek took in 50 US cities. Ms Turner then took her farewell tour across Europe without him. His fan base there was relatively strong and loyal, so he could headline his own tour without too much problem. Indeed, Britain was now considered to be his second home, where he was guaranteed regular work thanks to his management team of John Reid, David Croker and Melanie Greene being based in London. In the USA, supporting Tina Turner was regarded by many as him making a comeback, whereas across the Atlantic he'd never really gone away! Naturally, Richie was thrilled to be working with the superstar diva again, and, of course, having access to the huge arena audiences she attracted. 'She's one of a kind, and she's been through all of the stuff I have,' he raved. 'She knows what highs and lows make up this business. She's a comfort and a thrill to watch, all at the same time...Tina used my tour to launch her renaissance – her rebirth – and I used Tina's tour to launch mine. She's still the greatest pair of legs in the business.' Jon Pareles of the *New York Times* wrote that Lionel Richie was oil to Ms Turner's vinegar,

> unctuously flattering the audience for remembering his songs after he disappeared for most of the 1990s. He sang his hits from the 70's and 80's, skilful genre exercises that never shied away from a romantic bromide; the one new song was 'Cinderella'. The set was a reminder of Mr Richie's variety, from the nasal funk of the Commodores' 'Brick House' to the heartland rock of 'Dancing On The Ceiling', to countryish ballads like 'Easy' to his anticipation of current Latin pop 'All Night Long'. His voice was warm and the band helped him milk the songs, changing them from promises of romance to an unabashed courting of the crowd and his dormant career.

Of the star herself, Pareles glowed,

> Indomitable and indefatigable, Tina Turner reigned at Madison Square Garden, defying time, pop fashion and any man who would try to hold her down...the strong, lusty woman who has grown tougher with every setback and every betrayal...her leathery voice and her leonine presence. Strutting across the stage in spike heels, shaking her blonde tousled mop top, she sang, 'I may be bruised but I ain't broken'.

As Lionel Richie began his fourth decade in the music-making business, his first major contribution to the new millennium was his much-awaited album *Renaissance* (the word means 'rebirth'), which he promised 'would be full of surprises, certainly a fresh challenge. Every album is a rebirth, a new beginning, but certainly this album was even more so. Every now and then you feel like you've been through a tunnel and come out the other side and *Renaissance* was definitely that feeling.' Recording it was a joy, he enthused, as he sought out producers Walter Afanasieff, Rodney Jerkins (known for his work with Whitney Houson and Madonna, among others), Mark Taylor, and British producer Brian Rawling (who had recently worked with Cher and Enrique Iglesias), with whom he worked in London.

> I really enjoyed it. We were in this little studio away from all the glitter and nonsense of a Hollywood recording studio. It had this little recording board downstairs. Before, if I needed a European feel or a dance mix I'd add it later. Here I wanted to do things differently. Sometimes you have to go where the vibe is the strongest. I also love to collaborate as it's a chance to really test your skills both as a writer and performer.

Mark Taylor told BBC Radio 2,

> The aim was simply to try to capture Lionel Richie but to try and bring some sort of up-to-date themes to some of the stuff. Wanting to have a current sound, and an up-to-date feeling about the tracks. I think 'Angel' feels like a Lionel Richie song so the idea was to make it a full, proper song with a much more dancy upbeat feel to it. It started to have feeling, sort of Latin element coming through, so when it was time to make the record it seemed obvious to have a flavour of it which is something he's hinted at before anyway on stuff like 'All Night Long'… It was good fun.

As it turned out, 'Angel' was the biggest hit from the album, a far cry from the singer's never-ending, unrelenting success during the 1980s, when platinum sales were an everyday occurrence. The music business had changed; fans had moved on while those who stayed loyal weren't enough to sustain high-charting places anymore. Yet, Lionel Richie could still play to full arena audiences, particularly in Britain, which must have given him some comfort. Indeed, in 1992, when his compilation *Back To Front* sat at the top of the album chart, he recognized the country's fans for helping 'forgotten black artists'. Was he now one of those acts? Sceptics thought so, but Richie always bounced back.

Working with Rodney Jerkins was also a wonderful learning experience for him, as he elaborated, 'It reminded me of the early days with the Commodores, the way they are having fun, knowing that whatever they are involved with they can do no wrong. There was a spirit and attitude there that I could relate to. It was also fantastic working with Walter again as he has so much experience and we were really able to bounce ideas off each other.'

Released in Europe during October 2000, *Renaissance* attracted negative reviews from critics. Bill Buckley was typical.

> It was with high expectations that I approached this brand new album. Had good ol' Lionel reinvented himself? Has he taken his music into the new millennium?...The answer, sadly, is no. Lionel hasn't been reborn, he's simply retreading all his old ideas and style clichés. That's not to say this is a bad album. Indeed there are some pleasant moments here and it's clearly a package that'll sell by the boatload to the man's faithful fans. Those very fans will delight in the ballads like 'Tender Heart', 'How Long', 'Just Can't Say Goodbye' and the Daryl Simmons produced 'Piece Of My Heart' which is possibly the best of the bunch.

The remaining tracks, he felt, were almost nondescript: 'Dance With The Night' was as mundane as the title suggested; 'Cinderella' banal; 'Angel' and 'Don't Stop The Music' emulated Cher's international chart-topper 'I Believe', because both were composed and produced by Brian Rawling; and Rodney Jerkins was unsuccessful in trying to spice up 'Tonight'. For his parting shot, Buckley wrote, and quite rightly so, 'In the press release Lionel claims he wanted to create something new here, but somewhere along the way he and his several producers and collaborators have lost that particular plot. *Renaissance* is not really new – it's just another Lionel Richie solo album and if that's your thing – fine!'

*Billboard* held the view that '*Renaissance* finds Richie in an oh-so-contemporary setting, encompassing uptempo dance, Latin-hued and funky pop, and power ballads...While this may sound like a far-fetched concept on paper, it works surprisingly well on disc – albeit without breaking any new ground.' *Rolling Stone* believed the album should be 'filed between Eric Clapton's work with Babyface and the last Tina Turner album'. It was expected that this album would, like his previous two, fade without trace, but his loyal fans proved otherwise by giving him a top-ten UK album. In the USA, his fans were less devoted, as the album peaked in the top seventy.

Fighting off negative responses to the album, the unblinkered Lionel Richie was convinced he'd taken the right musical direction: he had to move with the times, keep abreast of the changing demands. And his indomitable curiosity in experimenting with new ideas, and his staunch refusal to be pigeon-holed have stood him in good stead throughout his career so far. 'I had to get out of my comfort zone,' he told *Blues & Soul*.

> I was taught the hardest lessons about this business as a young cat by the likes of Marvin Gaye and I still take heed of those lessons today. What applied then, applies now. Some things never change. I can't do what Sisqó does or what D'Angelo does because for them it's old school. If B. B. King plays the blues,

it's 'the blues'. If Mariah does the blues it's fresh. That is the dilemma so I had to think about what my best next move would be. And this, I believe, is it!

Making music is always a mystery. It's an affirmation into the unknown and I'll never forget when I was with the Commodores. We were straight ahead R&B and the people and the record company expected that from us. And that was that. In the middle of the dance craze I wrote 'Three Times A Lady', and they said I was out of my mind. I'll never forget a radio programmer looked me right in the eye and said, 'You're the craziest man who ever lived, or the bravest, for releasing this song now.'

*Renaissance*, released on Island Records, was a brave move.

Four extracted tracks became British hit singles. 'Angel' was a top-twenty entrant in October 2000 and top-forty US entrant in May 2001. It was also nominated for a Grammy Award in the Best Dancing Recording category, but lost to Janet Jackson with 'All For You'. The rousing anthemic 'Don't Stop The Music' followed two months later to peak in the top forty, while 'Tender Heart' was in the top-thirty in March 2001. Long-time admirers of Lionel Richie, teenage idols the Backstreet Boys were featured on 'Cinderella', released Stateside only, while the top-forty British hit 'I Forgot' was the final single to be lifted from the album during 2001.

'I've been doing this for thirty-plus years. I'm now on my third generation of fans and I also have a seven-year-old not only singing "Angel" but also singing "Easy". He wasn't even born when I put that record out! …The old sound is the new sound.' It would, however, be two years before Richie released another album but it was hardly new! Commodore William King said on BBC Radio 2, 'He's had a couple of albums out that didn't do as well as any of us wished…[but] it's part of the business.' He thought Richie should now perhaps consider expanding into film soundtracks or Broadway productions but that if he was to make huge inroads into American pop music again, he would need to work harder. 'Harder than he's worked in a while and I don't know if he's willing to do that.' This was a feeling shared by others in the business, like Nelson George, who said, 'It would take a certain commitment to being popular and it would require a lot of work. But it doesn't seem that he wants to do it.'

Having British management allowed him to become more involved in activities outside his home country, and being involved in the September 2000 'Party In The Park' (prior to the release of *Renaissance*) was a good indication of this. This annual event is organized by the Capital Radio Corporation, and held in Hyde Park before audiences of roughly 100,000. All concerts are fundraisers for the Prince's Trust, which was set up by the Prince of Wales in 1976 to help young people overcome barriers and get their lives working. Through practical support that includes training, mentoring and financial help, the Trust helps 14- to 30-year-olds realize their potential and, hopefully, transform their lives. To date, it has helped over half a million young people and operates in Scotland, Wales, Northern Ireland and every English region. On the 2000 stage Lionel Richie joined an immensely star-studded bill that included Elton John, Kylie Minogue, Ronan Keating and Christina Aguilera. Also that year, Richie performed at the highly prestigious Royal Variety Performance at London's Dominion Theatre before the Prince of Wales and other family members. Comic and author Ben Elton compèred the show, which again included Ronan Keating and Kylie Minogue, along with Dame Shirley Bassey, Elaine Paige and Westlife among others. He guested on high-profile television programmes like *The Des O'Connor Show* (slanted towards middle-aged viewers), and on the musical tribute *A Song for Jill*, in memory of Jill Dando, one of Britain's most popular television presenters, who was brutally murdered on her doorstep in West London on 26 April 1999.

During April 2001 plans were under way for a European tour, which included nine British performances. In Birmingham, on 5 May, all the lights dimmed as a synthesizer note reverberated through the sold-out NEC auditorium, before the soft chords of a lazy piano joined in. The singer sang 'Hello' as he walked on stage, whereupon the audience, ranging from teenagers to middle-agers, went wild in an unashamed show of welcome and love. As the stage lights hit full and the curtains drew open, a six-piece band and a trio of huge screens were revealed, enabling artist and musicians to be seen in all quarters of the huge venue. Revisiting the Commodores' material, along with the best of his own work, the performance was balanced between romantic ballads and uptempo dancers, new and old, which Richie delivered with the excitement and enthusiasm of a well-practised performer. Sincerity blended with schmaltz to great effect, and with a rousing finale of 'All Night Long (All Night)' it was clear the Lionel Richie magic had not faded. It was performances like this that inspired his 2002 top-ten British album *Encore*, recorded live at three concerts in London's Wembley Arena.

> I wanted to do this live greatest hits collection for a very simple reason. For the past thirty years I've been enjoying a show the crowd has never heard. The performance the audience puts on along with me. Playing live is my chance to be completely wild and crazy. It's like time disappears and I'm in my living room, playing with a bunch of friends who stopped by for the afternoon. The larger the crowd, the more fun I have.

He blissfully continued, 'The live experience is so universal. The audience knows every lyric, every guitar solo, every drumbeat. It's like the most elaborate karaoke night you could ever imagine. But that's what's so amazing about performing because in every country around the world, regardless of their language, people sing my songs along with me.' He was concerned about what tracks to use, as his live show covers twenty-eight songs and the album held just more than half that number. 'While certain songs represent cornerstones of my career, a live album without "Easy", "Three Times A Lady", "Hello" and "All Night Long" just cannot happen. And when it comes to bringing in some of my newer songs or older Commodores tracks, it got to the point where we were having anxiety attacks over which ones to leave out.' In the end he left the decision-making to others. An aspect he did have control over was the sound, because he felt the album represented a command performance for his fans, 'in that it's a chance for them to hear what I've been hearing for the last twenty-five years of my life, which is their performance. So I decided that instead of turning them down and only having them come up at the end for the applause, I wanted them to hear themselves...For example, on "Three Times A Lady", which is normally a very quiet song, the crowd's singing is so loud it sounds like a soccer chant.' And it was to these fans that he paid homage.

> I was the one who stayed away for a while, not the fans. Normally that's the kiss of death and they forget you. But here it was years later and they showed up louder and stronger than ever. I thought they were there to hear me sing. Instead I discovered the greatest compliment is when the audience wants to sing with you. All I did was show up. The performance was in the audience.

In his review of *Encore* Charles Waring wrote,

> Lionel Richie could be regarded as black music's answer to Barry Manilow. But the erstwhile Commodores man writes infinitely better tunes than Manilow, and sings with a lot more soul. He's also, as this energetic new live collection reveals, an exuberant live performer. Basically nothing more than an in-concert greatest hits package, *Encore* will be a mandatory purchase for his many fans and especially those who attended his Wembley concerts last year.

An added attraction to this album was a pair of studio tracks – 'To Love A Woman', a duet with Enrique Iglesias (son of heart-throb crooner Julio), and 'Goodbye', a companion piece to 'Hello'. The former song, Richie explained to WorldNow, sprang from the mutual admiration the two composers had for each other. 'Enrique wanted to work with me and I was really honoured and flattered by that. I have lots of respect for him. "To Love A Woman" sounds like we've been singing together for years. We have our own styles but our voices blend together.' Charles Waring disagreed:

> The moment you hear Enrique's quivering musings in the opening moments you envisage mothers losing their minds and possibly knickers everywhere...Then your own convulsions kick in and shit starts to get ugly. This is hideous...I like

Lionel as much as the next bloke and I do indeed love a woman. But this is too much!

Despite Richie's enthusiasm at the time, by 2004 he had forgotten the young Latin hunk. The story goes that he was dining in the London restaurant Nobu when Enrique spotted him and dashed up to say 'Hello'. Richie replied, 'Nice to meet you' and autographed a napkin, whereupon an embarrassed Enrique bid a hasty retreat! The single peaked in the British top ten, but failed to register when issued in the USA. Of the sombre 'Goodbye', he said it addressed the untimely death of a loved one, and was the bookend to 'Hello'. 'It addresses the unexpected reality that the word "forever" can come to an end, and that is a very difficult feeling to put into words.'

Raised in London by Nigerian parents, Lemar (Obika) had been knocking on the music industry's door for eight years and had supported acts like Destiny's Child on tour. After recording material for BMG Records which wasn't later released, he was on the verge of abandoning his dream when a telephone call asked him to attend auditions for *Fame Academy*, BBCTV's attempt to rival ITV1's highly watchable *Pop Idol*, where the television audiences voted for and against contestants. Lemar did not win *Fame Academy* but his duet with Lionel Richie was the series' highlight. However, prior to Richie joining the programme, the young contender was on the verge of walking out because he was homesick. 'Lionel came on at just the right time, exactly half-way through. I was finding it hard being away from my family. Then I did the duet with Lionel. I was very nervous, but the performance went down really well. He inspired me to stay longer but not to win.' Apparently Richie advised him, 'I do believe you've got what it takes, but don't win the show. The minute you win, the pressure's on to bring out an album which will be commercially controlled.' He later told Jeremy Vine,

> I knew it from the first second I heard him that this kid not only had potential but, if managed the proper way, had a career. When you don't have to coach a person, you just have to let them know the rules of how to perform. Lemar was absolutely electrifying and as I told him – 'The loser has a chance to use the time for experience, go back and refine your craft, and then record.' And that's exactly what happened.

Richie's advice was spot-on: by 2006 Lemar had enjoyed six British top-ten singles and scooped two Brit Awards, a pair of MOBO (Music of Black Origin) awards, and record sales in excess of 1.5 million.

Around this time *Lionel Richie* and *Dancing On The Ceiling* were re-released as a double CD in Britain. In a review Bill Buckley noted that the singer was now considered something of a soul oddity. 'Over here, he's now condemned to wander the music limbo-land that is Radio 2, but he deserves much more (*B&S*). It contained previously unreleased items, like the demo version of 'Endless Love', showing an unhealthy country and western influence, while on the second CD, listeners were invited to hear four 12-inch versions of the hit singles! Now that's dedication!

A deluxe version of the twenty-year-old *Can't Slow Down* followed in August 2003. Now remastered to audiophile standards, *Can't Slow Down* took up the first disc of the lavishly packaged double CD set and was supplemented by a clutch of contemporaneous 12-inch remixes. The second disc was more interesting because it contained twelve previously unissued demo recordings, alternative mixes, working masters and so-called 'jam sessions'. The embryonic tracks were a quick peek into Richie's working methods and doubtless were a major selling point. It is interesting to note that he believes there is no such creature as a demo record, a point he pushed home when he said, 'The demo is the real track. Some of the greatest songs in the world were lost in the demo stage because they couldn't recreate it in the studio. If I'm grooving with something, then that's the record.' In the opening CD notes Richie recalled the album's original release in 1983, when the world had discovered Madonna and Tom Cruise, and when Michael Jackson's *Thriller* was exploding worldwide. 'It was like being in a car going 300 miles an hour and sticking your head out the window.' He also remembered he was then Motown's main man after the departure of Diana Ross, Marvin Gaye and Michael Jackson, and with no Stevie Wonder project due. 'Berry Gordy had a phrase that would drive me mad. I'd run into him in the hallway at Motown and say, "Mr Gordy, I've got another hit record." The response was "Congratulations" but with "Great, what's next?" And he was right. It's always about what's next.' While the singer's fans were grateful for these new musical insights, Richie himself enjoyed a personal highlight. On his fifty-fourth birthday, Friday, 20 June 2003, he was honoured with a star on the Hollywood Walk of Fame. As a youngster he had hopped from one star's name to the other, daydreaming of having one of his own some day. His star was number 2229 on this most famous street in Hollywood history, and doubtless other youngsters will now skip across it with ambitions of becoming famous.

During Richie's promotion of *Encore* he mentioned several times that a reunion with the Commodores was in the pipeline for 2003. The group had, by all accounts, recently reunited for one show at the Anselmo Valencia Amphitheatre in Tucson, Arizona. From raucous disco hits like 'Brick House' to beautiful love ballads such as 'Three Times A Lady' to the retrospective musical tribute to the late Marvin Gaye and Jackie Wilson in 'Nightshift', the Commodores managed to cross over into several musical formats. It was an enjoyable performance. Richie admitted it wouldn't be an easy task to get the group together because members now lived in Auckland, Los Angeles, Florida and Atlanta. 'It may be ironic but what I'm finding out now is that if there's something harder than being in a group it's putting that group back together,' he laughed. 'So, where we're at right now is me saying to the promoters "You get the Commodores together, and I'll join you".' The intention was the group would be introduced on stage during a Lionel Richie tour to perform their songs together – fans dismissed the idea as poppycock. Meanwhile, compilations kept their music alive, like *The Best Of The Commodores*, which for the first time featured all ten of the group's top-ten singles. Still harbouring fond memories of his time as a Commodore, Richie admitted Clyde Orange was the funkiest in the membership.

> Everybody's giving me credit for singing 'Brick House' but that's not me. That's Clyde. The story is that there was no song written to complement what Clyde does. Since 'Brick House' we didn't follow up with him, because quiet as it was kept, Clyde was the one who wrote most of the lyrics and melody to that song. That was his style and we just never went back as a group and followed up on it. But Clyde is the funkiest little creature on the planet…It's very easy to drive a car if it's built like the Commodores' machine because I could go out and sing any song in the world with those four guys playing. They made it so simple to sit in the driver's seat.

This was also the year when 'Brick House' was featured in Rob Zombie's movie *House of 1000 Corpses*. Richie said he had known Zombie for two years.

> He's just a guy, but he's also one of us. By that I mean one of us in this business. Fans show up in all sizes, shapes and characters. I have been absolutely shocked throughout my career by people who've come backstage and say 'Man, I'm a huge fan of yours.' Fifteen years ago, I started receiving Christmas cards from Alice Cooper and to this day we're very close. You're sitting at a restaurant one night and Marilyn Manson walks over. At some point you have to go – 'What's this all about?' And the answer is – music!

He drew on his memory to recall his first introduction to George Clinton and his Parliament/Funkadelic family of artists. 'I was like a kid walking into *The Rocky Horror Show*! These guys had a look. In the corner is a grown man, sitting there, with a diaper on, and that's when I knew I was in a different kind of business.'

With no news of an imminent album to follow *Encore*, Motown/UK decided to bridge the gap by releasing *Lionel Richie & The Commodores – The Definitive Collection*. Richie said at the time of its release,

> Putting this together with the company has been a labour of love. It's not only brought back some amazing memories, but some amazing pictures. I've dug up

some pictures that I would never want to see again. Where that Afro came from I'll never know! But, again, what a great time in life and I can celebrate it. I can laugh about it and joke about platform shoes all the way through.

His loyal public, however, didn't joke about it, they moaned that this was the singer's third compilation following *Back To Front* (1992) and *Truly – The Love Songs* (1997). Twelve tracks featured on both albums were included, but 'Dancing On The Ceiling' and 'You Are' were not. Fans also wondered why five Commodores tracks were included, yet two of Richie's top-selling titles ('My Love' and 'Love Will Conquer All') were omitted. Nonetheless, it was representative of his best work and included contributions from his most recent projects. The top-ten charting album in 2003 was a timely Christmas present for two years running, and for Valentine's Day and Mother's Day in between!

# 11 just for you

'If Nicole Richie doesn't kill me, nothing will!'   Lionel Richie

'I spend in excess of $50,000 a month for my own personal services, entertainment and shopping.'   Diane Richie

'He was once, twice, three times a brother and we love him.'   Clyde Orange, of the late Milan Williams

At the start of 2003 the Richie name was once again hitting the headlines. However, it wasn't the singer this time, but his adopted daughter Nicole, now a socialite and television star thanks to *The Simple Life*, a highly rated reality series loosely based on the 1960s US sitcom *Green Acres*, where a city couple experienced culture shock when they moved into a rural area. Nicole's co-star was her best friend Paris Hilton (whom she had known since she was two years old), and the series followed the exploits of the two young heiresses as they coped extremely badly with life on an Arkansas farm. 'The show is hilarious,' Lionel Richie told Nina Myskow. 'It's like a Lucille Ball comedy but unscripted. When Nicole first told me about it I was not thrilled. I told her, "If you want to be an actress, be a serious actress, let's not play around"' (*Daily Mirror*).

But Nicole *was* playing around in her personal life. As the headline screamed, she had been arrested by Los Angeles sheriff's deputies in Malibu, California, and charged with possession of heroin. She was also charged with driving her car while her licence was suspended. After spending five hours in custody, Nicole was released on $10,000 bail. However, after she was formally charged, she apparently failed to appear for her April arraignment, whereupon the judge forfeited her bail and issued a warrant for her immediate arrest. Within two days of this judgement Nicole's lawyer appeared in the Malibu courthouse, with the result that the arrest order was rescinded and her arraignment rescheduled for June. The young woman admitted that she started taking heavy-duty drugs when she was thirteen years old because she kept company with older children. 'I had the freedom to do what I wanted,' she divulged to *Jet* magazine. 'My dad wasn't really around and my mom was just doing her thing. When you're a girl and you're thirteen, you're at a rebellious stage anyway. And I definitely wasn't listening to my parents anyway. From the time I was nine through to thirteen nobody was around.' Richie blamed himself for his daughter's transgression by admitting he was indeed an absentee father.

> Was I there for my kid during the recitals? Was I there for my kid's graduation? Was I there? And a lot of the times the answer was – especially in Nicole's case, no...I was trying my best at the time to be Lionel Richie. I wasn't Lionel Richie yet. I was an ex-Commodore. I wasn't focusing at all on what Nicole was doing but where do I go next with 'Hello' or 'All Night Long'. I wasn't there.

He had also secretly prayed she wouldn't touch drugs, but sighed, 'I guess she thought she had to live a bit. What was she doing? A little bit of everything. Mostly pills. I think Zanax was her thing. She's reported to have been doing heroin, but she wasn't. It was just in her car, and it belonged to one of her friends.' He also told broadcaster Michael Parkinson, 'You say the word "drugs" and you immediately think about every gig you've ever played in your life and what you knew about them, what you experimented with, and what you did.'

However, Richie made up for lost time. When Nicole checked herself into a drug rehabilitation clinic in Arizona, he took two weeks out of his schedule to support her. 'She came out of that programme so clear as to who she was and where she wanted to go. She wanted to be the best she could be for the show. Now I'm just delighted for her and her success, and it's not because she's off my American Express bill, or that daddy gets to keep his hair.' He confirmed father and daughter were closer than ever before, and that he did not intend to repeat his mistake with Nicole with his two younger children, Miles and Sofia. 'I want to make as many memories for them as I can. Nicole is a great big sister for them and I know now that the key word in the family is "communicate".' He went on to say that he thought the most terrifying part of life was offstage, away from the public spotlight. 'I have no rehearsal for [offstage]. But onstage I know what I'm gonna sing. I know the band. I know the crowds – you don't have to worry about any kind of introductions. Once I step off that stage I turn into daddy and life is terrifying.'

With Nicole no longer attracting adverse headlines, Richie flew to Europe for selected dates, dropped into Britain for a quick promotional round of interviews, before returning to the USA for television spots in New York City and Los Angeles. He also ploughed his energies into completing material for a new album. However, before he could release the result, he and his second wife, Diane, announced their separation. A shocked Richie told Nina Myskow, 'It's like somebody took my heart out and stepped on it. Divorce? Not yet. I don't want to put the kids through this. They are innocent, and they have no idea what's going on because daddy's not home... We're still trying to work out what happened, but it was mutual.' It's true to say that when the couple first met the singer was at home every day, but when he later returned to work, whether it was recording or touring, they would, he said, be apart for two weeks at a go. 'And, absence is not healthy. Much as I wanted to be home I love what I do. Sitting at home is not my greatest pastime. I'm bored at the beach, bored at the club. I'm excited in the studio, excited performing. That's what I do.'

Despite Richie's optimism that divorce was some way off, on 28 October 2003 his wife filed a petition for a legal separation, but this did not become public knowledge for at least two months. They had been married for seven years. As an aside, an American magazine reported Diane had been spotted in the company of an Argentinian plastic surgeon on several occasions, which seemed to fuel the divorce rumours until the story broke. Meantime, as his marriage collapsed around him, Richie's career upturned with the unexpected runaway success of the before-mentioned *Lionel Richie & The Commodores – The Definitive Collection*, surprising both the singer and his record company, which, quite frankly, was not expecting such heavy sales even though television advertising was prolific. 'I saw the numbers,' a happy artist explained.

> And when you hear that it entered the chart higher than *Dancing On The Ceiling*, you have to ask 'Where am I?'...This is not a business of logic; it's a business of people liking it, and there's no logical reason why people [do]. I have seen great songs like "Easy"...you can't get it off the radio...and 'Three Times A Lady' has got weddings wiped out for the next two hundred years...I wrote those songs thinking they were going to be hit records, not knowing they were going to be part of people's lives forever. I keep waiting for somebody to tap me on the shoulder and say, 'You're grown up now, you have to leave the playground.'

A month after a review for *The Definitive Collection* was printed, recommending it as a highly desirable 2004 Valentine's Day present, Richie released his brand-new single 'Just For You', which was practically buried underneath the recent family publicity. The soft-rock slice of sophisticated commercial soul – so typical of Richie's musical styling – was welcomed by his eager public, who pushed it into the British top ten during March 2004, although in his home country his fans were less supportive. The title struggled into the top one hundred – an extremely poor showing for a star of his status. As the album of the same name hit the British stores, details of Richie's broken marriage were awash in the tabloids. But music first. Reviewer Charles Waring believed the project to be 'a turgid platter of vapid, rock-tinged, pop-cum-MOR that pales in comparison with the recently reissued "Can't Slow Down"' (*B&S*). Richie responded 'I wanted to be as organic as possible. No gimmicks, nothing flowery. It's kind of an old-fashioned way of doing things, but I wanted a kind of rawness and natural sound to everything.' The album was crammed with those 'organic' influences, from the ebb and flow of 'Ball And Chain', which kicked in with the singer's voice against an acoustic guitar, before building to an electrified rock bridge, to the folky flavour of 'Just To Be With You Again', and the Eastern-tinged 'She's Amazing'. 'I've never gone into politics or religion that much, but on this album it was necessary for me to say the phrases that people are thinking,' he explained at the time of the CD's release. 'Here we are again. The world seems to be in turmoil, but the world has always been in turmoil. The more things change, the more they stay the same. I want to send a message to the world that says, "People, as critical as it looks, we're OK, we're in control, whether we feel it or not!"' And 'One World', written by Richie, Paul Barry and Mark Taylor, with its social/political slant appeared to house all his observations.

> I started out with this album writing songs like 'Just For You', 'I Still Believe' and 'One World', and I was going in a very positive direction. Then, all of a sudden my marriage fell apart. It's hard to live with yourself when you're feeling certain things personally. I found myself writing 'Ball And Chain', and these other songs based on sheer emotion. The album got more and more honest as it kept going along. By the time I ended [it], it was a pure album that came straight from the heart.

With these words, Richie could well have echoed one of his musical hero's statements. When the marriage of Marvin Gaye and his wife Anna ended in divorce in 1977, the settlement was unusual, to say the least. His ex-wife asked for $1 million and, knowing he was bankrupt, agreed that he could pay a total of $600,000 to her with his next album. Gaye was in no hurry to finish his 'divorce settlement' album because

> I was involved in some political fighting with Motown and then the Federal Court felt the album was part of my estate for bankruptcy. At first I thought I'd put out a lot of garbage for the album because all I had to give was one album. There was no stipulation that it had to be a good one, so Anna was taking her chances here. (*I Heard It Through the Grapevine*)

Partway through the recording, Marvin changed his mind: 'I thought of my fans [and] the more I cut, the more I got involved. After a certain point I forgot I was mad and angry, and did some decent work. The result was, I think, pretty fair. I listened to it for over a year and I felt poor when I realized I wasn't going to make any money from it.' Titled *Here, My Dear* and released in 1978, the remarkable, soul-searching album was a poor seller at the time.

For the album track 'Do Ya', Lionel Richie teamed up with teen idol Daniel Bedingfield; the result was an infectious combination. Lenny Kravitz worked with the singer on three tracks, two of which appeared on *Just For You*, with the remaining title, 'Destiny', earmarked for Kravitz's next album. The two had met in Florida. 'And Lenny said, "So, we're not gonna do anything together?" The next thing I know, we recorded these songs, "Road To Heaven" [produced by Kravitz and 7 Aurelius, known best for working with Mariah Carey] and "Time Of Our Life".' Finally, the singular superior ballad, 'She's Amazing', hinted at past glory, as did the passing R&B message in 'The World Is A Party'.

Richie commented,

> Simplicity is the key to what I do. I want to find the simplest phrase that everybody says, no matter what language you speak. At one point I was actually going to make the title of this album *Simplicity*. So much of my career has been about saying things the way people say them, using melodies not that I can sing but that the people can sing. 'All Night Long' will always be 'All Night Long'. 'Easy Like Sunday Morning' will always be [that]...'Truly', or 'Still' or 'Endless Love' – if you look at the titles, they say the entire thought before you even go into the story. And that's why music has stayed around so long.

Charles Waring wrote, 'This is a singularly unremarkable effort and one that confirms that these days Richie is a mere artisan rather than a bona fide artist.' Artisan or artist, the *Just For You* album was a top-fifty US title but again it was left to Britain to show its strength by elevating it into the top five during March 2004.

Lionel Richie planned to support the release by hitting the touring trail. He often remarked that travelling the world was a huge influence on his composing abilities and cited his current album as a home for dozens of such inspirations.

> Taking time to sit back and watch and think about what you've seen is important. I found that when I travel and just sit in the corner and watch, a million ideas come to me. The new tour will start in July and will just keep going. I'm going to be off and on to make the next record and stuff like that, but basically I'm going to be a touring, writing and performing artist for a while. And I can't think of anything better.

He also gave an insight into his tough schedule while on the road:

> *It is crazy!* I have breakfast at noon, lunch at 6 in the evening and dinner at 11.30 p.m. I end up going to bed at 4 or 5 in the morning because I am so charged with adrenaline. It takes three hours to wind down...Touring takes a lot of energy; you are exhausted afterwards, but it's great...Not a day goes by when I am not excited by what I do. I feel I'm the luckiest human on the planet because I am in the most exciting business in the world.

Five months after her filing for a legal separation, on 3 March 2004, Diane Richie's divorce documents were lodged at the Los Angeles Superior Court. She was demanding at least $300,000 in monthly support payments, and went to extreme lengths to detail their highly extravagant lifestyle. Of course, the media lapped up every word. The *Daily Mirror* was typical, with a two-page spread under the heading 'For Richie...For Poorer', but generally speaking British journalists were quick to support the singer, probably because of the easy relationship he now enjoyed with the majority of them. In the documents, Richie's wife declared she had had no limit to her spending power. She detailed the size of their home and items of furniture. Located on Copely Place, Beverly Hills, it was the original Guggenheim estate, which the Richies had owned for five years but lived in for only eighteen months. It was worth $40 million – the Richies had purchased it for $6 million and spent a further $7 million on restoration and improvements. The mansion had thirty rooms, including seven bedrooms, seventeen bathrooms, music room, library, dining room, family room, multiple offices, a safe room and staff room. Diane Richie also claimed she oversaw all aspects of the restoration for four years after finding the mansion while her husband was touring. With the help of distinguished interior designers, their home had been beautifully and tastefully decorated and furnished. In the petition it was also stated that some pieces of furniture were worth between $10,000 and $25,000 each, while a single chandelier was worth $35,000; a tapestry was valued at $50,000, with $150,000 worth of oriental rugs. Works of art ranged from $10,000 to $25,000 each.

She further claimed that her husband never had a problem earning money, citing a monthly pay cheque of $300,000, which they comfortably spent in the same time span. At least twice monthly he performed at private functions, with a price tag of up to $1 million for a single performance. He received regular record royalties, a huge income from touring, and had a long-standing relationship with the Mercedes-Benz car company, for which he undertook promotional work. Prior to their marriage, Diane Richie had her own clothing-manufacturing business and retail shop, 'Alexander Brown'. She co-owned the company but decided to sell her shares to become a full-time wife and mother. 'The Respondent constantly reassured me that I had nothing to worry about financially and that there was no need for me to earn an income.' She also sold the house in which she and Richie had lived for a year prior to their marriage. The proceeds of $600,000, she said, were placed into her husband's account. 'That was the only separate money which I had.' Even before they were married, Richie had financially supported her and bought her cars and expensive gifts.

The paperwork also, rather surprisingly, gave details about their staff, which included eight full-time members – a house manager and assistant (who spent at least $1000 a week on food and drink for the entire household), head housekeeper, three housekeepers (two of whom also worked as nannies), a gardener and Richie's secretary – with a total monthly salary bill of $45,000.

The court papers then detailed Diane Richie's maintenance requirements, which, of course, the tabloids gleefully relished: 'I spend in excess of $50,000 a month for my own personal services, entertainment and shopping.' Her personal services included massages, dermatology, hairdressers, nail care, electrolysis, laser hair removal, facials, Pilates classes and therapy. In addition, she spent at least $20,000 a year on plastic surgery, claiming, 'The Respondent has always encouraged me to spend as much money as I want on beauty treatments.' One newspaper, perhaps a little too unkindly, suggested she must look like *Star Wars*' Chewbacca!

Entertainment included the cinema, theatre, restaurants like Spago, Mr Chow, the Ivy and La Dome, and so on, while her shopping took her to designer establishments like Jimmy Choo, Gucci, and Dolce & Gabbana. She spent thousands of dollars every month on their two children, Miles and Sofia. Miles currently attended a boarding school in Colorado where the tuition was $125,000 annually, and Diane visited him at least once a month at a cost of between $15,000 and $20,000 because other family members and friends accompanied her. They travelled always with a nanny, flew first class and stayed in expensive hotels. Tuition fees for Sofia were estimated at $16,000 a year. One journalist suggested, 'You may want to get on Sofia's birthday list because it turns out she spends at least a thousand dollars a month on birthday presents!'

There was even a section in the court papers devoted to family holidays, where Richie's wife advised,

> We vacationed several times a year at the most popular resorts and on exclusive yachts. We went on family vacations at least two or three times a year to such places as New York, Colorado, the Caribbean, Hawaii, as well as to Europe. In addition, the Respondent and I went at least one time a year by ourselves, usually to a city in Europe or to Hawaii. We always stayed at the best hotels and resorts.

On holiday they often jet-skied, went horseriding, skiing, swam with dolphins and purchased expensive souvenirs for themselves and their family. Naturally, they stayed in the most expensive hotel suites and ate at the most fashionable restaurants.

It was a hugely extravagant bill and when it was published alongside details of their astronomical use of money it appeared ludicrous to the everyday person. British journalists attempted to offer a shocked Richie some solace by indicating that Tom Cruise's divorce from Nicole Kidman cost him £46 million ($83 million), while Demi Moore was awarded £38 million ($69 million) from Bruce 'Diehard' Willis. However, the most expensive divorce package in 2004 was Melissa Mathison, whose divorce from Harrison Ford cost him a cool £50 million ($90 million)!

Estimated to be worth £200 million ($363 million), Lionel Richie could face a yearly settlement of £2 million ($3.6 million) to run for as long as the presiding judge decreed. If the ruling was for life, it would make it one of the costliest divorce settlements of the decade.

First to Richie's defence was his daughter Nicole, who publicly blasted her stepmother's demands, saying she could always work for a living! The *Daily Mirror* had reported that one of Diane Richie's friends said, 'One reason for the request is she wants her kids to be raised normally, not like Nicole...' In reply, Nicole was reputed to have said, 'If you want a normal life, go get a fucking job and stop asking for $300,000 a month!'

Meanwhile, a shocked, yet calm, husband admitted, 'I remember calling up my accountant and asking him "Am I worth a billion?" And he said, "Of course, you're not." I'd added up the figures and worked out I'd need to have a billion to pay that kind of money. The numbers are not real. I was impressed though.' Broadly speaking, he had sold over 100 million records but had lost a chunk of his fortune following his first divorce. He further told viewers on Michael Parkinson's chat show that Diane's settlement 'scared me to death' and joked he would need

> several hits to pay for her amazing demands! I did call her on the phone after I had read this. I said, 'That's a lot of money' and she said, 'I didn't say that.' 'But, yes, did you speak to someone?' She said, 'I didn't say that' and I told her 'Welcome to public life'. It does have to be the end but I'm keeping my fingers crossed and hope that we are friends at the end. Because we have kids we have to be friends.

He claimed that when his personal life crumbled around him, it forced him to return to his work, to escape from a situation he no longer controlled. Finding the right balance was what was needed.

> When I'm into an album or a tour, I either have to focus all the way or I can't do it. And that's one thing I've learned on this whole journey of celebrity. When I first went to Hollywood I thought what is this? Marriage is so fickle? They're getting married on Monday, getting a divorce on Friday. Then I realized how typical it is. Having a relationship and doing what we do in public life is absolutely the hardest juggling act in the world. You'll see me do a lot more work now than you'll see me in relationships!

When asked about the insane monthly amount his ex-wife claimed they had spent so easily, all Richie would admit was 'I'm a hopeless romantic. Always was, always will be. We've given ourselves time and space to figure this out. Diane is a great mom and we talk on a daily basis. The kids and I see each other every other day and I'm going to be there for them, like I am for Nicole.' Never once did he place any blame for the divorce on Diane; he took full responsibility, claiming his long absences from home were to blame.

> You try to scale it down. You say, 'I'm only going to do six weeks' and then people say, 'But that is only America'. Or something amazing comes up. They go 'The Queen wants you.' Or you get a call – 'Lionel, great news, they want you to come to the Olympics.' Great! What's the date? Ah, that happens to be my wedding anniversary. There's a huge party set up. The ideal thing would be the whole family goes on tour, but on a school day it becomes another animal.

And he did get a call to co-host *Motown 45* with Justin Timberlake, to be screened by the ABC network during May 2004. The two-hour special was to be taped at Los Angeles' Shrine Auditorium, with ticket proceeds going to the United Negro College Fund. Immediately the show was announced, US black activist groups made heavy representations to Motown regarding Justin Timberlake's involvement in a programme devoted to black music. After further discussion, a press release later announced that Timberlake was unable to appear due to a previous engagement. When screened, *Motown 45* featured company superstars like Gladys Knight and Smokey Robinson, alongside Britain's new R&B star Joss Stone (who is white!) and of course Lionel Richie, who hosted the show with Cedric the Entertainer. Opening the show with a poor version of 'All Night Long (All Night)', before duetting with Kelly Rowland on 'Endless Love' (she went on to perform in a mock-up of the Supremes with Mary Wilson and Cindy Birdsong), he interacted with the Commodores, who had reunited for the programme. Richie said at the time that he believed their much-promised tour was possible. 'In fact, the conversation is in full force. The healing is going to be something else. I'm loving where we are. We're too old to lie to one another.' And further, 'Right now there are only two original Commodores and the big task would be to get the original Commodores back together, and then maybe that might happen. I've always believed sometimes that the mystique is better than the reality.'

Meanwhile a solo tour beckoned, and in July 2004 Lionel Richie confirmed his intention to tour the world, including British dates during October, when 'I Still Believe' was extracted as a single from the *Just For You* album. The *Blues & Soul* reviewer suggested the title of the single could refer to his career of late, before adding, 'The song is tired and too middle of the road…still there are plenty of people who disagree and they'll most likely make this a top ten record.' They didn't. So, 'Long, Long Way To Go' followed in November 2004. Previously recorded by Def Leppard, this tepid rock track benefited from Richie's power-pumped vocals and soulful delivery. It sounded a little out of place in the (then) current market, but confirmed his ability not to conform.

To ensure he stayed in the public arena, he then lent his support to Britain's Sport Relief, before cheating death when he appeared as a guest on BBC2 television's motoring programme *Top Gear*. In the segment where celebrities compete for the fastest lap time around the Dunsfold Park circuit, the singer drove a Suzuki Liana. When he reached 80 mph on a practice lap, a wheel came off his car in the middle of a fast corner. Thankfully, he wasn't hurt, but had it happened five seconds earlier, he could have suffered fatal injuries. Two months later he again appeared on a primetime television show, where the results were equally disastrous, as critic Ian Hyland described in the *Sunday Mirror*.

> Excitement at the end of *All Time Greatest Love Songs Mania* as Tess Daly revealed her co-host Lionel Richie was about to perform a greatest hits medley. So there I was, ready to join in with 'Dancing On The Ceiling' (literally) having spent the last hour climbing the walls while watching this late-summer leftover. But no, Lionel could only manage the slow ones – which perhaps explains why he agreed to work with Tess. Not sure whose idea this show was. But given the plugs for his new album (which actually came out last March) I'm guessing Lionel's PR was involved. Not that I'm knocking Lionel. I lost my virginity to him. Well, one of his songs was on in the background – although I'd rather not dwell on the title, 'Stuck On You'.

Other artists performing included Elaine Paige and Barbara Dickson, Ronan Keating, Mick Hucknall and Tony Hadley.

As he became a television entertainer, his ex-group the Commodores released a trio of albums on the Sound Barrier label. With tracks like 'The First Noel', 'The Christmas Song' and 'Jerry The Elf', one album was appropriately titled *Commodores Christmas*; *Commodores Hits Volume 2* spoke for itself with titles like 'Still', 'Sail On' and 'Nightshift'; while *No Tricks* proved more interesting, with tracks like 'Shut Up And Dance', 'Missing You' and 'Take My Hand'. No further information was forthcoming about a possible joint tour.

Then, once again, Lionel Richie's private life was dragged into the public arena when his ex-wife Diane was arrested for allegedly allowing her boyfriend, an Argentinian doctor named Daniel Serrano, to turn her Beverly Hills bathroom into an illegal cosmetic surgery clinic. She was charged with aiding and abetting Serrano, who apparently injected patients with anti-wrinkle drugs that were not approved by the US health authorities. Diane Richie spent a night in jail and was released on $25,000 bail following a court hearing. The police also reputedly seized jewellery, cash and amounts of a liquid substance, believed to be used in the manufacture of the illegal anti-wrinkle drug connected to the case. While Diane Richie was bailed, Serrano – known as Dr Daniel and licensed to practise medicine in Argentina but not in California – was held in custody. It was reported that Lionel Richie, allegedly a client of Dr Daniel, had alerted investigators to possible malpractice when he became suspicious of the doctor's methods. He had also suspected Serrano was having an affair with his ex-wife. When Serrano was jailed, actor Walter Matthau's niece Michelle, who was at one point married to him, told the media he was innocent of the charges.

As the battle of words continued across the Atlantic, Lionel Richie was wowing audiences on his world tour. Matilda Egere-Cooper attended his performance at London's Wembley Arena on 4 October 2004.

> Lionel Richie will never go broke...and is staying relevant thanks to his slacker daughter, and can still manage to pack out an arena that Mary J. Blige only managed to half-fill earlier this year...Though the five-time Grammy winner has got the kind of hits catalogue you can't help but subconsciously hum along to, seeing him encourage a geriatric on the front row to clap along to 'Just For You' and grab his mic stand like a black Mick Jagger is oddly hilarious. Even hearing Richie encourage the ladies to 'Work that body, baby' as he lays into 'Outrageous' would have put Mutley in double-stitches – not to mention his dancing that makes Chris Rock's quip about Richie not being black since the Commodores seem like gospel. He jumped up on the piano to play classics like 'Easy' and 'Three Times A Lady' reminding all present of his superstar status, although some of the eighties material began to sound dated. (*B&S*)

But, she continued,

> Groups of teenagers mouth the words of 'Running With The Night' and 'I Still Believe' like they were written last week by the Busted boys...The rest of the show goes down a storm – his performance of 'Say You, Say Me' sparks off massive hand-waving. 'Dancing On The Ceiling' is simply electric, and the finale 'All Night Long' even had me flapping my wings in front of a woman old enough to be my grandmother. Richie will be laughing all the way to the bank when he cashes tonight's cheque, of course, but he's a bona fide star alright and one who always gives his fans exactly what they want. (*ibid.*)

The touring circus then rolled on across the world.

The Commodores were also on the road but their US dates were rather low-key compared to those graced by their ex-lead singer. Nevertheless, their reviews were always highly favourable. For example, after a performance at the Indianapolis Jazz Fest in 2005, an unknown US reviewer wrote,

> The Commodores brought lawn-chair sitters to their feet at Military Park, where opening number 'Brick House' featured a pyrotechnic blast – perhaps the first in

the festival's seven-year history. The 1977 girl-watching anthem also warranted a bass solo, and the audience was chanting the name of the backing band's bass player by the song's end. Today's front line Commodores consist of original members William King and Walter Orange, plus Lionel Richie's successor, J. D. Nicholas. The trio sang 'Just To Be Close To You' with coordinated harmonies and dance steps reminiscent of the Temptations and the Four Tops, the Commodores' forefathers at Motown Records. Of course, the Commodores are best known as a two-pronged hit machine of funk numbers and Richie's ballads. When King, Orange and Nicholas sang the funk numbers in unison or round-robin, the good times rolled. When 'Easy' and other ballads received a patchwork vocal treatment, Richie's distinctive drawl was missed.

This year saw Lionel Richie as a high-profile performer. In July 2005, for instance, he smiled non-stop at Silverstone's Grand Prix Ball when he was paid a handsome £250,000 to perform a 45-minute set. Tickets for the ball were £8,000 for a table seating eight, and attending celebrities included Caprice, Peter Stringfellow and drivers from the world of Formula I motor racing. He then performed with Kenny Rogers on a *Country Music Television Crossroads* special, where the US programme gave an informative insight into their friendship both in and out of the music business. Richie was also in the planning stages of a new album which would, like his most recent studio projects, include input from third parties in vogue with the current music scene. He appeared to shy away from his tested composing talent, perhaps not trusting his individual approach to music any more. Maybe he wasn't confident he could capture the imagination of the young record-buying market as a soloist? Or perhaps he had just lost confidence in himself. For some reason he seemed to be hell-bent on avoiding the middle-of-the-road market in order to take up the musical gauntlet in the younger arena. Whatever the reasoning, he was recruiting help with his new project.

Twenty years before, in December 1985, USA For Africa had released 'We Are The World' – a record spearheaded by Quincy Jones to raise funds for the starving populations in Africa. To celebrate its twentieth anniversary, a benefit DVD was released, capturing the all-night recording session, with Jane Fonda as narrator. It included four hours of footage and two of bonus material, such as solo sessions by Bob Dylan, Michael Jackson and Bruce Springsteen. Also at this time in 2005 Michael Jackson was apparently locked into litigation over his involvement with the charity single, although Richie told reporter Chuck Creekmur that, because of Jackson's recent high-profile child molestation court case (when he was found not guilty of all charges), his friend was 'a magnet to anything that had lawsuit written on it'. He elaborated on the subject. 'We had eleven lawsuits for "We Are The World"…Quincy Jones told me "You can always tell when you have a smash record – you get sued!" ...There's always somebody who wakes up one morning [and says] "They stole my song". And you literally have to go through and deal with it.'

And then Lionel Richie visited China, where he had always enjoyed a huge fan base, to host the fifty-fourth annual Miss World contest on the tropical island of Sanya. The southern Chinese province was so thrilled with its celebrity visitor that the government declared 3 December to be National Lionel Richie Day. The Miss World contest was one of the most-watched annual events on a worldwide basis. In 2003, for instance, 162 nations screened it, with an audience of 2.3 billion. Richie said, 'I want to find local artists in China and would love to do a song with that person. Then Lionel Richie will become part of the culture!'

Headlining the Barbados Jazz Festival began 2006 on a musical high for the singer. It was his first visit to the country since 1978, when he was still a member of the Commodores. It was the thirteenth festival, and he was joined by saxophonist Bony James and jazz artist Jill Scott. In previous years performers included Luther Vandross and Patti LaBelle. His next significant appearance was on 20 May, when he participated in the Prince's Trust's thirtieth anniversary concert at Tower Hill, London. Richie joined the Bee Gees, Annie Lennox, McFly, and Will Young, among others, but reviewers agreed he was the musical highlight of the evening, which raised £3 million in aid of the Trust. The concert was screened live on ITV1 and could be viewed in 3D through specially designed glasses! 'I met Charles and Diana some years ago,' he told reporter Zoe Nauman. 'It was an honour to be asked to get involved. Diana came to a concert and I have such fond memories of meeting her. She came backstage and wanted to hang out. But Charles was saying – "We have to go, they have shut twenty streets for us to get home!"' (*Sunday Mirror*).

During his trip to Britain, the singer took the opportunity to talk to the press, and mentioned his concern about Nicole's health, a matter already discussed quite openly in fashion glossies, teen magazines and gossip columns in the tabloids. In true Richie fashion, he blamed himself for her weight loss, saying how upset she was over his expensive divorce case, not to mention the adverse publicity surrounding the break-up. 'When I saw how thin she was, I was concerned and worried. I would love to see her with more meat on her...When Nicole worries, she doesn't eat. She is very sensitive and has been through a very tough time. Our divorce was difficult for her.' Now weighing six stone, twenty-four-year-old Nicole admitted she was too thin, but insisted she had no eating disorder. 'I'm not happy with the way I look. I have a problem and I want to fix it.' Although she was not his biological daughter, daddy Richie admitted they both suffered from anxiety and a fast metabolism. 'When I was younger, I was very skinny.

People would ask, "Are you OK?" [because] they thought I was ill. I was like a string bean. I have always struggled to maintain my weight.'

Through the publicity that followed Nicole from her American sitcom success with *The Simple Life* and her parents' divorce, she inadvertently opened up a new audience for her father. He laughed at the new situation. 'I am now known as Nicole Richie's dad, and a whole other generation has discovered me who wouldn't have done so, if it hadn't been for her.' It's this fact alone that may have led him to seek out younger artists to work with him on his albums. As time passed, Nicole became stronger and weathered the storm of her personal life, and her father had nothing but admiration for her strength. 'I'm a big fan of hers just watching her go through this, although she will call me two or three times a week with one more major crisis, which makes me feel good as a dad. Because dads always like to have things that they can solve with the kids.' Besides, this is the little girl who grew up in an unusual household, where the people she mixed with were international stars. 'She referred to her uncles as uncle Michael, uncle Kenny Rogers and uncle Lenny Kravitz...So she kinda grew up into the show-business thing. What's shocking all of us is that [now] she's emerging unscathed from her tabloid press, which normally would have unnerved me if I had had only two years in the business and had to face this kind of press.' Of himself, he said, he too felt stronger, and more able to cope with the aftermath of his disastrous personal life, thanks to his – genetics. 'I would love to say it's yoga or it's a vegetarian diet. My grandmother lived to be 104. I am banking on those genes coming through to save me. And...if Nicole Richie doesn't kill me, nothing will!'

Following the Prince's Trust anniversary gala, John Berman reported for ABC News that during the time he had been in Iraq reporting on the US-led invasion, he had seen 'bombs and blood, rebuilding and restructuring, death and democracy'. And Lionel Richie! 'Grown Iraqi men get misty-eyed by the mere mention of his name. "I love Lionel Richie," they say. Iraqis who do not understand a word of English can sing an entire Lionel Richie song.' Berman later asked the singer if he was aware of his popularity in Iraq. 'The answer is, I'm huge, huge in the Arab world. The answer as to why is, I don't have the slightest idea!' Richie told the journalist that he had performed in Morocco, Qatar, Libya and Dubai and felt the reason his music could be so popular was because it carried the simple message – love.

> I've stayed in the middle ground called love. Love falls into three categories. You lost someone, you found someone, you're love-ly. That's love. But now I've taken love to another stage. Love is the one remedy that will solve the world's problems. Throughout my career the words corny, syrupy, schmaltzy,

have covered my songs but I've found out over the years that the only word that does not go out of style is – love!

He added that he had been told the Iraqis were playing 'All Night Long (All Night)' on the streets during the night US tanks rolled into the country in 2003, and that he fully intended to perform there as soon as the tension eased sufficiently. In April 2006, that time was right.

Radiating charm and wit, Lionel Richie won over a soberly dressed audience by singing a selection of his hit material during a concert to mark the twentieth anniversary of a US raid on Libya. Bombing Benghazi and Tripoli in the early hours of 15 April 1986 had been President Reagan's retaliation for what he claimed was Libyan complicity in the bombing of a Berlin nightclub where a US serviceman was one of three killed. Using Colonel Gaddafi's shell-pitted home as a backdrop, the singer roared, 'Libya, I love you' to over one thousand senior officials and diplomats who were gathered in front of the building. Some laughed when he joked that he believed members of the audience knew the words to his songs better than he did. Organizers of the celebration, called 'Hanna Peace Day' in tribute to one of several children killed in the raid, wanted an upbeat commemoration of the raid, with Richie's star input to highlight Libya's intention to promote a message of international goodwill. Opera stars José Carreras and Ofelia Sala shared the bill, and the event closed with a group of children dressed as angels singing 'We Are The World'.

From Libya to New Orleans, where Richie headlined the 2006 Jazz Fest with Bob Dylan, Bruce Springsteen and Paul Simon, among others, before joining in the 4th of July celebrations of Independence Day in Philadelphia, where he shared the billing with the 2004 *American Idol* winner Fantasia Barrino. Their performances were supported by one of America's most prestigious orchestras, the Philly Pops under conductor Peter Nero. Richie then debuted his new single 'I Call It Love' on NBC's broadcast of *Macy's 4th of July Fireworks Spectacular*, saying the song was lifted from his pending *Coming Home* album.

Five days after Lionel Richie's sensational Philadelphia performances, Commodore Milan Williams died. The keyboard genius, whose searing riffs were the very backbone of the group's funk sound, had been fighting cancer for a while. As time was running out for him, his wife arranged a last surprise when the existing group members (apparently excluding Richie) called Williams on a conference phone. Commodores News reported,

> He sounded really up and although we could hear the weakness in his voice, the content of the conversation was very strong. One of the most profound things he said to us was 'Gentlemen, whatever grudges you may have between yourselves or anyone else in the world, let them go, shake hands and move on with the precious life God has given you. Life is too short.'

When Commodores fans were alerted of his failing health via the SoulfulDetroit website, countless messages were sent to him through one host, who reported back, 'They definitely put a smile on his face to know that so many people cared.' Milan Williams died on the afternoon of 9 July 2006 at the University of Texas M. D. Anderson Cancer Center in Houston, Texas. He was survived by his wife Melanie, two sons from previous marriages, two brothers and one sister. The funeral took place on 14 July in Okolona, Mississippi, his birth town, followed by a memorial service in Los Angeles in August. Clyde Orange said, 'He was once, twice, three times a brother and we love him. He gave all he could give to the Commodores. He'll always be remembered.'

On the Monday after Milan Williams's funeral, Lionel Richie's single 'I Call It Love', written and produced by Taj and Stargate, was scheduled for release. It was the taster for an album that played host to several in-vogue all-star names. For instance, 'I'm Coming Home', 'I Love You' and 'Outta My Head' were Richie compositions, but he co-produced them with his musical director of five years, Chuckii Booker, also an accomplished composer in his own right. He collaborated with Richie on three further tracks – 'I'm Missing Her', 'Keep Me Up All Night' and 'Why' – the latter two co-produced and co-written with Sean Garrett, who had enjoyed recent hits with Beyoncé and Usher. Raphael Saadiq wrote and produced 'Sweet Vacation', Jermaine Dupri penned 'You Are', while the singer co-wrote 'Reason To Believe' with the track's producer Dallas Austin, known for his work with Pink and TLC. 'All Around The World', jointly credited to Richie and Montreal-based Quicksand, rounded off the album.

Recording with a new and younger generation of artists prompted Richie to tell Chuck Creekmur that being referred to as 'Mr Richie' 'was the only thing I had to get used to working with Jermaine Dupri and Sean Garrett. They kept saying, "You know, Mr Richie" [and] I said, "Guys, just say yo Rich or something"...I was totally respected on this album.' One of the guidelines laid down by him during the recording of 'I Call It Love' was to develop a sound that was believable. 'If it doesn't we are definitely going down the wrong road.' Thankfully, he knew he was on the right track when an outsider chanced to come into the studio when the single was being mixed, and asked him if it was one of his (Richie's) songs. 'And that was the compliment because it sounded that comfortable. That's the selling point to me – how do you pull off Lionel Richie to be contemporary in 2006? It's got to be real.'

Of the album itself, he admitted he gave his collaborators a free hand, a move that could prove dangerous because the result often represented everything but the actual artist. Not so here, he said.

It was a mutual admiration society because I actually gave them permission to mess me up. What I said was 'What does Lionel Richie sound like in 2006? Right, take all I've done. Take "Sail On", "Brick House", "Zoom", take all this stuff. What do I sound like?' ... We didn't have to go that far in left field. We discovered that actually they know more about the old school than I can remember.

As his promotional touring circus swung into top gear in support of *Coming Home*, one of his collaborators, Dallas Austin, was arrested for carrying 1.36 grams of cocaine into Dubai. Having pleaded guilty to possession of the drug, while claiming that he was unaware he had violated the laws of the country, he was sentenced to four years in prison by a Dubai court. That same court later pardoned and deported the disgraced Austin back to the USA. According to the *New York Times*, the pardon was given courtesy of high-level string-pulling including Lionel Richie, who received a call from the United Arab Emirates consul in Washington asking him for a reference. Richie reported, 'It was ...tell me what kind of guy is Dallas Austin? I said, "Listen, this is a guy who's done a great job for the community. A gangster, a hoodlum, a thug, he's not".' Austin stated, 'This unfortunate experience has had a profound effect on me and I regret any grief caused to friends and business associates.'

From his earliest introduction to music as a saxophonist in a Tuskegean funk group, Lionel Richie's career has trodden a bumpy, yet totally fulfilling, road. With his innate talent to write near-perfect love songs, he readily admits he got lucky when he chose to write about the greatest emotion ever, because 'Love is the only thing that doesn't go out of style!' He steered the Commodores through various musical avenues and shrugged off adversity, to climax with 'Three Times A Lady', before branching out as a soloist to enjoy his current world iconic status. Despite his respected position, Richie maintains he's still a country boy at heart, who loves life, music and his public. 'After all this time my career is not a job. It's the greatest hobby I've ever had, and it just happens to be the way I make my living.'

To date he's made a good living too! Selling more than 100 million records worldwide, he is the winner of five Grammy Awards, one Oscar, has a star in a Hollywood pavement, hundreds of honours, achievements, and countless silver, gold and platinum discs both as a Commodore and as a soloist. It's a remarkable story of success and struggle, personal heartbreak and joy, but one that any artist of this era would love.

When Lionel Richie was asked how he would like to be remembered, he said, 'I don't want to be the greatest black singer of all time. I just want to be the greatest singer of all time!'

# discography

## British hit albums

| Year | Title | Record number | Chart position |
|---|---|---|---|
| The Commodores with Lionel Richie ||||
| 1978 | Commodores Live! | TMSP 6007 | 60 |
| 1978 | Natural High | STML 12087 | 8 |
| 1978 | Greatest Hits | STML 12100 | 19 |
| 1979 | Midnight Magic | STMA 8032 | 15 |
| 1980 | Heroes | STMA 8034 | 50 |
| 1981 | In The Pocket | STML 12156 | 69 |
| 1982 | Love Songs | K-TEL 1171 | 5 |
| 1985 | Nightshift (without Richie) | ZL 72343 | 13 |
| 1985 | The Very Best Of The Commodores – 16 Classic Tracks | TELSTAR STAR 2249 | 25 |
| 1995 | The Very Best Of The Commodores | MOTOWN 5305472 | 26 |
| 2003 | The Definitive Collection – Lionel Richie & The Commodores | UNIVERSAL TV 9861394 | 10 |
| Lionel Richie as solo artist ||||
| 1982 | Lionel Richie | STMA 8037 | 9 |
| 1983 | Can't Slow Down | STMA 8041 | 1 |
| 1986 | Dancing On The Ceiling | ZL 72412 | 2 |
| 1992 | Back To Front | MOTOWN 5300182 | 1 |
| 1996 | Louder Than Words | MERCURY 5322412 | 11 |
| 1998 | Truly – The Love Songs | MOTOWN 5308432 | 5 |
| 1998 | Time | MERCURY 5585182 | 31 |
| 2000 | Renaissance | ISLAND 5482222 | 6 |
| 2002 | Encore | MERCURY 0633482 | 8 |
| 2004 | Just For You | MERCURY 9861710 | 5 |
| 2006 | Coming Home | ISLAND 000648402 | 15 |

## British hit singles

| Year | Title | Record number | Chart position |
|---|---|---|---|
| The Commodores with Lionel Richie | | | |
| | | *Tamla Motown* | |
| 1974 | 'Machine Gun' | TMG 902 | 20 |
| 1974 | 'The Zoo (The Human Zoo)' | TMG 924 | 44 |
| | | *Motown* | |
| 1977 | 'Easy' | TMG 1073 | 9 |
| 1977 | 'Sweet Love'/'Brick House' | TMG 1086 | 32 |
| 1978 | 'Too Hot Ta Trot'/'Zoom' | TMG 1096 | 38 |
| 1978 | 'Flying High' | TMG 1111 | 37 |
| 1978 | 'Three Times A Lady' | TMG 1113 | 1 |
| 1978 | 'Just To Be Close To You' | TMG 1127 | 62 |
| 1979 | 'Sail On' | TMG 1155 | 8 |
| 1979 | 'Still' | TMG 1166 | 4 |
| 1980 | 'Wonderland' | TMG 1172 | 40 |
| 1981 | 'Lady (You Bring Me Up)' | TMG 1238 | 56 |
| 1981 | 'Oh No' | TMG 1245 | 44 |
| 1985 | 'Nightshift' (without Richie) | TMG 1371 | 3 |
| 1985 | 'Animal Instinct' (without Richie) | ZB 40097 | 74 |
| | | *Polydor* | |
| 1986 | 'Goin' To The Bank' (without Richie) | POSPA 826 | 43 |
| | | *Motown* | |
| 1988 | 'Easy' | ZB 41793 | 15 |
| Lionel Richie as solo artist | | | |
| | | *Motown* | |
| 1981 | 'Endless Love' (with Diana Ross) | TMG 1240 | 7 |
| 1982 | 'Truly' | TMG 1284 | 6 |
| 1983 | 'You Are' | TMG 1290 | 43 |
| 1983 | 'My Love' | TMG 1300 | 70 |
| 1983 | 'All Night Long (All Night)' | TMG 1319 | 2 |
| 1983 | 'Running With The Night' | TMG 1324 | 9 |
| 1984 | 'Hello' | TMG 1330 | 1 |
| 1984 | 'Stuck On You' | TMG 1341 | 12 |
| 1984 | 'Penny Lover' | TMG 1356 | 18 |
| 1985 | 'Say You, Say Me' | ZB 40421 | 8 |
| 1986 | 'Dancing On The Ceiling' | LIO 1 | 7 |
| 1986 | 'Love Will Conquer All' | LIO 2 | 45 |

Lionel Richie as solo artist *(continued)*

| Year | Title | Record number | Chart position |
| --- | --- | --- | --- |
| 1986 | 'Ballerina Girl'/'Deep River Woman' | LIO 3 | 17 |
| 1987 | 'Sela' | LIO 4 | 43 |
| 1992 | 'Do It To Me' | TMG 1407 | 33 |
| 1992 | 'My Destiny' | TMG 1408 | 7 |
| 1992 | Love Oh Love | TMG 1413 | 52 |
|  | *Mercury* |  |  |
| 1996 | 'Don't Wanna Lose You' | MERC 461 | 17 |
| 1996 | 'Still In Love' | MERC 477 | 66 |
| 1998 | 'Closest Thing To Heaven' | Mercury 5661312 | 26 |
| 2000 | 'Angel' | Mercury 5726702 | 18 |
| 2000 | 'Don't Stop The Music' | Mercury 5688992 | 34 |
| 2001 | 'Tender Heart' | Mercury 5728462 | 29 |
| 2001 | 'I Forgot' | Mercury 5729922 | 34 |
| 2003 | 'To Love A Woman' (with Enrique Iglesias) | Mercury 0779082 | 19 |
| 2004 | 'Just For You' | Mercury 9862071 | 20 |

# bibliography

The following books, newspapers, magazines, articles, fanzines and websites have been consulted during the writing of this book, and I am extremely grateful to all those authors, journalists, website owners and Lionel Richie fans. Unfortunately, there are some I cannot thank because the printed sources have suffered through time and are in a bad state, particularly photocopies, which seem to disintegrate at the merest touch. So, I apologize profusely if by chance anyone is omitted from this list.

## Books

Armani, Eddy, *The Real T* (London: Blake Publishing, 1998).

Ashford, Jack, *Motown: The View from the Bottom* (East Grinstead: Bank House Books, 2003).

Betts, Graham, *Complete British Hit Singles 1952–2004* (London: Collins, 2004).

Bronson, Fred, *The Billboard Book of Number One Hits*, 3rd edition (London: Guinness Publishing, 1992).

Davis, Sharon, *Motown: The History* (London: Guinness Books, 1988).

Davis, Sharon, *I Heard It Through the Grapevine* (Edinburgh: Mainstream Publishing, 1991).

George, Nelson, *The Death of Rhythm & Blues* (London: Omnibus Press, 1989).

Gordy, Berry, *To Be Loved* (New York: Warner Books, 1994).

Gordy-Singleton, Raynoma, *Berry, Me and Motown* (Contemporary Books, 1990).

Jackson, Michael, *Moonwalk* (London: Heinemann, 1988).

Nathan, David, *Lionel Richie: An Illustrated Biography* (New York: McGraw-Hill, 1984).

Ritz, David, *Divided Soul: The Life of Marvin Gaye* (London: Michael Joseph, 1985).

Smith, Joe, *An Oral History of Popular Music: Off the Record* (London: Pan Books, 1990).

Taraborrelli, J. Randy, *Call Her Miss Ross* (London: Sidgwick & Jackson, 1989).

White, Adam, and Bronson, Fred, *The Billboard Book of Number One R&B Hits* (New York: Billboard Books, 1993).

## Publications and CDs featuring interviews, reviews and news items

ABC News: John Berman (19 May 2006)

*Billboard*: Paul Grein, Nelson George, Roberta Plutzik (undated items)

*Blues & Soul*
- G of Abbey: April 1977; September 1979
- John Abbey: July 1979; March 1983; December 1984; March 1985; November 1986
- Bill Buckley: November 2000; July 2003
- Sharon Davis star interviews: 1982, 1983, 1986, 1987 in particular, together with reviews, news items and articles
- Matilda Egere-Cooper: October 2004
- Frank Elson: November 1986; June 1987
- Pete Lewis: April 1996
- David Nathan: October 1988; June 1992
- Charles Waring: May 2001; September 2003; May 2004
- Peter Antal, Mick Clark, Dave Godin, Bob Killbourn, Jeff Lorez, Justin Lubbock, Ralph Tee, Pete Tong: additional information, reviews and conversations (undated)

*Can't Slow Down* deluxe edition (440018120-2) CD notes – Steven Ivory (2003)

*Chatbuster* (2004 onwards)

*Commodores Anthology* CD notes: A. Scott Galloway (2001)

*Daily Express*: Lizzie Catt (4 December 2004)

*Daily Mail*: Mark Reynolds and Laura Benjamin (4 March 2004)

*Daily Mirror*: Nina Myskow (14 February 2004); Anthony Harwood (4 March 2004)

*Daily Times* (USA): journalist unknown (18 November 2004)

*Ebony*: Robert L. Johnson (January 1985)

*Hello!*: Sue Russell (1996)

Island Records press releases (June 2006)

*Melody Maker*: Dessa Fox (1984)

Mercury/Universal press releases (2000)

Motown Records press releases (UK & US) (1974 onwards)

*National Enquirer*: Alan Braham Smith and David Perel (19 July 1988)

*New York Times*: James Berardinelli and John Pareles (11 April 2000)

*Rolling Stone*: Andrew Dansby (12 March 2003)

*The Sun*: Clarkson on Saturday (10 July 2004)

*Sunday Mirror*: Ian Hyland (19 September 2004); Zoe Nauman (7 May 2006)

*Sunday Telegraph Magazine*: Marianne Macdonald (4 July 2004)

*Woman*: David Ragan (date unknown)

## TV and radio

BBC Radio 2, *The Lionel Richie Story – Parts 1 & 2*, Robin Quinn and Wayne Imms (writers/presenters), broadcast 30 September and 7 October 2003. Contributors included Michael Boddicker, James Carmichael, Sharon Davis, Bob Giraldi, Calvin Harris, William King, Ken Kragen, Suzanne de Passe, Greg Phillinganes, Lionel Richie, Cynthia Weil, Milan Williams. (Some quotations from every contributor are included in the present work.)

BBC1, *The Jeremy Vine Show* (11 May 2004) (used for reference purposes)

ITV1, *The Michael Parkinson Show* (6 March 2004) (used for reference purposes)

## Websites

Alabama Music Hall of Fame
allhiphop.com (Lionel Richie interview by Chuck 'Jigsaw' Creekmur)
commodoresnews.com
davidwolper.com/shows
firstuniversal
indystar.com
lionelrichie.com
manchesteronline.co.uk ('That's Richie' by Eddie Rowley, 28 October 2004)
MSNBC.com (15 April 2006)
princeofwales.gov.uk/trusts
thesmokinggun.com/archive (Diane Richie's Petition for Dissolution of Marriage)
tinaturnerfanclub.com
tuskegee.edu/global
usaforafrica.org/shows
washingtonpost.com

And all the reviewers, critics, authors and journalists who have helped shape the continuing successful professional life of Lionel Richie.

# index

'L.' indicates Lionel Richie. Figures in italics indicate captions.

3 Ounces of Love  39–40, 41
7 Aurelius  153
7th Wonder  51

A&M Studios, Hollywood  95
Abba  45
Abbey, Gof  50
Abbey, John  52–3, 54, 59, 60, 66–7, 71, 74, 90, 98
ABC News  162
ABC-TV  65, 85, 136
Actors Fund, The  77
Acu-Acu club, near Cannes  9
Adidas  88
Afanasieff, Walter  140
African famine relief  94–7
Aguilera, Christina  143
Alabama  9, 41, 63, 74, 105, 109, 132
Alabama Hall of Fame  99
Alabama State University  8
Ales, Barney  31
Alexander, Diane, *see* Richie, Diane
'Alexander Brown' (company)  154
All Saints  136
*All Time Greatest Love Songs Mania* (television programme)  158
American Academy Awards  64, 100
*American Idol* (television show)  163
American Music Association  59
American Music Awards  45, 51, 59, 84–5, 95, 129
Amsterdam  127
Anaid Film Productions  93
Andrews, Julie  120
Anselmo Valencia Amphitheatre, Tucson, Arizona  146
Ant, Adam  73

Antal, Peter  104
anti-apartheid groups  118, 121
Armani, Eddy: *The Real T*  89
ASCAP (American Society of Composers, Authors and Publishers)  97
Ashburn, Benjamin  38, 42
   public relations firm  5
   contacted by Milan Williams  5, 6
   becomes the Commodores' manager  6
   Commodores Entertainment Corporation formed  8
   secures Commodore bookings in Europe  9
   Commodores showcased in New York  11
   defends the group  45–6
   1984 Olympics  56, 81
   death  64–5
   L. on  67
   issue of L's leaving the group  70
*Associate, The* (film)  37
Astaire, Fred  104
Atlanta  147
Atlantic Records  6, 7, 30, 50
Auckland, New Zealand  106, 147
Austin, Dallas  164, 165
Australasia  46
Australia  97, 109–10
Austria  97

B*Witched  136
Babyface  130, 131, 141
Backstreet Boys  142
Bailey, Philip  35
Baird, Tom  21
Ball, Lucille  149

172

Ballard, Florence 93
Band Aid 94
Bar-Kays 7
Barbados Jazz Festival 161
Barbiero, Michael 111
Barrino, Fantasia 163
Barry, Paul 152
Baryshnikov, Mikhail 99, 100
Bassey, Dame Shirley 143
BBC 97
    BBC2 television 158
    BBCTV 145
    Radio 2 70, 77, 80, 83, 87, 91, 94, 106, 114, 119, 120, 137, 140, 142, 146
Beach Boys, the 121
Beatles, the 2, 7, 8, 48, 49, 121
Bedingfield, Daniel 153
Bee Gees, the 45, 48, 56, 161
Belafonte, Harry 94
Belgium 46
Bell, Robert 'Kool' 25–6
Benghazi, Libya 163
Benny, Jack 6, 43
Benson, George 86
Berardinelli, James 135
Berlin, Irving 87
Berman, John 162
Berry, Chuck 48, 49, 112
Beverly Hills 117
Beyoncé 164
*Billboard* 47, 55, 59, 81, 88, 91, 94, 98, 101, 109, 141
*Billboard Book of Number One Hits, The* 20
*Billboard Book of Number One R&B Hits, The* 31
*Billboard Book of Top 40 Hits* 98
Birdsong, Cindy 73, 157
Birmingham 41, 111, 143
Birmingham Odeon 32
Birmingham Radio/Midlands Broadcasting: 'People's Party' 136
*Bishop's Wife, The* (film) 135
Blige, Mary J. 159
Bloom, Howard 102
Blow, Kurtis 56, 57
Blue Moon 107

*Blues & Soul* magazine viii, 19, 25, 33, 34, 50, 57, 59, 61, 67, 73, 76, 91, 106, 110, 118, 123, 125, 127, 141–2, 146, 157, 159
BMG Records 145
Bob Marley & the Wailers 56
Bobby M 70
Boddicker, Michael 63, 83, 113–14
Bogart, Neil 51
Bolan, Marc 36
Boogie Man, The 138
Booker, Chuckii 164
Boomtown Rats 94
Boseman, Jesse 88
Boston, Massachusetts 11
Boston Ventures 115
Bowen, Jeffrey 19
Bowie, David 97
Boy George 79, 94, 126
Brick Hall of Fame 123
Brighton 41
Brit Awards 145
Britain
    Commodore tours in 32, 41, 46, 50, 117, 128
    London gigs, *see under* London
    music industry 48
    radio stations 49
    and Live Aid 96–7
    and terrorist threat 102, 109, 112
    'Outrageous Tour' 111–12
    and the Motown sale 116
    L.'s loyal fan base in 138, 140
    L.'s 2001 tour 143
    L. as a high-profile performer (2005) 160
    L. talks to the press 161
Brockman Music 93, 97
Brooks, Pattie 38
Brown, Gerry 77
Brown, James 4, 34
Buckley, Bill 141, 145–6
Budokan, Tokyo 51
Busby, Jheryl 116, 123
Busted 159
Butler, Jerry 32
Butler, Lanette 72
Byrd, Gary 70

index **173**

California 63
Callaghan, Andre 4, 5, 7
Cameo 38, 77
Campbell, Glen 13
Canada 117
Capital Radio Corporation 142
Capitol Records 33, 89, 93
Capra, Frank 135
Caprice 160
*Car Wash* (film) 38
Carey, Mariah 58, 142, 153
Carmichael, James Anthony 42, 55, 72, 107
    introduced to the Commodores 21
    and the group sound 21–2
    and 'Fancy Dancer' 31–2
    on 'Zoom' 35
    on 'Three Times A Lady' 42–3
    and 'Sail On' 46–7
    and L.'s first solo album 63, 64, 67–8
    and L.'s second solo album 73
    on 'All Night Long (All Night)' 79–80
    unusual recording techniques 83
    and *Can't Slow Down* 91
    and 'Missing You' 93
    plagiarism case 93
    Grammy Award 97
    and 'Say You, Say Me' 100
    pressure on the successful 106
    and L.'s personal problems 125–6
    and *Louder Than Words* 131
    L. on 132–3
Carreras, José 163
Carrington, Laura 86
Casablanca Records 38, 51
Cash, Alvin 7
CBS Records 27, 53, 59, 69
Cedric the Entertainer 157
Chandler, Jordy 121
Charles, HRH The Prince of Wales 111, 142, 143, 161
Charles, Ray 94
Cheetah Club, New York 6
Cher 140
China 136, 161
Citizens' Band (CB) radios 43
Civic Auditorium, Santa Monica 45

Clapton, Eric 97, 141
Clark, Dick 85
Clark, Mick 61
Clarke, Stanley 77
Clay, Tom 18
Clayton, Merry 53
Clinton, George 15, 147
Coca-Cola 88, 121
Cochrane, David 32, 39, 49
Cocker, Joe 71
Cole, Natalie 121
Coliseum, Los Angeles 82
Collins, Mick 92
Collins, Phil 94, 97, 100
*Color Purple, The* (film) 95–6
Coltrane, John 132
Columbia Pictures 99
Commodores, the
    formed 2
    personnel 5, 7
    choice of name 5
    perform in New York (1969) 5–6
    appearance 5, 21, 32, 41
    first album shelved 6–7, 23
    management plan 8
    showcased in New York 11–12
    first tours supporting the Jackson 5 (1970) 12–15
    invited to become a Motown act 15
    and Motown method of working 19
    debut on the Mowest label 19
    Gloria Jones on 19–20
    first single on the Motown label 21
    first golden disc 21
    the group sound 21–2, 29, 31, 35
    success of 'Machine Gun' 22–3
    *Machine Gun* released 23
    first Far East tour 24
    supports Rolling Stones in USA 24–5
    musical changeover 26, 28, 30, 32
    members complete degree courses 27
    start of their funkless material 28
    touring with the O'Jays 28
    second consecutive gold disc 31
    first British tour (1977) 32
    logo 35, 44, 49

    most popular black unit in the USA
       35
    as 'a huge melting pot'  36
    decision-making  36
    debut in British album chart  38
    'The Black Beatles'  42
    songwriting  42
    and American Music Awards  45,
       51
    Grammy Award nominations  45
    loss of their black base  46
    number-one titles  47
    the biggest black group earners  47
    exclusive recording contract with
       Motown  49
    L.'s last single with the group  61–2
    loss of Benny Ashburn  64, 65
    L. on their 'non-success'  67
    European tour (1983)  70–1, 74–5
    Motown twenty-fifth anniversary
       show  72
    release of first album without L.
       73–4
    'Only You' stalls  80–1
    McClary leaves  90–1, 98
    J.D. Nicholas recruited  98
    Alabama Hall of Fame  99
    move from Motown  106
    dissatisfied with Polygram  107
    and Bruce Willis  110
    cancelled South African tour
       117–18
    digital recordings  118–19
    Britain toured with ex-Supreme
       members  128
    reunite for one show in Tucson  146
    reunite for Motown 45  157
    favourable reviews  159–60
Commodores Entertainment Corporation
   8, 39, 40–1, 53
Commodores Moving On Company  41
Commodores News  163
Commodores Records & Entertainment
   119
Connors, Jimmy  63–4
Cooke, Sam  34, 52
Cooper, Alice  147
Copely Place, Beverly Hills  154
Corporation, the  12

Corvettes, the  7
Cosby, Hank  17
Cotillion Records  6
Country Music Television Crossroads
   special (2005)  160
Creekmur, Chuck  160, 164
Croker, David  139
Crouch, Andrea  95
Cruise, Tom  146, 156
Culture Club  79
Curtis, Lieutenant Robert  116

da Costa, Paulinho  63
Daily Mirror  149, 154, 156
Daisy nightclub, Beverly Hills  12
Daly, Tess  158
dance  45
Dance Theatre of Harlem  77
Dando, Jill  143
D'Angelo  141
Dansby, Andrew  37
Davis, Hal  19
Davis, Henry  76–7
Dazz Band, the  66, 70
de Passe, Suzanne  11, 12, 20, 21, 22,
   36, 55, 63, 69, 72, 105–6, 120
De-Lite Records  26
DeBarge  70, 72
Dee, Kiki  97
Def Leppard  158
Des O'Connor Show, The (television
   programme)  143
Destiny's Child  145
Detroit, Michigan  9, 16–17
Detroit Sound  17
Devastating Affair  18
Diana, Princess of Wales  111, 161
Dickens, Charles: A Christmas Carol  135
Dickson, Barbara  158
Dire Straits  97
Disco Aid  97
disco music  27, 35–6, 41, 45, 51
Disco-Tex and the Sex-O-Lettes  27
Dominion Theatre, London  143
Donen, Stanley  104
Dozier, Lamont  10
Drifters, the  121
Dubai  162, 165
Duke, George  96

index   175

Dunsfold Park circuit  158
Dupri, Jermaine  164
Dylan, Bob  94, 95, 97, 121, 126, 160, 163

Earl Van Dyke and the Soul Brothers  9
Earth, Wind & Fire  21, 35
Edwin Hawkins Singers  53
Egere-Cooper, Matilda  159
Elizabeth Taylor AIDS Foundation  127
Ellington, Duke  2
Elson, Frank  103–4, 109
Elton, Ben  143
EMI Records  10, 20, 25, 59
Emotions, the  50
*Endless Love* (film)  57
Escovedo, Sheila  77, 106
Ethiopia  94
Ethiopian Fund  97
Eurovision Song Contest  45
Eurythmics  121

Fair, Yvonne  18, 21, 53
Falcons, the  12
*Fame* (film)  86
*Fame Academy* (television series)  145
Far East tours  24, 32, 76
Faye, Kathy  32, 35, 41
Fields, Venetta  53
Fitzgerald, Ella  49
Fleetwood Mac  93
Florida  74, 147
Fonda, Jane  160
Fontana label  10
Forbes, Dr James  134
Ford, Harrison  156
Formula 1 motor racing  160
Foster, David  97, 130, 137
Four Tops, the  36, 47, 72, 84, 115, 136, 160
Fox, Dessa  86
France  46
*France, SS*  9
Frenchick, Michael  113
Funk Brothers  10
Funkadelic  15

Gaddafi, Colonel Muammar  163
Galloway, A. Scott  35, 71

Garrett, Sean  164
Gary, Indiana  12
Gary Byrd and the GB Experience  73
Gaye, Anna  152
Gaye, Marvin  19, 21, 33, 84, 100, 104, 105
  becomes an A-list performer  16
  personal control of his career  36
  number-one titles  47
  duet with Tammi Terrell  58
  leaves Motown  59, 146
  recalls the roots of black music  72
  clashes with Diana Ross  92–3
  influences L.  92, 131, 141
  retains his soulful feeling  104
  release of *What's Going On*  138
  divorce settlement  152
  shot dead by his father  69, 92
  tributes to  92, 98
Gaynor, Gloria  27
Geldof, Bob  94, 96
George, Nelson  109, 125, 131, 142
  *The Death of Rhythm & Blues*  91, 103
Georgia Mass Choir  136
Germany  46
Getz, Stan  132
Gibb, Barry  80
Gilbert, Michael  5, 7
Giraldi, Bob  83, 86–7
Gladys Knight and the Pips  16, 18, 21
glam rock  45
Glasgow  46
Godin, Dave  29, 34
Goldberg, Whoopi  127
Golde, Franne  98
Golden Globe Awards  100
Goldsmith, Harvey  96
Gordon, Keith  12
Gordy, Berry, Jr  10, 19, 50, 127
  education  9
  creates Motown Records  9
  first Motown Revue  9
  and the Jackson 5  12
  success of  16
  anxious to expand into television and films  16, 17
  the move to Los Angeles  17, 18
  and 'Endless Love'  58

Gaye's *What's Going On* project 138
Diana Ross and Marvin Gaye leave 58–9
and twenty-fifth anniversary of Motown 72, 73
*Can't Slow Down* project 79
and artists' failure to deliver albums on time 101–2
puts Motown up for sale 114
sells the company 115–16
maddening phrase 146
*To Be Loved* 22
Gordy-Singleton, Raynoma: *Berry, Me and Motown* 79
Grammy Awards 70, 87, 96, 97, 98, 159, 165
nominations 45, 55, 59, 85, 142
Grant, Cary 135
Grapevine Advertising 16
Green, Al 89, 121
*Green Acres* (US sitcom) 149
Greene, Melanie 139
Greig, Dr Byron 79
Grein, Paul 55

Hackford, Taylor 99
Hadley, Tony 158
Halifax Building Society 33, 118
Hall & Oates 97
Hamburg 127
Hammer, MC 120
Hammersmith Odeon, London 70–1, 74, 90
Hammerstein Ballroom, New York: 'Ultimate Dance Party' 136
*Hands Across America* benefit event 96, 102
'Hanna Peace Day' 163
Harris, Calvin 'Razor Black' 22, 31–2, 83, 107
Harris, Eddie 4
Harrison, George 7
Harvey-Richie, Brenda (L.'s first wife)
L. first sees her 3–4
relationship with L. 4
marries L. 28
and 'Three Times A Lady' 42
and *Share Your Love* 55

L. travels with her instead of the group 56, 70
and Sheila Escovedo 77
and *Can't Slow Down* 84
meets Tina Turner 89
and 'Penny Lover' 91
'We Are The World' project 94
marital breakdown and divorce 116–17
L. inspired by her 126
Hawaii 46, 85
Hayvenhurst, Encino, California 94
Heatwave 98
*Hello!* magazine 119, 120, 122, 128
High Inergy 72
Hilton, Paris 149
Hines, Gregory 99, 100, 135
Hitsville USA, Detroit 9, 72
Holiday, Billie 27
Holland 46
Holland, Brian 10
Holland, Dozier and Holland 19
Holland, Eddie 10
*Hollywood Palace Show* (television programme) 12
Hollywood Walk of Fame 146
*House of 1000 Corpses* (horror film) 37, 147
Houston, Cissy 136
Houston, Texas 41
Houston, Thelma 18, 19, 38, 47
Houston, Whitney 121, 131, 134, 135, 136, 140
Hudson, Harold 32, 39, 68, 73
Hungary 136
Hutch, Willie 19, 79
Hutton, Michael 82
Hyde Park, London
'Party In The Park' (2000) 142–3
Prince's Trust charity gala 136
Hyland, Ian 158

Iggy Pop 36
Iglesias, Enrique 140, 144, 145
Iglesias, Julio 88, 144
Ike & Tina Turner Revue 89
Ikeda, Suzee 55
Indianapolis Jazz Fest (2005) 159
Intruders, the 7

index 177

Iraq 162–3
Island Records 142
*It's a Wonderful Life* (film) 135
ITV1 145, 161
Ivey, Clayton 21
Ivory, Steven 22, 80

J-Notes 7
Jabara, Paul 38
Jackson, Jackie 12, 13
Jackson, Janet 142
Jackson, Jermaine 12, 13, 65–6, 92
Jackson, Joe 12
Jackson, Latoya 94–5
Jackson, Marlon 12, 13
Jackson, Michael 47, 54, 59, 61, 75, 79, 81, 82, 83, 162
  on Diana Ross 12
  a child superstar 13
  friendship with L. 14
  first solo album 53
  hugely successful *Thriller* 53, 69, 84, 85, 86, 91, 93, 97, 105, 146
  and Motown twenty-fifth anniversary show 72
  disguised, watches L. perform a "Billie Jean' rap 78
  burnt while filming Pepsi Cola commercial 87
  'We Are The World' project 94–5, 160
  awards 97
  godfather to Nicole Richie 105, 121
  hyperbaric chamber story 110
  plastic surgery on his face 121
  L. on 121
  found not guilty of child molestation 121, 160
  Neverland 121
  *Moon Walk* 96, 121
Jackson, Tito 12, 13
Jackson 5, the 19, 21, 22, 25, 27, 47, 54, 84, 91, 100
  first tour 11
  original members 12
  and Berry Gordy 12
  and the Corporation 12
  debut album 12
  J5-mania 12, 14
  first tour with the Commodores as support act (1970) 12–15
  earnings 2, 14
  leave Motown 36, 53
  number-one titles 47
  name owned by Motown 53
  and Motown twenty-fifth anniversary show 72
  'Victory' tour 87, 88
Jacksonville, Florida 34
Jagger, Mick 25, 74, 97, 159
Jam, Jimmy 130, 131
Jamerson, James 17–18
James, Bony 161
James, Rick 66, 78
Japan 23, 24, 46, 51, 71, 72, 97, 117
Jays, the 4–5
jazz 132
Jerkins, Rodney 140, 141
*Jet* magazine 117, 149
Jive Records 91
Jobete 16, 115
Joel, Billy 78, 94
John, Elton 34, 97, 109–10, 127, 132, 143
Johnson, Gary 32
Johnson, Jimmy 5, 7
Johnson, Marv 10
Johnson, Robert E. 129
Johnson Publishing 44
Jones, Darrell 32
Jones, Father 2
Jones, Gloria 16, 18, 19–20
Jones, Quincy 68, 77, 85, 91, 94, 95, 114, 160–1
Jordan, Michelle 117
Jr Walker and the All Stars 18

K-Tel Records 65
KC and the Sunshine Band 13, 27
Keating, Ronan 143, 158
Kelly, Gene 104
Kemp, Martin 94
Kendricks, Eddie 18, 47, 97
Kidman, Nicole 156
Killbourn, Bob 118
King, B. B. 48, 126, 141–2

King, Ben E. 123
King, Carole 64
King, Clydie 53
King, William 2, 56, 72, 107, 118, 160
    in the Mystics 4
    a founder member of the Commodores 5
    at Small's Paradise 5–6
    education 8
    on band bonding 8
    lessons from touring with the Jackson 5 13
    on Sawyer and Jones 19
    on the failure of 'Sanctified' 24
    and lyrical content 25
    getting airplay and recognition 26
    on 'Sweet Love' 27
    the group as 'a huge melting pot' 36
    on 'Brick House' 37
    on the group's clothes 41
    CB radio nickname 43
    on US stadium tours 46
    disagrees with outside commitments 51
    on *Heroes* 52
    on L.'s leaving the group 69, 92, 98
    records a gospel album 82
    and *Nightshift* 98–9
    L.'s need to work harder 142
Kissoon, Katie 91
Klique 90
Knight, Gladys 16, 157
    *see also* Gladys Knight and the Pips
Kool & the Gang 25–6
Korea 117
Kostelanetz, André 43
Kragen, Ken 1, 54, 55, 56, 99–100
    and Kenny Rogers 54, 55
    manages L.'s solo projects 56, 70
    and L.'s first solo world tour 76
    colour issues 88
    'We Are The World' project 94, 95
    and L.'s Oscar for 'Say You, Say Me' 100
    split with L. 101, 102
    'Dancing On the Ceiling' video 104
    and plagiarism claims 113
    and L.'s inability to decline work 119
Kravitz, Lenny 153, 162
Kubinec, Betty 116

LaBelle, Patti 97, 102, 161
Lake Tahoe, Nevada 76, 80
Lambert, Dennis 91, 98, 107
Landover, Washington, DC 38
LaPread, Ronald 49, 51
    joins the Commodores 7
    education 8
    into rock and funk 31
    death of his wife 32, 35, 41
    and 'Zoom' 35
    CB radio nickname 43
    forms Shaggy Dog Inc 51
    and A Taste of Honey 59
    shares the vocals 71
    leaves the group 106
    moves to New Zealand 106
Las Vegas 54, 58
Lauper, Cyndi 94
Laurence, Lynda 128
Layton, Joe 76
Le Bon, Simon 94
Led Zeppelin 8
Leeds 32
Lemar (Obika) 145
LeMel, Gary 99–100
Lendl, Ivan 109
Lennon, John 7, 80, 132
Lennox, Annie 161
Levi Jeans 123
Levine, Stewart 126
Lewis, Pete 122, 127, 132, 133
Lewis, Terry 130, 131
Libya 102, 112, 162, 163
*Lionel Richie Story, The* (BBC Radio 2) 11
Live Aid (1985) 96–7
Lloyd Price's Turntable Club, New York 11
London
    Commodore dates 32, 41, 46, 70–1, 74–5, 90
    L.'s solo concerts *108*, 111–12, 126, 134, 159
London-American label 10

index   179

Lorez, Jeff 130–1
Los Angeles 16, 17, 38, 41, 63, 64, 78, 80, 92, 147, 150, 164
  Federal District Court 93
  Supreme Court 154
Los Angeles Memorial Coliseum: Olympics (1984) 1, 56
L.T.D. (Love, Togetherness, and Devotion) 45, 46, 77
Lubbock, Justin 75

McCartney, Linda (née Eastwood) 7
McCartney, Paul 59, 80, 87, 132
McClary, Thomas 28, 46, 49
  meets L. 4
  on the Jays 4–5
  a founder member of the Commodores 5
  education 8
  on first Far East tour 24
  on 'too black' singles 30
  into acid rock 36
  CB radio nickname 43
  debuts a new guitar tone 44
  shares the vocals 71
  new ingredients to the group 73–4
  Michael Hutton project 82
  leaves the Commodores 90–1, 98
  first solo single 90
McCoy, Van 24, 36
Macdonald, Marianne 122
McFly 161
*Macy's 4th of July Fireworks Spectacular* (NBC broadcast) 163
Madison Square Garden, New York 14, 41, 45, 56–7, 109, 127, 139
Madonna 97, 131, 140, 146
Malibu, California 149
Manchester 32, 41
Mandela, Nelson: 70th Birthday Party 121
Manila 24
Manilow, Barry 79, *82*, 103, 144
Mann, Barry 83
Manson, Marilyn 147
Marley, Bob 57, 79
Marshall, Penny 135
Martha and the Vandellas 9, 10, 97
Martin, Marilyn 100

Marvelettes, the 10, 16, 18, 47
Mary Jane Girls, the 70, 78
Mathieson, Greg 107
Mathis, Johnny 43
Mathison, Melissa 156
Matthau, Walter 159
Maxims, Wigan 74
Mayfair Hotel, London viii
MCA Records 85, 90, 115, 116
Mean Machine, the 32, 39, 41, 68, 71, 74, 118
Melbourne Entertainment Centre 109
*Melody Maker* 86
Mercury Records 127, 128
Mercury/Phonogram Records 94
Metropolitan Club, New York 133
Mexico 117
Michael, George 94, 121, 127
Midler, Bette 95
Miller, Skip 76, 80
Minelli, Liza 27
Minneapolis 139
Minogue, Kylie 143
Miracles, the 9, 16, 27, 47, 72, 107, 129
  see also Smokey Robinson and the Miracles
Miss World contest 161
Mississippi 5
Monkees, the 80
Montgomery, Alabama 5, 71
Moore, Demi 156
Morney, Lester 56
Morocco 162
'Motown 25: Yesterday, Today, Forever' spectacular 72, 73
*Motown 40: The Music Is Forever* (documentary special) 136
*Motown 45* (television special) 157
Motown label 10, 16, 21
Motown Productions Inc. 16
Motown Records 8
  created by Berry Gordy 9
  Revues 9–10
  image 9
  plagiarism case 93
  and *Back To Front* 127
Motown Sound 10, 17, 19, 34, 37
Motown/Casablanca Filmworks 38

Motown/UK 61, 71–2, 76, 78, 85, 99, 102, 111, 136, 147
Mowest label 18, 19, 20, 21, 23
Mr Lucky's nightclub, Gary, Indiana 12
Mucknall, Mick 158
*Muppets from Space* (film) 37
Muscles 32
Music of Black Origin (MOBO) awards 145
    award ceremony (Covent Garden, London, 1996) 134
Myskow, Nina 149, 150
Mystics, the 4

Nashville, Tennessee 105
Nathan, David 39, 40–1, 45, 57, 65, 89–90, 107, 118
    *Lionel Richie: An Illustrated Biography* 21–2, 28, 47–8, 123
National Association for Sickle Cell Disease 72
National Association of Brick Distributors 123
*National Enquirer* 115, 116
National Exhibition Centre (NEC), Birmingham 111, 143
National Lionel Richie Day (3 December, China) 161
Nauman, Zoe 161
Navratilova, Martina 109
NBC 163
Nero, Peter 163
Nesmith, Mike 80
Nevada 77
New Connaught Rooms, London 134
New Orleans, Louisiana 5
New Orleans Jazz Fest (2006) 163
New Wave 35
New York City 5–6, 11–12, 56–7, 109, 111, 150
New York *Daily News* 58
New York Dolls, the 36
New York Philharmonic Orchestra 43
*New York Times* 115, 139, 165
New York Town Hall 5
Newcastle 41
*News of the World* 117
Nicholas, J.D. (James Dean) 91, 99, 106, 107, 160
    recruited to the Commodores 98
    shares lead vocals 118
Nigeria 23–4
Noah, Yannick 109
Nobu restaurant, London 145
Northeastern High School, Detroit 9
northern soul circuit 74
Norway 97, 111

Ocean Way Studios, Hollywood 78
Ohio Players, the 15, 21, 24
O'Jays 24, 28
Okolona, Mississippi 164
Olympic Committee 81
Olympics (Los Angeles, 1984) 1, 56, 81–2
Omni Auditorium, Atlanta, Georgia 38
Ono, Yoko 7
Orange, Walter 'Clyde' 23, 49, 73, 107, 160
    joins the Commodores 7
    education 8, 27
    on L. as the band's focal point 14
    splits vocals with L. 28
    on the Motown family 31
    prefers black music for the group 34
    into big band and jazz 36
    and 'Three Times A Lady' 42
    and group songwriting 42
    CB radio nickname 43
    motorcycle accident 54
    the only trained musician in the group 60
    L. on 62, 74, 135, 147
    European tour (1983) 70
    debut as lead vocalist 70, 71
    debut solo project 82
    and 'Nightshift' 98
    and the Motown sale 115
    shares lead vocals with Nicholas 118
    on Milan Williams 164
Oriole label 10
Osaka, Japan 51
Oscars 100, 119, 165
    galas 64
    nominations 59
'Outrageous Tour' *108*, 109, 111–13

Page, Gene  64
Paige, Elaine  143, 158
Pareles, Jon  139
Parfitt, Rick  94
Paris  111, 127
Paris, Mica  136
Parker, Ray, Jr  91, 98
Parkinson, Michael  104, 150, 156
Parliament/Funkadelic  147
Parliaments, the  23
Parton, Dolly  82
Parton, Stella  82
'Party In The Park' (Hyde Park, London, 2000)  142
Pasadena Civic Auditorium, Los Angeles  72
Payne, Scherrie  128
Pepsi Cola  87–8, 108
Perel, David  116
Philadelphia  25, 163
Philadelphia International Records  28
Phillinganes, Greg  63, 76, 77, 127, 129
Philly Pops  163
Phoenix, Arizona  78, 109
Pickett, Wilson  34
Pine, Courtney  127
Pink  164
Platinum Hook  39–40, 53
*Playboy* magazine  70
Plutzik, Roberta  47, 81
Pointer Sisters  76, 91, 94
Poland  136
Polydor Records  117, 118, 119
Polygram  57, 58, 106, 107
Porter, Cole  87
*Preacher's Wife, The* (film and album)  135–6
Presley, Elvis  36
Preston, Billy  66
Prince  91, 102
Prince's Trust  111, 136, 142–3, 161, 162
Promoters Association  88
punk  35

Qatar  162
Queen  97
Quicksand  164

Radio City Music Hall, New York  58, 77
Rafelson, Bob  80
Railroad  4
Randle, Vickie  111
rap  120, 131–2
Rawling, Brian  140, 141
RCA Records  93, 101
RCA/Capitol Records  58
Reagan, Ronald  102
Redding, Otis  34, 103
Reeves, Martha  17, 72
Regal nightclub, Chicago  12
Reid, John  139
Richie, Alberta (L.'s mother)  2, 42, 78, 120
Richie, Brenda, *see* Harvey-Richie, Brenda (L.'s first wife)
Richie, Deborah (L.'s sister)  3
Richie, Diane (née Alexander; L.'s second wife)  115, 122, 136
    Brenda's attack  116, 117
    children by L.  122
    time of readjustment  127–8
    marries L. (1996)  133–4, 137
    marital breakdown and divorce  150–1, 154–7, 161
    'Alexander Brown' company  154
    Serrano case  158–9
Richie, Lionel Brockman, Jr
    birth (20 June 1949)  2
    childhood  2–3
    saxophone  2, 3, 4, 8, 132
    influence of Uncle Bertram  2
    grandmother (Adelaide)  2–3, 8, 63, 77–8, 137, 162
    early song-writing  3
    family background  3
    education  3, 4, 8, 107–8
    first sees his future wife  3–4
    in the Mystics  4
    a founder member of the Commodores  5
    nicknames  6, 43, 47, 79, *82*
    tells his father of his career move  8
    on touring with the Jacksons  13
    the group's focal point  14, 34, 74
    friendship with Michael Jackson  14
    networking  14–15
    discovers a talent for songwriting  19

first composition to be recorded 21
marries Brenda Harvey 28
distinctive voice and styling 28
on a 'closed-minded society' 30
established as the group's lead
   singer 43
uses Tuskegee as a safe haven 43
duet with Diana Ross 45, 57–8,
   64, 76, 136
health 51, 120, 161–2
steals the limelight in the group 54
first production work outside the
   group 55–6
issue of his leaving the Commodores
   56, 59, 60, 62, 63, 69–70, 74,
   92, 98
practice of composing in the
   bathroom 57
last single with the group 61–2
first solo album 63–8, 66, 90
death of Benny Ashburn 64–5
awards 70, 97, 100, 114, 119,
   134, 159, 165
first solo world tour (1983) 76–8,
   80
plane crash 78
secures six number-one singles in six
   years 80
Olympic Games closing ceremony
   81, 82
promotional videos 86–7, 104,
   111
Pepsi Cola deal 87–8
and McClary's first solo single 90
Marvin Gaye's influence 92, 131,
   141
'We Are the World' project 94–5,
   96
concern for the state of the world 96
leaves Motown 101–2
charitable services 107
education campaign 107–8
as a potential target for personal
   attack 112
on fame 113
most successful year (1987) 114
marital breakdown and divorce
   (Brenda) 116–17, 122, 123,
   125, 128

enormous workload 119
death of his father 120, 125, 126,
   128
loses a friend through AIDS 122,
   128
comeback campaign 126–7
joins Mercury Records 127
on writing love songs 128–9,
   162–3, 165
Phillinganes praises his composing
   talent 129
marries Diane 133–4, 137
first serious acting debut 134, 135
and Tina Turner's farewell tour
   (2000) 139
and Nicole's behaviour 150–1
marital breakdown and divorce
   (Diane) 150–1, 154–8
popularity in the Arab world 162
records with a younger generation
   164
current world iconic status 165
aims to be the greatest singer of all
   time 165
personality
   amiability 120
   charm 120, 163
   an easy conversationalist 34,
      120
   highly opinionated 34
   shyness 3
   wit 163
Richie, Lyonel (L.'s father) 2, 8, 34, 42,
   120, 122, 125, 126, 128
Richie, Miles Brockman (L.'s son) 136,
   150
   birth (1994) 122
   attends L.'s and Diane's wedding
      134
   education 155
Richie, Nicole (L.'s adopted daughter)
   136
   on stage at a Prince concert 104–5
   adopted by the Richies 105
   Michael Jackson her godfather 105,
      121
   and parents' divorce 122, 162
   in *The Simple Life* 149, 162
   drug abuse 149–50

index **183**

and her stepmother's demands 156, 161
weight loss 161–2
Richie, Sofia (L.'s daughter) 150
birth (1998) 122
education 155
Rios, Carlos 77
Ritz, David: *Divided Soul: The Life of Marvin Gaye* 69
Ritz Club, New York 127
Robinson, William 'Smokey' 8, 16, 21, 27, 61, 74, 84, 107
and Gordy 9
and Wanda Rogers 18
leaves the Miracles 27
Motown twenty-fifth anniversary show 72
and Marvin Gaye 92, 93
'We Are The World' project 94
erratic sales 115
distinctive R&B edge 129
*Motown 45*, 157
Rock, Chris 159
Rock and Roll Hall of Fame 121
Rogers, Kenny 45, 57, 61, 62, 80, 81, 112, 162
wants to record with L. 47, 51, 54
*Share Your Love* album 55
relationship with L. 56, 160
and 'My Love' 64
and the 1984 Olympics 81
'We Are The World' project 94
version of 'Lady' 138
Rogers, Wanda 18
*Rolling Stone* magazine 37, 38, 141
Rolling Stones, the 24–5, 74, 88, 114
Rollins, Sonny 132
Ronnie Scott's Club, Soho, London 7, 18
Rose, Howard 88
Rose Royce 36
Ross, Diana 19, 22, 38, 47, 52, 76, 81, 84, 85–6, 97, 98, 112, 121
and the Commodores' introduction to the public 12
leaves the Supremes 16, 37
movies 27
*Blues & Soul* award 33
personal control of her career 36

duet with L. 45, 57–8, 64, 76, 136
number-one titles 47
Radio City incident 58
leaves Motown 58–9, 146
and Motown's twenty-fifth anniversary 71, 72, 73
on Michael Jackson 85
'Missing You' 92, 93, 97
and Marvin Gaye 92–3
'We Are The World' project 94, 95
visits Britain 102
Rossi, Francis 94
Rowland, Kelly 157
Royal Variety Performance (Dominion Theatre, London, 2000) 143
*Royal Wedding, The* (film; Br. title *Wedding Bells*) 104
Ruffin, David 97
Russell, Sue 119, 122
Russia 97, 113

Saadiq, Raphael 164
Sade 97
St Maarten island 22
St Tropez, French Riviera 9
Sala, Ofelia 163
Santa Barbara County Sheriff's Department 121
Sanya, China 161
Sarm Studios, London 94
*Saturday Night Fever* (film) 38, 45
Sawyer, Pam 18, 19
Scandinavia 117
Schlitz Beer 41
Schneider, John 62
Scott, Jill 161
Seattle 48
Serrano, Daniel 158, 159
Sex Pistols, the 36
Shaggy Dog Inc 51
Sharpton, Reverend Al 88
Shepherd, Cybill 110
Shields, Brooke 57
*Showtime At The Apollo* 138
Shrine Auditorium, Los Angeles 157
Shriver, Pam 109
Silver Convention 27
Silverstone: Grand Prix Ball (2005) 160

Simon, Paul  163
*Simple Life, The* (reality series)  149, 162
Simply Red  126
Sims, Winston  32
Sinatra, Frank  41, 132
Singleton, Jeffrey  71
Sisqó  141
Sly & the Family Stone  7, 24
Small's Paradise nightclub, New York  5–6
Smalls, Pete  5–6
Smiley, Charles 'Chuck'  65, 69, 70
Smith, Alan Braham  116
Smith, Joe  18
Smith, Kevin  71
Smith, William  47
Smokey Robinson and the Miracles  8, 16, 84
    *see also* Miracles, the
*Song for Jill, A* (musical tribute)  143
Songwriters Hall of Fame twentieth anniversary gala  119
Soul label  16, 18
SoulfulDetroit website  164
Sound Barrier label  158
*Sound of Motown, The* (British television show)  9
South Africa  117–18, 121
South America  46
Sport Relief  158
Sports Aid  97
Springfield, Dusty  9–10, 48
Springsteen, Bruce  84, 94, 95, 160, 163
Stafford  46
Stallone, 'Wimpo'  102
Starr, Edwin  47, 92
Starr, Ringo  7
Stateside (EMI Records subsidiary)  10
Staton, Candi  33
Status Quo  97
Steeltown label  12
Stern, Randy  77
Stewart, Rod  88
Sting  94, 97
Stockholm  46
Stone, Joss  157
Stone City Band, the  84

Stone Diamond  115
Streisand, Barbra  68, 132
Stringfellow, Peter  160
Sugarhill Gang  120
Sullivan, Charles  88
Sullivan, Ed  9
Summer, Donna  36, 38, 75
*Sunday Mirror*  158, 161
Sunshine  38
Supremes, the  8, 9, 10, 16, 18, 19, 33, 36, 47, 72, 73, 93, 121, 128, 136, 157
Sweden  46, 111
Switzerland  46
Symphony Space  77
Syreeta  27, 115

Taj (Jackson) and Stargate  164
Tamla label  10, 16, 18
Tamla Motown (Motown Records)
    launch of  10
    the largest independent record company in the world  10
    family-based  10
    Quality Control Department  10
    training of acts  13
    invites the Commodores to be a Motown act  15
    subsidiary labels  16, 18
    outgrows its Detroit roots  16
    transfers to Los Angeles  16, 17–18
    expands into an entertainment complex  17
    L. on  29
    the Motown family  31
    makes inroads into television films  36
    first British 12-inch single  39
    the top black-owned company in the USA  44
    Commodores' exclusive recording contract  49
    twentieth anniversary  51, 52
    'Endless Love' as the most successful Motown single (1981)  59
    pressurizes L. to release solo work  63, 70
    and *Love Songs*  65
    twenty-fifth anniversary  71–3

index  185

'All Night Long (All Night)' becomes the most successful Motown single 78
   L. leaves 101–2
   Commodores leave 106
   new male superstar launched (Bruce Willis) 110
   put up for sale 114
   sold (1988) 115
   see also all entries under Motown
Taraborrelli, J. Randy: *Call Her Miss Ross* 58, 93
Taste of Honey, A 59
Taupin, Bernie 132
Tavares 33, 36
Taylor, Bobby 12
Taylor, Johnnie 7
Taylor, Mark 140, 152
*Teachers Only* (US television sitcom) 71
Tee, Ralph 99
Teena Marie 92
Temperton, Rod 96
Temptations, the 7, 8, 9, 12, 13, 16, 18, 19, 30, 33, 47, 50, 72, 92, 93, 97, 110, 115, 136, 160
Terrell, Tammi 58
Tex, Joe 36
*Thank God It's Friday* (film) 38
Thompson, Gene 93–4
Thompson, Steve 111
Three Dog Night 13
3 Ounces of Love 39–40, 41
Timberlake, Justin 157
TLC 164
'To Give Is To Love' concert (Madison Square Garden, New York, 1992) 127
Tokyo Music Festival 24, 51, 71
Toledo, Ohio 77
Tong, Pete 61
*Top Gear* (motoring programme) 158
*Top Ten* television show (US) 119
tour sponsorship 88
Town and Country Club, Camden Town, London 126–7
Trammps 36
Tripoli, Libya 163
Tucker, Sundray 128
Turner, Ike 89

Turner, Tina 89–90, 91, 94, 97, 109, 135, 139, 141
Tuskegee, Alabama 2, 7, 13, 41, 43, 63, 65, 69, 77, 120
Tuskegee Institute/University, Alabama 2–6, 8, 11, 27, 97, 132
'Twenty Four Seven Tour' (Tina Turner, 2000) 139
Tymes, the 27

*Undercover Brother* (film) 37
*Underground Aces* (film) 53
United Arab Emirates 165
United Negro College Fund 157
United States
   Commodores' first US tour 24
   Commodores' triumphant sell-out tour (1978) 38
   King on US stadium tours 46
   religious radio stations 53
   well-planned 1980 tour 54, 55–6
   L.'s solo tours 76–8, 89–90, 101, 109, 110
   black radio stations 88
   *Hands Across America* benefit event 96, 102
   and Live Aid 96–7
University of Texas M. D. Anderson Cancer Center, Houston, Texas 164
Ure, Midge 94
USA For Africa 96, 112, 160
Usher 164

Vance, Courtney B. 135
Vancouvers, the 12
Vandross, Luther 58, 161
Vanilla Ice 120
Vega, Tata 95–6
Velvettes, the 10
Vietnam War 7, 96
Village People, the 136
Vine, Jeremy 86, 117, 121, 145
VIP label 16
Virgin Records 115
Virginia 11

Walker, Junior 72, 74, 84
Walsh, Joe 63
War 20

Ware, Leon  92
Waring, Charles  144–5, 151, 153
Warnes, Jennifer  71
Warren, Diane  137
Warwick, Dionne  94
Washington, Booker T.  3
Washington, Denzel  134, 135
Waters, Muddy  48
Waters, Oren  53
Watts, Nathan  63
Wayne, John  102
'We Are The World' project  94–6, 101
Web 4 Studios, Atlanta  71
Weil, Cynthia  83–4, 105, 125
Weller, Paul  94
Wells, Mary  10, 47, 72, 85
Wembley Arena, London  46, 50, 111, 143, 159
Wembley Stadium, London  96, 121
West Germany  111
Westlife  143
Weston, Jay  53
White, Adam  19, 31, 38
White, Marjorie  87
White, Maurice  35
*White Nights* (film)  99–100
Whitfield, Norman  19, 91
Williams, Jerry 'Swamp Dog'  6, 7
Williams, John  1
Williams, Melanie  164
Williams, Milan  23, 27, 30, 49, 107
   in the Jays  4
   a founder member of the Commodores  5
   contacts Ashburn  5, 6
   education  8
   the 'University of Motown'  21
   on 'Easy'  33
   into jazz and country and western  36
   CB radio nickname  43
   air accident  56
   on L.'s leaving the group  69, 74
   Orange on  74
   works with Stella Parton  82
   and Commodores move from Motown  106
   'a fresh start'  106
   leaves the Commodores  118
Williams, Paul  93
Williams, Vesta  75
Willingham, Cecil  39
Willis, Bruce  110, 156
Wilson, Jackie  98, 146
Wilson, Mary  36, 73, 157
WOBS radio station  34
Wolper, David  81–2
Wonder, Stevie  9, 16, 21, 23, 70, 76, 93, 97, 107, 121, 132, 146
   Motown company heavyweight  23
   and Motown's poor British strength (1975)  27
   L. on his status  30
   *Blues & Soul* award  33
   his commercial *Hotter Than July*  52
   personal control of his career  36
   number-one titles  47
   and Paul McCartney  59
   Motown twenty-fifth anniversary show  72
   compliments L.  81
   and Marvin Gaye  92
   'We Are The World' project  94, 95
   retains his soulful feeling  104
   erratic sales  115
Woodford, Terry  21
WorldNow  144
Wyoming Seminary  3

YMCA, 135th Street, New York  6
Young, Paul  99
Young, Will  161
Yugoslavia  97

Zeffirelli, Franco  57
Zombie, Rob  37, 147

# index of songs and albums

Figures in italics indicate captions.

'12.01 A.M.' 49
*13* 73
*25 Number One Hits From 25 Years* 72

'All Around The World' 164
'All Night Long (All Night)' 1, 77–81, 84, 85, 89, 91, 97, 111, 125, 127, 139, 140, 143, 144, 150, 153, 157, 159, 163
*All The Great Hits* 68, 71
'All The Way Down' 52
'Angel' 140, 141, 142
'Animal Instinct' 99
'Are You Happy' 21

*Back To Front* 123, *124*, 125, 126, 127, 140, 148
'Ball And Chain' 152
'Ballerina Girl' 104, 106
'Beat It' 75
*Best Of The Commodores, The* 71, 147
'Brick House' 35, 37–8, 46, 50, 72, 74, 131, 138, 139, 146, 147, 159–60, 165
'Bump, The' 23

'(Can I) Get A Witness' 25
'Can't Get Over You' 132
'Can't Let You Tease Me' 29
*Can't Slow Down* [first titled *Positive Force*] 22, 68, 76, 77, 79, 80, 82–6, *82*, 91, 93, 97, 99, 105, 114, 137, 146, 151
'Captured' 73

*Caught In The Act* 24, 25, 35
'Cebu' 25
'Change' 131
'Christmas Song, The' 158
'Cinderella' 139, 142, *141*
'Climbing' 132, 133
*Climbing Higher* 51
'Closest Thing To Heaven' 137
'Cloud Nine' 13
'Come Inside' 28, 29
*Coming Home* 163, 164–5
*Commodores* [British title *Zoom*] 33–7, *33*, 52
*Commodores Anthology* [2001] 35
*Commodores Christmas* 119, 158
*Commodores Hits, Vol. 1* 119
*Commodores Hits, Vol. 2* 119, 158
*Commodores Live!* 38–9
*Commodores XX – No Tricks* 119, 158

'Daisy Lady' 51
'Dance With The Night' 141
*Dancing On The Ceiling* 100, 101, 103–6, 112, 114, 127, 139, 145, 151
'Dancing On The Ceiling' 103, 104, 106, 109, 113, 125, 148, 158, 159
'Deep River Woman' 105, 106, 109, 110
'Do It To Me' 126, 127
'Do Ya' 153
'Don't Stop' 105, 112
'Don't Stop The Music' 141, 142
'Don't Wanna Lose You' 129–30, 131
'Don't You Be Worried' 21

*Easy* 33–4
'Easy' 32, 35, 36, 44, 50, 118, 125, 139, 142, 144, 151, 153, 159, 160
*Encore* 143, 144, 146, 147
'Endless Love' 57–64, 67, 68, 76, 78, 80, 100, 112, 125, 136, 146, 153, 157
'Everytime' 138

'Fancy Dancer' 29, 31–2, 35
'Fire Girl' 44
'First Noel, The' 158
'Flying High' 42, 43, 44, 50
'Forever' 137
'Forever Came Today' 72
'Free' 25
'Funky Situation' 35
'Funny Feelings' 34

'Gettin' It' 49
'Gimme My Mule' 25
'Girl, I Think The World About You' 29
'Goin' Back To Alabama' 54, 55
'Goin' To The Bank' 106, 107, 118
'Goodbye' 144, 145
'Got To Be Together' 52
*Greatest Hits* 44
'Grrip' 118

'Heaven Knows' 35
'Hello' 84–7, 93, 109, 111, 125, 132, 136, 143, 144, 145, 150
*Heroes* 51–4
'Heroes' 51–3, 61
'High On Sunshine' 28, 29, 32
'Hold On' 25
*Hot On The Tracks* 28–9, 30–1, 33, 43
'How Long' 141

'I Call It Love' 163, 164
'I Feel Sanctified' 24, 32, 50
'I Hear Your Voice' 137
'I Like What You Do' 50
'I Love You' 164
'I Still Believe' 152, 157, 159
'I Wanna Take You Down' 131
'I'm Coming Home' 164
'I'm In Love' 73
'I'm Missing Her' 164

'I'm Ready' 24
*In The Pocket* 60, 61, 62, 65

'Janet' 99
'Jerry The Elf' 158
'Jesus Is Love' 52, 53
'Just Can't Say Goodbye' 141
*Just For You* 151–2, 153, 157
'Just For You' 151, 152, 159
'Just To Be Close To You' 28–33, 35, 44, 50, 67, 130, 160
'Just To Be With You Again' 152

'Keep Me Up All Night' 164
'Keep On Dancing' 7
'Keep On Taking Me Higher' 61

'Lady (You Bring Me Up)' 54–5, 60–3, 67, 68, 109, 112
'Lay Back' 99
'Let's Do It Right' 24
'Let's Get Started' 29, 32
'Liar' 13
*Lionel Richie* 63–8, 66, 68, 71, 114, 119, 145
*Lionel Richie – The Composer: Great Love Songs With The Commodores And Diana Ross* 102
*Lionel Richie & The Commodores – The Definitive Collection* 147–8, 151
'Long, Long Way To Go' 158
*Louder Than Words* 128, 130–4, 135, 136, 137
'Love, Oh Love' 126
*Love Songs* 65
'Love Will Conquer All' 105, 106, 111–12, 148
'Lovers At First Sight' 132, 133
'Lovin' You' 49
'Lucy' 65

*Machine Gun* 23, 24, 35
'Machine Gun' [previously 'The Ram'] 21–4, *23*, 30, 32, 39, 44, 50, 52
'Mary Mary' 25
*Midnight Magic* 46, *48*, 49, 50–1
'Midnight Magic' 49, 50
'Mighty Spirit' 52, 53

'Miss Celie's Blues (Sister)'  96
'Missing You'  92, 93, 97, 158
*Motown 20th Anniversary Album, The*  52
*Motown Story – The First Twenty-Five Years, The*  72, 107
*Motown Superstars Sing Motown Superstars*  72
*Movin' On*  25
'My Destiny'  126, 136
'My Love'  64, 67, 71, 148

*Natural High*  42, 43, 45, 46, 52, 85
*Nightshift*  98–9, 106, 118, 146
'Nightshift'  98, 99, 118, 158
'Nothing Else Matters'  132
'Nothing Like A Woman'  73

'Oh No'  61, 62
'Old-Fashioned Love'  51, 52
'One World'  152
'Only You'  73, 74, 80–1
'Ooo, Woman You'  73
'Ordinary Girl'  131
'Outrageous'  159
'Outta My Head'  164

'Painted Picture'  68
'Patch It Up'  35
'Penny Lover'  83, 84, 91, 125
'Piece Of Love'  132
'Piece Of My Heart'  141

'Quick Draw'  29, 43

'Rapid Fire'  23
'Reach High'  71
'Reason To Believe'  164
*Renaissance*  139–42
'Right Here And Now'  118
*Rise Up*  107
'Rise Up'  7
'Road To Heaven'  153
*Rock Solid*  117, 118
'Round And Round'  67
'Running With The Night' [previously 'Strangers In The Night']  83, 84, 85, 111, 125, 159

'Sail On'  46–7, 49, 50, 52, 67, 106, 125, 136, 158, 165
'Say I Do'  131, 132, 134
'Say Yeah'  44
'Say You, Say Me'  99, 100, 101, 107, 109, 111, 119, 125, 136, 159
'Sela'  105, 111, 119
'Serves You Right'  63, 64, 67, 90
'Sexy Lady'  49
'She Works Hard For The Money'  75
'She's Amazing'  152, 153
'Shut Up And Dance'  158
'Slip Of The Tongue'  99
'Slippery When Wet'  24, 25, 32
'So Nice'  118
'Special Service To Country Radio, A'  106
'Squeeze The Fruit'  34
'Stay'  138
'Still'  47, 49, 50, 52, 67, 80, 89, 125, 136, 153, 158
'Still In Love'  132, 134
'Stuck On You'  84, 91, 93, 106, 125, 158
'Such A Woman'  44
'Superman'  23
'Sweet Love'  25, 26, 27–8, 32
'Sweet Vacation'  164

'Take My Hand'  158
'Tell Me'  64, 67
'Tender Heart'  141, 142
'Thank You'  118
'There's A Song In My Heart'  21, 23
*13*  73–4
'Thin Walls'  90
'This Is Your Life'  24, 32, 138
'This Love'  61
'Three Times A Lady'  27, 41–7, 49, 50, 52, 59, 80, 85, 90, 118, 125, 136, 138, 142, 144, 146, 151, 159, 165
'Thumpin' Music'  29
*Time*  136–8
'Time'  25, 28
'Time Of Our Life'  153
'To Love A Woman'  144–5
'To The Rhythm'  138

190  index of songs and albums

'Tonight' 141
'Too Hot Ta Trot' 38, 39, 50
'Touch' 138
'Touchdown' 73
'Truly' 67, 68, 70, 76, 80, 90, 125, 153
*Truly – The Love Songs* 136, 148
'Turn Off The Lights' 73, 75
'12.01 A.M.' 49
*25 Number One Hits From 25 Years* 72

'Underground Aces' 53
*United* 107

*Very Best Of The Commodores, The* 99
'Visions' 43

'Wandering Stranger' 64, 67, 123
'Way I Feel, The' 138
'We Are The World' 94–6, 101, 105, 112, 119, 160–1, 163

'Welcome Home' 73
'Why' 164
'Why You Wanna Try Me' 61–2
'Wichita Lineman' 13
'Wide Open' 24
'Woman In My Life, A' 99
'Wonderland' 49, 50–1
'Won't You Come Dance With Me' 35
'World Is A Party, The' 153

'X-Rated Movie' 44

'You Are' 69, 70, 148, 164
'You Mean More To Me' 67, 72
'Young Girls Are My Weakness' 23
'You're Special' 49

'Zoo (The Human Zoo), The' 19, 20
'Zoom' 35, 39, 50, 123, 138, 165
*Zoom*, see *Commodores* 33
'Zoomin'' 137

index of songs and albums 191